The Quran With Tafsir Ibn Kathir
Part 3 of 30:
Al Baqarah 253 To
Al Imran 092

The Quran With Tafsir Ibn Kathir
Part 3 of 30:
Al Baqarah 253 To
Al Imran 092

With
Arabic Script, Transliteration of Arabic, Meaning in English
and Ibn Kathir's Abridged Tafsir (Explanation)

Muhammad Saed Abdul-Rahman

BSc, DipHE

© Muhammad Saed Abdul-Rahman,2012
ISBN 978-1-86179-834-3

All Rights reserved

British Library Cataloguing in Publication Data. A Catalogue record for this book is available from the British Library

Designed, Typeset and produced by:
MSA Publication Limited, 4 Bello Close, Herne Hill,
London SE24 9BW
United Kingdom

Cover design: Houriyah Abdul-Rahman

TABLE OF CONTENTS

TABLE OF CONTENTS V

PRELUDE XI

OPENING SERMAN XI
OUR MISSION XII
BIOGRAPHY OF HAFIZ IBN KATHIR (701 H - 774 H) XII
    Ibn Kathir's Teachers xii
    Ibn Kathir's Students xiii
    Ibn Kathir's Books xiii
    Ibn Kathir's Death xiv

PREFACE XV

ABOUT THIS BOOK XV
PERFORMING PROSTRATION WHILE READING THE QUR'AN XV

PART 3 FULL ARABIC TEXT 1

INTRODUCTION TO CHAPTER (SURAH) 2: AL-BAQARAH (THE COW) 12

IBN KATHIR'S INTRODUCTION 12
    The Virtues of Surat Al-Baqarah 12
    Virtues of Surat Al-Baqarah and Surat Al `Imran 14
    Surat Al-Baqarah was revealed in Al-Madinah 16

CHAPTER (SURAH) 2: AL-BAQARAH (THE COW), VERSES 253-286 17

Surah: 2 Ayah: 253 17
    Tafsir Ibn Kathir 18
        Allah Honored Some Prophets Above Others 18
Surah: 2 Ayah: 254 19
    Tafsir Ibn Kathir 20
Surah: 2 Ayah: 255 20
    Tafsir Ibn Kathir 21
        The Virtue of Ayat Al-Kursi 21
        Allah's Greatest Name is in Ayat Al-Kursi 22
        Ayat Al-Kursi has Ten Complete Arabic Sentences 23
    Tafsir Ibn Kathir 26
        No Compulsion in Religion 26
        Tawhid is the Most Trustworthy Handhold 27
Surah: 2 Ayah: 257 29
    Tafsir Ibn Kathir 29
Surah: 2 Ayah: 258 30
    Tafsir Ibn Kathir 30
        The Debate Between Ibrahim Al-Khalil and King Nimrod 30
Surah: 2 Ayah: 259 32

Tafsir Ibn Kathir	32
The Story of `Uzayr	32
Surah: 2 Ayah: 260	**34**
Tafsir Ibn Kathir	34
The Khalil Supplicates to Allah to Show Him How He Resurrects the Dead	34
The Answer to Al-Khalil's Request	35
Surah: 2 Ayah: 261	**36**
Tafsir Ibn Kathir	36
Rewards of Spending in Allah's Cause	36
Surah: 2 Ayah: 262, Surah: 2 Ayah: 263 & Surah: 2 Ayah: 264	**38**
Tafsir Ibn Kathir	39
To Remind About Charity Given is Forbidden	39
Surah: 2 Ayah: 265	**40**
Tafsir Ibn Kathir	41
Surah: 2 Ayah: 266	**41**
Tafsir Ibn Kathir	42
The Example of Evil Deeds Nullifying Good Deeds	42
Surah: 2 Ayah: 267, Ayah: 268 & Ayah: 269	**43**
Tafsir Ibn Kathir	44
The Encouragement to Spend Honest Money for Allah's Sake	44
Shaytanic Doubts Concerning Spending in Charity	45
The Meaning of Al-Hikmah	46
Surah: 2 Ayah: 270 & Ayah: 271	**47**
Tafsir Ibn Kathir	48
The Virtue of Disclosing or Concealing Charity	48
Surah: 2 Ayah: 272, Ayah: 273 & Ayah: 274	**49**
Tafsir Ibn Kathir	50
Giving Charity to Polytheists	50
Who Deserves Charity	52
Praise for those who Spend in Charity	53
Surah: 2 Ayah: 275	**54**
Tafsir Ibn Kathir	54
The Punishment for Dealing with Riba (Interest and Usury)	54
Surah: 2 Ayah: 276 & Ayah: 277	**58**
Tafsir Ibn Kathir	59
Allah Does Not Bless Riba	59
Allah Increases Charity, Just as One Raises His Animal	59
Allah Does not Like the Disbelieving Sinners	60
Praising Those Who Thank Allah	60
Surah: 2 Ayah: 278, Ayah: 279, Ayah: 280 & Ayah: 281	**60**
Tafsir Ibn Kathir	61
The Necessity of Taqwa and Avoiding Riba	61
Riba Constitutes War Against Allah and His Messenger	62
Being Kind to Debtors Who Face Financial Difficulties	63
Surah: 2 Ayah: 282	**65**

| Table of Contents | vii |

    Tafsir Ibn Kathir 66
        The Necessity of Writing Transactions That Take Effect Later on 66
        Witnesses Should Attend the Dictation of Contracts 68
Surah: 2 Ayah: 283 72
    Tafsir Ibn Kathir 72
        What is the `Mortgaging' Mentioned in the Ayah 72
Surah: 2 Ayah: 284 74
    Tafsir Ibn Kathir 74
        Would the Servants be Accountable for What They Conceal in Their Hearts 74
Surah: 2 Ayah: 285 & Ayah: 286 77
    Tafsir Ibn Kathir 78
        The Tafsir of the Last Two Ayat of Surat Al-Baqarah 78

CHAPTER (SURAH) 3: AL-I-'IMRAN (THE FAMILY OF 'IMRAN), VERSES 001-092 81

Surah: 3 Ayah: 1, Ayah: 2, Ayah: 3 & Ayah: 4 81
    Tafsir Ibn Kathir 81
Surah: 3 Ayah: 5 & Ayah: 6 83
    Tafsir Ibn Kathir 83
Surah: 3 Ayah: 7, Ayah: 8 & Ayah: 9 83
    Tafsir Ibn Kathir 84
        The Mutashabihat and Muhkamat Ayat 84
        Only Allah Knows the True Ta'wil (Interpretation) of the Mutashabihat 86
Surah: 3 Ayah: 10 & Ayah: 11 88
    Tafsir Ibn Kathir 89
        On the Day of Resurrection, No Wealth or Offspring Shall Avail 89
Surah: 3 Ayah: 12 & Ayah: 13 90
    Tafsir Ibn Kathir 91
        Threatening the Jews With Defeat and Encouraging Them to Learn a Lesson From the Battle of Badr 91
Surah: 3 Ayah: 14 & Ayah: 15 92
    Tafsir Ibn Kathir 93
        The True Value of This Earthly Life 93
        The Reward of the Those Who Have Taqwa is Better Than All Joys of This World 95
Surah: 3 Ayah: 16 & Ayah: 17 95
    Tafsir Ibn Kathir 96
        The Supplication and Description of Al-Muttaqin 96
Surah: 3 Ayah: 18, Ayah: 19 & Ayah: 20 97
    Tafsir Ibn Kathir 98
        The Testimony of Tawhid 98
        The Religion with Allah is Islam 99
        Islam is the Religion of Mankind and the Prophet Was Sent to all Mankind 100
Surah: 3 Ayah: 21 & Ayah: 22 101
    Tafsir Ibn Kathir 101

Chastising the Jews for Their Disbelief and for Killing the Prophets and Righteous People 101

Surah: 3 Ayah: 23, Ayah: 24 & Ayah: 25............ 102
   Tafsir Ibn Kathir 102
      Chastising the People of the Book for Not Referring to the Book of Allah for Judgment 102

Surah: 3 Ayah: 26 & Ayah: 27............ 103
   Tafsir Ibn Kathir 104
      Encouraging Gratitude 104

Surah: 3 Ayah: 28............ 105
   Tafsir Ibn Kathir 105
      The Prohibition of Supporting the Disbelievers 105

Surah: 3 Ayah: 29, Ayah: 30............ 106
   Tafsir Ibn Kathir 107
      Allah Knows What the Hearts Conceal 107

Surah: 3 Ayah: 31 & Ayah: 32............ 108
   Tafsir Ibn Kathir 108
      Allah's Love is Attained by Following the Messenger 108

Surah: 3 Ayah: 33, Ayah: 34............ 109
   Tafsir Ibn Kathir 110
      The Chosen Ones Among the People of the Earth 110

Surah: 3 Ayah: 35 & Ayah: 36............ 110
   Tafsir Ibn Kathir 111
      The Story of Maryam's Birth 111

Surah: 3 Ayah: 37............ 112
   Tafsir Ibn Kathir 113
      Maryam Grows Up; Her Honor is with Allah 113

Surah: 3 Ayah: 38, Ayah: 39, Ayah: 40 & Ayah: 41............ 114
   Tafsir Ibn Kathir 115
      The Supplication of Zakariyya, and the Good News of Yahya's Birth 115

Surah: 3 Ayah: 42, Ayah: 43 & Ayah: 44............ 116
   Tafsir Ibn Kathir 117
      The Virtue of Maryam Over the Women of Her Time 117

Surah: 3 Ayah: 45, Ayah: 46 & Ayah: 47............ 119
   Tafsir Ibn Kathir 120
      Delivering the Good News to Maryam of `Isa's Birth 120
      `Isa Spoke When He was Still in the Cradle 120
      `Isa was Created Without a Father 121

Surah: 3 Ayah: 48, Ayah: 49, Ayah: 50 & Ayah: 51............ 121
   Tafsir Ibn Kathir 122
      The Description of `Isa and the Miracles He Performed 122

Surah: 3 Ayah: 52, Ayah: 53 & Ayah: 54............ 124
   Tafsir Ibn Kathir 124
      The Disciples Give Their Support to `Isa 124
      The Jews Plot to Kill `Isa 125

Table of Contents

Surah: 3 Ayah: 55, Ayah: 56, Ayah: 57 & Ayah: 58 126
    Tafsir Ibn Kathir 127
        Meaning of 'Take You' 127
        Altering the Religion of `Isa 127
        Threatening the Disbelievers with Torment in This Life and the Hereafter 129

Surah: 3 Ayah: 59, Ayah: 60, Ayah: 61, Ayah: 62 & Ayah: 63 129
    Tafsir Ibn Kathir 130
        The Similarities Between the Creation of Adam and the Creation of `Isa 130
        The Challenge to the Mubahalah 131

Surah: 3 Ayah: 64 134
    Tafsir Ibn Kathir 135
        Every Person Knows about Tawhid 135

Surah: 3 Ayah: 65, Ayah: 66, Ayah: 67 & Ayah: 68 136
    Tafsir Ibn Kathir 137
        Disputing with the Jews and Christians About the Religion of Ibrahim 137

Surah: 3 Ayah: 69, Ayah: 70, Ayah: 71, Ayah: 72, Ayah: 73 & Ayah: 74 139
    Tafsir Ibn Kathir 140
        The Envy the Jews Feel Towards Muslims; Their Wicked Plots Against Muslims 140

Surah: 3 Ayah: 75 & Ayah: 76 141
    Tafsir Ibn Kathir 142
        How Trustworthy Are the Jews 142

Surah: 3 Ayah: 77 143
    Tafsir Ibn Kathir 143
        There is No Share in the Hereafter for Those Who Break Allah's Covenant 143

Surah: 3 Ayah: 78 146
    Tafsir Ibn Kathir 146
        The Jews Alter Allah's Words 146

Surah: 3 Ayah: 79 & Ayah: 80 147
    Tafsir Ibn Kathir 147
        No Prophet Ever Called People to Worship him or to Worship Other Than Allah 147

Surah: 3 Ayah: 81 & Ayah: 82 148
    Tafsir Ibn Kathir 149
        Taking a Pledge From the Prophets to Believe in Our Prophet, Muhammad 149

Surah: 3 Ayah: 83, Ayah: 84 & Ayah: 85 150
    Tafsir Ibn Kathir 151
        The Only Valid Religion To Allah is Islam 151

Surah: 3 Ayah: 86, Ayah: 87, Ayah: 88 & Ayah: 89 152
    Tafsir Ibn Kathir 153
        Allah Does Not Guide People Who Disbelieve After they Believed, Unless They Repent 153

Surah: 3 Ayah: 90 & Ayah: 91 154
    Tafsir Ibn Kathir 154
        Neither Repentance of the Disbeliever Upon Death, Nor His Ransoming Himself on the Day of Resurrection Shall be Accepted 154

Surah: 3 Ayah: 92 156

Tafsir Ibn Kathir 157
    Al-Birr is Spending from the Best of One's Wealth 157

PRELUDE

Opening Serman

Indeed, all praise is due to Allah. We praise Him and seek His help and forgiveness. We seek refuge with Allah from our soul's evil and our wrong doings. He whom Allah guides, no one can misguide; and he whom He misguides, no one can guide

I bear witness that there is no (true) god except Allah – alone without a partner, and I bear witness that Muhammad (peace and blessings of Allah be upon him) is His 'abd (servant) and messenger.

$$\text{يَٰٓأَيُّهَا ٱلَّذِينَ ءَامَنُوا۟ ٱتَّقُوا۟ ٱللَّهَ حَقَّ تُقَاتِهِۦ وَلَا تَمُوتُنَّ إِلَّا وَأَنتُم مُّسْلِمُونَ}$$

O you who believe! Fear Allâh (by doing all that He has ordered and by abstaining from all that He has forbidden) as He should be feared. (Obey Him, be thankful to Him, and remember Him always), and die not except in a state of Islâm (as Muslims (with complete submission to Allâh)).

$$\text{يَٰٓأَيُّهَا ٱلنَّاسُ ٱتَّقُوا۟ رَبَّكُمُ ٱلَّذِى خَلَقَكُم مِّن نَّفْسٍ وَٰحِدَةٍ وَخَلَقَ مِنْهَا زَوْجَهَا وَبَثَّ مِنْهُمَا رِجَالًا كَثِيرًا وَنِسَآءً ۚ وَٱتَّقُوا۟ ٱللَّهَ ٱلَّذِى تَسَآءَلُونَ بِهِۦ وَٱلْأَرْحَامَ ۚ إِنَّ ٱللَّهَ كَانَ عَلَيْكُمْ رَقِيبًا}$$

O mankind! Be dutiful to your Lord, Who created you from a single person (Adam), and from him (Adam) He created his wife (Hawwâ (Eve)) and from them both He created many men and women; and fear Allâh through Whom you demand (your mutual rights), and (do not cut the relations of) the wombs (kinship). Surely, Allâh is Ever an All-Watcher over you.

$$\text{يُصْلِحْ لَكُمْ أَعْمَٰلَكُمْ وَيَغْفِرْ لَكُمْ ذُنُوبَكُمْ ۗ وَمَن يُطِعِ ٱللَّهَ وَرَسُولَهُۥ فَقَدْ فَازَ فَوْزًا عَظِيمًا}$$

He will direct you to do righteous good deeds and will forgive you your sins. And whosoever obeys Allâh and His Messenger (peace be upon him), he has indeed achieved a great achievement (i.e. he will be saved from the Hell-fire and will be admitted to Paradise).

Indeed, the best speech is Allah's Book and the best guidance is Muhammad's () guidance. The worst affairs (of religion) are those innovated (by people), for every such innovation is an act of misguidance leading to the Fire

Our Mission

Our mission is to gather in one place, for the English-speaking public, all relevant information needed to make the Qur'an more understandable and easier to study. This book tries to do this by providing the following:

1. The Arabic Text for those who are able to read Arabic
2. Transliteration of the Arabic text for those who are unable to read the Arabic script. This will give them a sample of the sound of the Qur'an, which they could not otherwise comprehend from reading the English meaning.
3. The meaning of the qur'an (translated by Dr. Muhammad Taqi-ud-Din Al-Hilali, Ph.D. and Dr. Muhammad Muhsin Khan)
4. Explanation (abridged Tafsir) by Ibn Kathir (translated by Safi-ur-Rahman al-Mubarakpuri)

We hope that by doing this an ordinary English-speaker will be able to pick up a copy of this book and study and comprehend The Glorious Qur'an in a way that is acceptable to the understanding of the Rightly-guided Muslim Ummah (Community).

Biography of Hafiz Ibn Kathir (701 H - 774 H)

By the Honored Shaykh `Abdul-Qadir Al-Arna'ut, may Allah protect him.

He is the respected Imam, Abu Al-Fida', `Imad Ad-Din Isma il bin 'Umar bin Kathir Al-Qurashi Al-Busrawi - Busraian in origin; Dimashqi in training, learning and residence.

Ibn Kathir was born in the city of Busra in 701 H. His father was the Friday speaker of the village, but he died while Ibn Kathir was only four years old. Ibn Kathir's brother, Shaykh Abdul-Wahhab, reared him and taught him until he moved to Damascus in 706 H., when he was five years old.

Ibn Kathir's Teachers

Ibn Kathir studied Fiqh - Islamic jurisprudence - with Burhan Ad-Din, Ibrahim bin `Abdur-Rahman Al-Fizari, known as Ibn Al-Firkah (who died in 729 H). Ibn Kathir heard Hadiths from `Isa bin Al-Mutim, Ahmad bin Abi Talib, (Ibn Ash-Shahnah) (who died in 730 H), Ibn Al-Hajjar, (who died in 730 H), and the Hadith narrator of Ash-Sham (modern day Syria and surrounding areas); Baha Ad-Din Al-Qasim bin Muzaffar bin `Asakir (who died in 723 H), and Ibn Ash-Shirdzi, Ishaq bin Yahya Al-Ammuddi, also known as `Afif Ad-Din, the Zahiriyyah Shaykh who died in 725 H, and Muhammad bin Zarrad. He remained with Jamal Ad-Din, Yusuf bin Az-Zaki AlMizzi who died in 724 H, he benefited from his knowledge and also married his daughter. He also read with Shaykh Al-Islam, Taqi Ad-Din Ahmad bin `Abdul-Halim bin `Abdus-Salam bin Taymiyyah who died in 728 H. He also read with the Imam Hafiz and historian Shams Ad-Din, Muhammad bin Ahmad bin Uthman bin Qaymaz Adh-Dhahabi, who died in 748 H. Also, Abu Musa Al-Qarafai, Abu Al-Fath Ad-Dabbusi and

'Ali bin `Umar As-Suwani and others who gave him permission to transmit the knowledge he learned with them in Egypt.

In his book, Al-Mu jam Al-Mukhtas, Al-Hafiz Adh-Dhaliabi wrote that Ibn Kathir was, "The Imam, scholar of jurisprudence, skillful scholar of Hadith, renowned Faqih and scholar of Tafsir who wrote several beneficial books."

Further, in Ad-Durar Al-Kdminah, Al-Hafiz Ibn Hajar AlAsqalani said, "Ibn Kathir worked on the subject of the Hadith in the areas of texts and chains of narrators. He had a good memory, his books became popular during his lifetime, and people benefited from them after his death."

Also, the renowned historian Abu Al-Mahasin, Jamal Ad-Din Yusuf bin Sayf Ad-Din (Ibn Taghri Bardi), said in his book, AlManhal As-Safi, "He is the Shaykh, the Imam, the great scholar `Imad Ad-Din Abu Al-Fida'. He learned extensively and was very active in collecting knowledge and writing. He was excellent in the areas of Fiqh, Tafsfr and Hadith. He collected knowledge, authored (books), taught, narrated Hadith and wrote. He had immense knowledge in the fields of Hadith, Tafsir, Fiqh, the Arabic language, and so forth. He gave Fatawa (religious verdicts) and taught until he died, may Allah grant him mercy. He was known for his precision and vast knowledge, and as a scholar of history, Hadith and Tafsir."

Ibn Kathir's Students

Ibn Hajji was one of Ibn Kathir's students, and he described Ibn Kathir: "He had the best memory of the Hadith texts. He also had the most knowledge concerning the narrators and authenticity, his contemporaries and teachers admitted to these qualities. Every time I met him I gained some benefit from him."

Also, Ibn Al-`Imad Al-Hanbali said in his book, Shadhardt Adh-Dhahab, "He is the renowned Hafiz `Imad Ad-Din, whose memory was excellent, whose forgetfulness was miniscule, whose understanding was adequate, and who had good knowledge in the Arabic language." Also, Ibn Habib said about Ibn Kathir, "He heard knowledge and collected it and wrote various books. He brought comfort to the ears with his Fatwas and narrated Hadith and brought benefit to other people. The papers that contained his Fatwas were transmitted to the various (Islamic) provinces. Further, he was known for his precision and encompassing knowledge."

Ibn Kathir's Books

1 - One of the greatest books that Ibn Kathir wrote was his Tafsir of the Noble Qur'an, which is one of the best Tafsir that rely on narrations [of Ahadith, the Tafsir of the Companions, etc.]. The Tafsir by Ibn Kathir was printed many times and several scholars have summarized it.

2- The History Collection known as Al-Biddyah, which was printed in 14 volumes under the name Al-Bidayah wanNihdyah, and contained the stories of the Prophets and previous nations, the Prophet's Seerah (life story) and Islamic history until his time. He also added a book Al-Fitan, about the Signs of the Last Hour.

3- At-Takmil ft Ma`rifat Ath-Thiqat wa Ad-Du'afa wal Majdhil which Ibn Kathir collected from the books of his two Shaykhs Al-Mizzi and Adh-Dhahabi; Al-Kdmal and Mizan Al-Ftiddl. He added several benefits regarding the subject of Al-Jarh and AtT'adil.

4- Al-Hadi was-Sunan ft Ahadith Al-Masdnfd was-Sunan which is also known by, Jami` Al-Masdnfd. In this book, Ibn Kathir collected the narrations of Imams Ahmad bin Hanbal, Al-Bazzar, Abu Ya`la Al-Mawsili, Ibn Abi Shaybah and from the six collections of Hadith: the Two Sahihs [Al-Bukhari and Muslim] and the Four Sunan [Abu Dawud, At-Tirmidhi, AnNasa and Ibn Majah]. Ibn Kathir divided this book according to areas of Fiqh.

5-Tabaqat Ash-Shaf iyah which also contains the virtues of Imam Ash-Shafi.

6- Ibn Kathir wrote references for the Ahadith of Adillat AtTanbfh, from the Shafi school of Fiqh.

7- Ibn Kathir began an explanation of Sahih Al-Bukhari, but he did not finish it.

8- He started writing a large volume on the Ahkam (Laws), but finished only up to the Hajj rituals.

9- He summarized Al-Bayhaqi's 'Al-Madkhal. Many of these books were not printed.

10- He summarized `Ulum Al-Hadith, by Abu `Amr bin AsSalah and called it Mukhtasar `Ulum Al-Hadith. Shaykh Ahmad Shakir, the Egyptian Muhaddith, printed this book along with his commentary on it and called it Al-Ba'th Al-Hathfth fi Sharh Mukhtasar `Ulum Al-Hadith.

11- As-Sfrah An-Nabawiyyah, which is contained in his book Al-Biddyah, and both of these books are in print.

12- A research on Jihad called Al-Ijtihad ft Talabi Al-Jihad, which was printed several times.

Ibn Kathir's Death

Al-Hafiz Ibn Hajar Al-Asqalani said, "Ibn Kathir lost his sight just before his life ended. He died in Damascus in 774 H." May Allah grant mercy upon Ibn Kathir and make him among the residents of His Paradise.

PREFACE

In the name of Allah, Most Gracious, Most Merciful.

About this book

The previous publication of this book included some background information to the chapters of the Qur'an by an Islamic scholar known as Abul Ala Maududi. This information was used to shed more light on the chapters by giving a summery of why each chapter was given its name, It's period of revelation and the circumstances surrounding its revelatiom. However, some Muslims objected to the inclusion of the contributions of Maududi.

In this new publication of Tafsir Ibn Kathir, we have removed all traces of the contribution of Abul Ala Maududi. Personally, I do not know the reasons for the objections to Maududi, but this work concerns only the tafsir of Ibn Kathir, so we have not included anything from Maududi in it. We have also corrected all the typing and formatting errors found in the previous publication. We have not alter the structure of the book. The reader is still able to read the full Arabic Text of the thirty Parts of the Qur'an and follow its meanings in the English language. The transliteration of the Arabic text should also give the reader a taste of the sound of the original Arabic.

May Almighty Allah accept this effort from us, and make it a source of blessings for us in this world and in the next. I bear witness that there is none worthy of worship but Allah and I bear witness that Muhammad (may the peace and blessings of Allah be upon him) is the slave and messenger of Allah.

Performing Prostration While Reading the Qur'an

Question:

Could you please give a list of the Qur'anic verses when a prostration is recommended? What happens if we read these verses and not perform a prostration?

A. Jalil

Answer:

There are 15 verses in the Qur'an that mention prostration before God Almighty as a good action by God-fearing believers. Therefore, it is strongly recommended to perform such a prostration when we read or listen to any of these verses, whether during prayer or in any situation.

Some scholars are of the view that even if one has not performed ablution, one should prostrate oneself. These verses are given here, starting with the Arabic title of the surah which is followed by two numbers, the first indicating the surah, and the second indicating the verse,: Al-Araf 7: 206; Al-Raad 13: 15; Al-Nahl 16: 50; Al-Isra 17: 109; Maryam 19: 58; Al-Hajj 22: 18 & 22: 77; Al-Furqan 25: 60; Al-Naml 27: 26;

Al-Sajdah 32: 15; Saad 38: 25; Fussilat 41: 38; Al-Najm 53: 62; Al-Inshiqaq 84: 21 and Al-Alaq 96: 19.

If you do not perform a prostration when you read or listen to any of these verses, you have done badly because you miss out on the reward of performing a prostration for God. You incur no sin and violate no divine order.

Reference:
http://archive.arabnews.com/?page=5&section=0&article=97811&d=1&m=7&y=2007

Tafsir Ibn Kathir Juz' 3 (Part 3):
Chapter (Surah) 2: Al-Baqarah (TThe Cow) 253 To Chapter (Surah) 3: Al-i-'Imran (The Family of Imran) 092

PART 3 FULL ARABIC TEXT

Chapter (Surah) 2: Al-Baqarah 253-286

بِسْمِ اللَّهِ الرَّحْمَٰنِ الرَّحِيمِ

﴿ ۞ تِلْكَ الرُّسُلُ فَضَّلْنَا بَعْضَهُمْ عَلَىٰ بَعْضٍ ۘ مِّنْهُم مَّن كَلَّمَ اللَّهُ ۖ وَرَفَعَ بَعْضَهُمْ دَرَجَاتٍ ۚ وَآتَيْنَا عِيسَى ابْنَ مَرْيَمَ الْبَيِّنَاتِ وَأَيَّدْنَاهُ بِرُوحِ الْقُدُسِ ۗ وَلَوْ شَاءَ اللَّهُ مَا اقْتَتَلَ الَّذِينَ مِن بَعْدِهِم مِّن بَعْدِ مَا جَاءَتْهُمُ الْبَيِّنَاتُ وَلَٰكِنِ اخْتَلَفُوا فَمِنْهُم مَّنْ آمَنَ وَمِنْهُم مَّن كَفَرَ ۚ وَلَوْ شَاءَ اللَّهُ مَا اقْتَتَلُوا وَلَٰكِنَّ اللَّهَ يَفْعَلُ مَا يُرِيدُ ۞ يَا أَيُّهَا الَّذِينَ آمَنُوا أَنفِقُوا مِمَّا رَزَقْنَاكُم مِّن قَبْلِ أَن يَأْتِيَ يَوْمٌ لَّا بَيْعٌ فِيهِ وَلَا خُلَّةٌ وَلَا شَفَاعَةٌ ۗ وَالْكَافِرُونَ هُمُ الظَّالِمُونَ ۞ اللَّهُ لَا إِلَٰهَ إِلَّا هُوَ الْحَيُّ الْقَيُّومُ ۚ لَا تَأْخُذُهُ سِنَةٌ وَلَا نَوْمٌ ۚ لَّهُ مَا فِي السَّمَاوَاتِ وَمَا فِي الْأَرْضِ ۗ مَن ذَا الَّذِي يَشْفَعُ عِندَهُ إِلَّا بِإِذْنِهِ ۚ يَعْلَمُ مَا بَيْنَ أَيْدِيهِمْ وَمَا خَلْفَهُمْ ۖ وَلَا يُحِيطُونَ بِشَيْءٍ مِّنْ عِلْمِهِ إِلَّا بِمَا شَاءَ ۚ وَسِعَ كُرْسِيُّهُ السَّمَاوَاتِ وَالْأَرْضَ ۖ وَلَا يَئُودُهُ حِفْظُهُمَا ۚ وَهُوَ الْعَلِيُّ الْعَظِيمُ ۞ لَا إِكْرَاهَ فِي الدِّينِ ۖ قَد تَّبَيَّنَ الرُّشْدُ مِنَ الْغَيِّ ۚ فَمَن يَكْفُرْ بِالطَّاغُوتِ وَيُؤْمِن بِاللَّهِ فَقَدِ اسْتَمْسَكَ بِالْعُرْوَةِ الْوُثْقَىٰ لَا انفِصَامَ لَهَا ۗ وَاللَّهُ سَمِيعٌ عَلِيمٌ ۞ اللَّهُ وَلِيُّ الَّذِينَ آمَنُوا يُخْرِجُهُم مِّنَ الظُّلُمَاتِ إِلَى النُّورِ ۖ وَالَّذِينَ كَفَرُوا أَوْلِيَاؤُهُمُ الطَّاغُوتُ يُخْرِجُونَهُم مِّنَ النُّورِ إِلَى الظُّلُمَاتِ ۗ أُولَٰئِكَ أَصْحَابُ النَّارِ ۖ هُمْ فِيهَا خَالِدُونَ ۞ أَلَمْ تَرَ إِلَى الَّذِي حَاجَّ إِبْرَاهِيمَ فِي

رَبِّهِ أَنْ ءَاتَىٰهُ ٱللَّهُ ٱلْمُلْكَ إِذْ قَالَ إِبْرَٰهِۦمُ رَبِّيَ ٱلَّذِى يُحْىِۦ وَيُمِيتُ قَالَ أَنَا۠ أُحْىِۦ وَأُمِيتُ ۖ قَالَ إِبْرَٰهِۦمُ فَإِنَّ ٱللَّهَ يَأْتِى بِٱلشَّمْسِ مِنَ ٱلْمَشْرِقِ فَأْتِ بِهَا مِنَ ٱلْمَغْرِبِ فَبُهِتَ ٱلَّذِى كَفَرَ ۗ وَٱللَّهُ لَا يَهْدِى ٱلْقَوْمَ ٱلظَّٰلِمِينَ ۝ أَوْ كَٱلَّذِى مَرَّ عَلَىٰ قَرْيَةٍ وَهِىَ خَاوِيَةٌ عَلَىٰ عُرُوشِهَا قَالَ أَنَّىٰ يُحْىِۦ هَٰذِهِ ٱللَّهُ بَعْدَ مَوْتِهَا ۖ فَأَمَاتَهُ ٱللَّهُ مِا۟ئَةَ عَامٍ ثُمَّ بَعَثَهُۥ ۖ قَالَ كَمْ لَبِثْتَ ۖ قَالَ لَبِثْتُ يَوْمًا أَوْ بَعْضَ يَوْمٍ ۖ قَالَ بَل لَّبِثْتَ مِا۟ئَةَ عَامٍ فَٱنظُرْ إِلَىٰ طَعَامِكَ وَشَرَابِكَ لَمْ يَتَسَنَّهْ ۖ وَٱنظُرْ إِلَىٰ حِمَارِكَ وَلِنَجْعَلَكَ ءَايَةً لِّلنَّاسِ ۖ وَٱنظُرْ إِلَى ٱلْعِظَامِ كَيْفَ نُنشِزُهَا ثُمَّ نَكْسُوهَا لَحْمًا ۚ فَلَمَّا تَبَيَّنَ لَهُۥ قَالَ أَعْلَمُ أَنَّ ٱللَّهَ عَلَىٰ كُلِّ شَىْءٍ قَدِيرٌ ۝ وَإِذْ قَالَ إِبْرَٰهِۦمُ رَبِّ أَرِنِى كَيْفَ تُحْىِ ٱلْمَوْتَىٰ ۖ قَالَ أَوَلَمْ تُؤْمِن ۖ قَالَ بَلَىٰ وَلَٰكِن لِّيَطْمَئِنَّ قَلْبِى ۖ قَالَ فَخُذْ أَرْبَعَةً مِّنَ ٱلطَّيْرِ فَصُرْهُنَّ إِلَيْكَ ثُمَّ ٱجْعَلْ عَلَىٰ كُلِّ جَبَلٍ مِّنْهُنَّ جُزْءًا ثُمَّ ٱدْعُهُنَّ يَأْتِينَكَ سَعْيًا ۚ وَٱعْلَمْ أَنَّ ٱللَّهَ عَزِيزٌ حَكِيمٌ ۝ مَّثَلُ ٱلَّذِينَ يُنفِقُونَ أَمْوَٰلَهُمْ فِى سَبِيلِ ٱللَّهِ كَمَثَلِ حَبَّةٍ أَنۢبَتَتْ سَبْعَ سَنَابِلَ فِى كُلِّ سُنۢبُلَةٍ مِّا۟ئَةُ حَبَّةٍ ۗ وَٱللَّهُ يُضَٰعِفُ لِمَن يَشَآءُ ۗ وَٱللَّهُ وَٰسِعٌ عَلِيمٌ ۝ ٱلَّذِينَ يُنفِقُونَ أَمْوَٰلَهُمْ فِى سَبِيلِ ٱللَّهِ ثُمَّ لَا يُتْبِعُونَ مَآ أَنفَقُوا۟ مَنًّا وَلَآ أَذًى ۙ لَّهُمْ أَجْرُهُمْ عِندَ رَبِّهِمْ وَلَا خَوْفٌ عَلَيْهِمْ وَلَا هُمْ يَحْزَنُونَ ۝ قَوْلٌ مَّعْرُوفٌ وَمَغْفِرَةٌ خَيْرٌ مِّن صَدَقَةٍ يَتْبَعُهَآ أَذًى ۗ وَٱللَّهُ غَنِىٌّ حَلِيمٌ ۝ يَٰٓأَيُّهَا ٱلَّذِينَ ءَامَنُوا۟ لَا تُبْطِلُوا۟ صَدَقَٰتِكُم بِٱلْمَنِّ وَٱلْأَذَىٰ كَٱلَّذِى يُنفِقُ مَالَهُۥ رِئَآءَ ٱلنَّاسِ وَلَا يُؤْمِنُ بِٱللَّهِ وَٱلْيَوْمِ ٱلْءَاخِرِ ۖ فَمَثَلُهُۥ كَمَثَلِ صَفْوَانٍ عَلَيْهِ تُرَابٌ فَأَصَابَهُۥ وَابِلٌ فَتَرَكَهُۥ صَلْدًا ۖ لَّا يَقْدِرُونَ عَلَىٰ شَىْءٍ مِّمَّا كَسَبُوا۟ ۗ وَٱللَّهُ لَا يَهْدِى ٱلْقَوْمَ ٱلْكَٰفِرِينَ ۝ وَمَثَلُ ٱلَّذِينَ يُنفِقُونَ أَمْوَٰلَهُمُ ٱبْتِغَآءَ مَرْضَاتِ ٱللَّهِ وَتَثْبِيتًا مِّنْ أَنفُسِهِمْ

كَمَثَلِ جَنَّةٍ بِرَبْوَةٍ أَصَابَهَا وَابِلٌ فَآتَتْ أُكُلَهَا ضِعْفَيْنِ فَإِن لَّمْ يُصِبْهَا وَابِلٌ فَطَلٌّ ۗ وَاللَّهُ بِمَا تَعْمَلُونَ بَصِيرٌ ۝ أَيَوَدُّ أَحَدُكُمْ أَن تَكُونَ لَهُ جَنَّةٌ مِّن نَّخِيلٍ وَأَعْنَابٍ تَجْرِي مِن تَحْتِهَا الْأَنْهَارُ لَهُ فِيهَا مِن كُلِّ الثَّمَرَاتِ وَأَصَابَهُ الْكِبَرُ وَلَهُ ذُرِّيَّةٌ ضُعَفَاءُ فَأَصَابَهَا إِعْصَارٌ فِيهِ نَارٌ فَاحْتَرَقَتْ ۗ كَذَٰلِكَ يُبَيِّنُ اللَّهُ لَكُمُ الْآيَاتِ لَعَلَّكُمْ تَتَفَكَّرُونَ ۝ يَا أَيُّهَا الَّذِينَ آمَنُوا أَنفِقُوا مِن طَيِّبَاتِ مَا كَسَبْتُمْ وَمِمَّا أَخْرَجْنَا لَكُم مِّنَ الْأَرْضِ ۖ وَلَا تَيَمَّمُوا الْخَبِيثَ مِنْهُ تُنفِقُونَ وَلَسْتُم بِآخِذِيهِ إِلَّا أَن تُغْمِضُوا فِيهِ ۚ وَاعْلَمُوا أَنَّ اللَّهَ غَنِيٌّ حَمِيدٌ ۝ الشَّيْطَانُ يَعِدُكُمُ الْفَقْرَ وَيَأْمُرُكُم بِالْفَحْشَاءِ ۖ وَاللَّهُ يَعِدُكُم مَّغْفِرَةً مِّنْهُ وَفَضْلًا ۗ وَاللَّهُ وَاسِعٌ عَلِيمٌ ۝ يُؤْتِي الْحِكْمَةَ مَن يَشَاءُ ۚ وَمَن يُؤْتَ الْحِكْمَةَ فَقَدْ أُوتِيَ خَيْرًا كَثِيرًا ۗ وَمَا يَذَّكَّرُ إِلَّا أُولُو الْأَلْبَابِ ۝ وَمَا أَنفَقْتُم مِّن نَّفَقَةٍ أَوْ نَذَرْتُم مِّن نَّذْرٍ فَإِنَّ اللَّهَ يَعْلَمُهُ ۗ وَمَا لِلظَّالِمِينَ مِنْ أَنصَارٍ ۝ إِن تُبْدُوا الصَّدَقَاتِ فَنِعِمَّا هِيَ ۖ وَإِن تُخْفُوهَا وَتُؤْتُوهَا الْفُقَرَاءَ فَهُوَ خَيْرٌ لَّكُمْ ۚ وَيُكَفِّرُ عَنكُم مِّن سَيِّئَاتِكُمْ ۗ وَاللَّهُ بِمَا تَعْمَلُونَ خَبِيرٌ ۝ ۞ لَّيْسَ عَلَيْكَ هُدَاهُمْ وَلَٰكِنَّ اللَّهَ يَهْدِي مَن يَشَاءُ ۗ وَمَا تُنفِقُوا مِنْ خَيْرٍ فَلِأَنفُسِكُمْ ۚ وَمَا تُنفِقُونَ إِلَّا ابْتِغَاءَ وَجْهِ اللَّهِ ۚ وَمَا تُنفِقُوا مِنْ خَيْرٍ يُوَفَّ إِلَيْكُمْ وَأَنتُمْ لَا تُظْلَمُونَ ۝ لِلْفُقَرَاءِ الَّذِينَ أُحْصِرُوا فِي سَبِيلِ اللَّهِ لَا يَسْتَطِيعُونَ ضَرْبًا فِي الْأَرْضِ يَحْسَبُهُمُ الْجَاهِلُ أَغْنِيَاءَ مِنَ التَّعَفُّفِ تَعْرِفُهُم بِسِيمَاهُمْ لَا يَسْأَلُونَ النَّاسَ إِلْحَافًا ۗ وَمَا تُنفِقُوا مِنْ خَيْرٍ فَإِنَّ اللَّهَ بِهِ عَلِيمٌ ۝ الَّذِينَ يُنفِقُونَ أَمْوَالَهُم بِاللَّيْلِ وَالنَّهَارِ سِرًّا وَعَلَانِيَةً فَلَهُمْ أَجْرُهُمْ عِندَ رَبِّهِمْ وَلَا خَوْفٌ عَلَيْهِمْ وَلَا هُمْ يَحْزَنُونَ ۝

ٱلَّذِينَ يَأْكُلُونَ ٱلرِّبَوٰا۟ لَا يَقُومُونَ إِلَّا كَمَا يَقُومُ ٱلَّذِى يَتَخَبَّطُهُ ٱلشَّيْطَـٰنُ مِنَ ٱلْمَسِّ ۚ ذَٰلِكَ بِأَنَّهُمْ قَالُوٓا۟ إِنَّمَا ٱلْبَيْعُ مِثْلُ ٱلرِّبَوٰا۟ ۗ وَأَحَلَّ ٱللَّهُ ٱلْبَيْعَ وَحَرَّمَ ٱلرِّبَوٰا۟ ۚ فَمَن جَآءَهُۥ مَوْعِظَةٌ مِّن رَّبِّهِۦ فَٱنتَهَىٰ فَلَهُۥ مَا سَلَفَ وَأَمْرُهُۥٓ إِلَى ٱللَّهِ ۖ وَمَنْ عَادَ فَأُو۟لَـٰٓئِكَ أَصْحَـٰبُ ٱلنَّارِ ۖ هُمْ فِيهَا خَـٰلِدُونَ ۝٢٧٥ يَمْحَقُ ٱللَّهُ ٱلرِّبَوٰا۟ وَيُرْبِى ٱلصَّدَقَـٰتِ ۗ وَٱللَّهُ لَا يُحِبُّ كُلَّ كَفَّارٍ أَثِيمٍ ۝٢٧٦ إِنَّ ٱلَّذِينَ ءَامَنُوا۟ وَعَمِلُوا۟ ٱلصَّـٰلِحَـٰتِ وَأَقَامُوا۟ ٱلصَّلَوٰةَ وَءَاتَوُا۟ ٱلزَّكَوٰةَ لَهُمْ أَجْرُهُمْ عِندَ رَبِّهِمْ وَلَا خَوْفٌ عَلَيْهِمْ وَلَا هُمْ يَحْزَنُونَ ۝٢٧٧ يَـٰٓأَيُّهَا ٱلَّذِينَ ءَامَنُوا۟ ٱتَّقُوا۟ ٱللَّهَ وَذَرُوا۟ مَا بَقِىَ مِنَ ٱلرِّبَوٰٓا۟ إِن كُنتُم مُّؤْمِنِينَ ۝٢٧٨ فَإِن لَّمْ تَفْعَلُوا۟ فَأْذَنُوا۟ بِحَرْبٍ مِّنَ ٱللَّهِ وَرَسُولِهِۦ ۖ وَإِن تُبْتُمْ فَلَكُمْ رُءُوسُ أَمْوَٰلِكُمْ لَا تَظْلِمُونَ وَلَا تُظْلَمُونَ ۝٢٧٩ وَإِن كَانَ ذُو عُسْرَةٍ فَنَظِرَةٌ إِلَىٰ مَيْسَرَةٍ ۚ وَأَن تَصَدَّقُوا۟ خَيْرٌ لَّكُمْ ۖ إِن كُنتُمْ تَعْلَمُونَ ۝٢٨٠ وَٱتَّقُوا۟ يَوْمًا تُرْجَعُونَ فِيهِ إِلَى ٱللَّهِ ۖ ثُمَّ تُوَفَّىٰ كُلُّ نَفْسٍ مَّا كَسَبَتْ وَهُمْ لَا يُظْلَمُونَ ۝٢٨١ يَـٰٓأَيُّهَا ٱلَّذِينَ ءَامَنُوٓا۟ إِذَا تَدَايَنتُم بِدَيْنٍ إِلَىٰٓ أَجَلٍ مُّسَمًّى فَٱكْتُبُوهُ ۚ وَلْيَكْتُب بَّيْنَكُمْ كَاتِبٌۢ بِٱلْعَدْلِ ۚ وَلَا يَأْبَ كَاتِبٌ أَن يَكْتُبَ كَمَا عَلَّمَهُ ٱللَّهُ ۚ فَلْيَكْتُبْ وَلْيُمْلِلِ ٱلَّذِى عَلَيْهِ ٱلْحَقُّ وَلْيَتَّقِ ٱللَّهَ رَبَّهُۥ وَلَا يَبْخَسْ مِنْهُ شَيْـًٔا ۚ فَإِن كَانَ ٱلَّذِى عَلَيْهِ ٱلْحَقُّ سَفِيهًا أَوْ ضَعِيفًا أَوْ لَا يَسْتَطِيعُ أَن يُمِلَّ هُوَ فَلْيُمْلِلْ وَلِيُّهُۥ بِٱلْعَدْلِ ۚ وَٱسْتَشْهِدُوا۟ شَهِيدَيْنِ مِن رِّجَالِكُمْ ۖ فَإِن لَّمْ يَكُونَا رَجُلَيْنِ فَرَجُلٌ وَٱمْرَأَتَانِ مِمَّن تَرْضَوْنَ مِنَ ٱلشُّهَدَآءِ أَن تَضِلَّ إِحْدَىٰهُمَا فَتُذَكِّرَ إِحْدَىٰهُمَا ٱلْأُخْرَىٰ ۚ وَلَا يَأْبَ ٱلشُّهَدَآءُ إِذَا مَا دُعُوا۟ ۚ وَلَا تَسْـَٔمُوٓا۟ أَن تَكْتُبُوهُ صَغِيرًا أَوْ كَبِيرًا إِلَىٰٓ أَجَلِهِۦ ۚ ذَٰلِكُمْ أَقْسَطُ عِندَ ٱللَّهِ وَأَقْوَمُ لِلشَّهَـٰدَةِ وَأَدْنَىٰٓ أَلَّا تَرْتَابُوٓا۟ ۖ إِلَّآ أَن تَكُونَ تِجَـٰرَةً حَاضِرَةً تُدِيرُونَهَا

بَيْنَكُمْ فَلَيْسَ عَلَيْكُمْ جُنَاحٌ أَلَّا تَكْتُبُوهَا ۗ وَأَشْهِدُوٓا۟ إِذَا تَبَايَعْتُمْ ۚ وَلَا يُضَآرَّ كَاتِبٌ وَلَا شَهِيدٌ ۚ وَإِن تَفْعَلُوا۟ فَإِنَّهُۥ فُسُوقٌۢ بِكُمْ ۗ وَٱتَّقُوا۟ ٱللَّهَ ۖ وَيُعَلِّمُكُمُ ٱللَّهُ ۗ وَٱللَّهُ بِكُلِّ شَىْءٍ عَلِيمٌ ۝ وَإِن كُنتُمْ عَلَىٰ سَفَرٍ وَلَمْ تَجِدُوا۟ كَاتِبًا فَرِهَٰنٌ مَّقْبُوضَةٌ ۖ فَإِنْ أَمِنَ بَعْضُكُم بَعْضًا فَلْيُؤَدِّ ٱلَّذِى ٱؤْتُمِنَ أَمَٰنَتَهُۥ وَلْيَتَّقِ ٱللَّهَ رَبَّهُۥ ۗ وَلَا تَكْتُمُوا۟ ٱلشَّهَٰدَةَ ۚ وَمَن يَكْتُمْهَا فَإِنَّهُۥٓ ءَاثِمٌ قَلْبُهُۥ ۗ وَٱللَّهُ بِمَا تَعْمَلُونَ عَلِيمٌ ۝ لِّلَّهِ مَا فِى ٱلسَّمَٰوَٰتِ وَمَا فِى ٱلْأَرْضِ ۗ وَإِن تُبْدُوا۟ مَا فِىٓ أَنفُسِكُمْ أَوْ تُخْفُوهُ يُحَاسِبْكُم بِهِ ٱللَّهُ ۖ فَيَغْفِرُ لِمَن يَشَآءُ وَيُعَذِّبُ مَن يَشَآءُ ۗ وَٱللَّهُ عَلَىٰ كُلِّ شَىْءٍ قَدِيرٌ ۝ ءَامَنَ ٱلرَّسُولُ بِمَآ أُنزِلَ إِلَيْهِ مِن رَّبِّهِۦ وَٱلْمُؤْمِنُونَ ۚ كُلٌّ ءَامَنَ بِٱللَّهِ وَمَلَٰٓئِكَتِهِۦ وَكُتُبِهِۦ وَرُسُلِهِۦ لَا نُفَرِّقُ بَيْنَ أَحَدٍ مِّن رُّسُلِهِۦ ۚ وَقَالُوا۟ سَمِعْنَا وَأَطَعْنَا ۖ غُفْرَانَكَ رَبَّنَا وَإِلَيْكَ ٱلْمَصِيرُ ۝ لَا يُكَلِّفُ ٱللَّهُ نَفْسًا إِلَّا وُسْعَهَا ۚ لَهَا مَا كَسَبَتْ وَعَلَيْهَا مَا ٱكْتَسَبَتْ ۗ رَبَّنَا لَا تُؤَاخِذْنَآ إِن نَّسِينَآ أَوْ أَخْطَأْنَا ۚ رَبَّنَا وَلَا تَحْمِلْ عَلَيْنَآ إِصْرًا كَمَا حَمَلْتَهُۥ عَلَى ٱلَّذِينَ مِن قَبْلِنَا ۚ رَبَّنَا وَلَا تُحَمِّلْنَا مَا لَا طَاقَةَ لَنَا بِهِۦ ۖ وَٱعْفُ عَنَّا وَٱغْفِرْ لَنَا وَٱرْحَمْنَآ ۚ أَنتَ مَوْلَىٰنَا فَٱنصُرْنَا عَلَى ٱلْقَوْمِ ٱلْكَٰفِرِينَ ۝

(Al-Baqarah 253-286)

Chapter (Surah) 3: Al-i-'Imran 001-092

بِسْمِ ٱللَّهِ ٱلرَّحْمَٰنِ ٱلرَّحِيمِ

الٓمٓ ۝ ٱللَّهُ لَآ إِلَٰهَ إِلَّا هُوَ ٱلْحَىُّ ٱلْقَيُّومُ ۝ نَزَّلَ عَلَيْكَ ٱلْكِتَٰبَ بِٱلْحَقِّ مُصَدِّقًا لِّمَا بَيْنَ يَدَيْهِ وَأَنزَلَ ٱلتَّوْرَىٰةَ وَٱلْإِنجِيلَ ۝ مِن قَبْلُ هُدًى لِّلنَّاسِ وَأَنزَلَ ٱلْفُرْقَانَ ۗ إِنَّ ٱلَّذِينَ كَفَرُوا۟ بِـَٔايَٰتِ ٱللَّهِ لَهُمْ عَذَابٌ شَدِيدٌ ۗ وَٱللَّهُ عَزِيزٌ ذُو ٱنتِقَامٍ ۝ إِنَّ ٱللَّهَ لَا يَخْفَىٰ عَلَيْهِ شَىْءٌ فِى ٱلْأَرْضِ وَلَا فِى ٱلسَّمَآءِ ۝ هُوَ

ٱلَّذِى يُصَوِّرُكُمْ فِى ٱلْأَرْحَامِ كَيْفَ يَشَآءُ ۚ لَآ إِلَٰهَ إِلَّا هُوَ ٱلْعَزِيزُ ٱلْحَكِيمُ ۝ هُوَ ٱلَّذِىٓ أَنزَلَ عَلَيْكَ ٱلْكِتَٰبَ مِنْهُ ءَايَٰتٌ مُّحْكَمَٰتٌ هُنَّ أُمُّ ٱلْكِتَٰبِ وَأُخَرُ مُتَشَٰبِهَٰتٌ ۖ فَأَمَّا ٱلَّذِينَ فِى قُلُوبِهِمْ زَيْغٌ فَيَتَّبِعُونَ مَا تَشَٰبَهَ مِنْهُ ٱبْتِغَآءَ ٱلْفِتْنَةِ وَٱبْتِغَآءَ تَأْوِيلِهِۦ ۗ وَمَا يَعْلَمُ تَأْوِيلَهُۥٓ إِلَّا ٱللَّهُ ۗ وَٱلرَّٰسِخُونَ فِى ٱلْعِلْمِ يَقُولُونَ ءَامَنَّا بِهِۦ كُلٌّ مِّنْ عِندِ رَبِّنَا ۗ وَمَا يَذَّكَّرُ إِلَّآ أُوْلُواْ ٱلْأَلْبَٰبِ ۝ رَبَّنَا لَا تُزِغْ قُلُوبَنَا بَعْدَ إِذْ هَدَيْتَنَا وَهَبْ لَنَا مِن لَّدُنكَ رَحْمَةً ۚ إِنَّكَ أَنتَ ٱلْوَهَّابُ ۝ رَبَّنَآ إِنَّكَ جَامِعُ ٱلنَّاسِ لِيَوْمٍ لَّا رَيْبَ فِيهِ ۚ إِنَّ ٱللَّهَ لَا يُخْلِفُ ٱلْمِيعَادَ ۝ إِنَّ ٱلَّذِينَ كَفَرُواْ لَن تُغْنِىَ عَنْهُمْ أَمْوَٰلُهُمْ وَلَآ أَوْلَٰدُهُم مِّنَ ٱللَّهِ شَيْـًٔا ۖ وَأُوْلَٰٓئِكَ هُمْ وَقُودُ ٱلنَّارِ ۝ كَدَأْبِ ءَالِ فِرْعَوْنَ وَٱلَّذِينَ مِن قَبْلِهِمْ ۚ كَذَّبُواْ بِـَٔايَٰتِنَا فَأَخَذَهُمُ ٱللَّهُ بِذُنُوبِهِمْ ۗ وَٱللَّهُ شَدِيدُ ٱلْعِقَابِ ۝ قُل لِّلَّذِينَ كَفَرُواْ سَتُغْلَبُونَ وَتُحْشَرُونَ إِلَىٰ جَهَنَّمَ ۚ وَبِئْسَ ٱلْمِهَادُ ۝ قَدْ كَانَ لَكُمْ ءَايَةٌ فِى فِئَتَيْنِ ٱلْتَقَتَا ۖ فِئَةٌ تُقَٰتِلُ فِى سَبِيلِ ٱللَّهِ وَأُخْرَىٰ كَافِرَةٌ يَرَوْنَهُم مِّثْلَيْهِمْ رَأْىَ ٱلْعَيْنِ ۚ وَٱللَّهُ يُؤَيِّدُ بِنَصْرِهِۦ مَن يَشَآءُ ۗ إِنَّ فِى ذَٰلِكَ لَعِبْرَةً لِّأُوْلِى ٱلْأَبْصَٰرِ ۝ زُيِّنَ لِلنَّاسِ حُبُّ ٱلشَّهَوَٰتِ مِنَ ٱلنِّسَآءِ وَٱلْبَنِينَ وَٱلْقَنَٰطِيرِ ٱلْمُقَنطَرَةِ مِنَ ٱلذَّهَبِ وَٱلْفِضَّةِ وَٱلْخَيْلِ ٱلْمُسَوَّمَةِ وَٱلْأَنْعَٰمِ وَٱلْحَرْثِ ۗ ذَٰلِكَ مَتَٰعُ ٱلْحَيَوٰةِ ٱلدُّنْيَا ۖ وَٱللَّهُ عِندَهُۥ حُسْنُ ٱلْمَـَٔابِ ۝ ۞ قُلْ أَؤُنَبِّئُكُم بِخَيْرٍ مِّن ذَٰلِكُمْ ۚ لِلَّذِينَ ٱتَّقَوْاْ عِندَ رَبِّهِمْ جَنَّٰتٌ تَجْرِى مِن تَحْتِهَا ٱلْأَنْهَٰرُ خَٰلِدِينَ فِيهَا وَأَزْوَٰجٌ مُّطَهَّرَةٌ وَرِضْوَٰنٌ مِّنَ ٱللَّهِ ۗ وَٱللَّهُ بَصِيرٌۢ بِٱلْعِبَادِ ۝ ٱلَّذِينَ يَقُولُونَ رَبَّنَآ إِنَّنَآ ءَامَنَّا فَٱغْفِرْ لَنَا ذُنُوبَنَا وَقِنَا عَذَابَ ٱلنَّارِ ۝ ٱلصَّٰبِرِينَ وَٱلصَّٰدِقِينَ وَٱلْقَٰنِتِينَ وَٱلْمُنفِقِينَ وَٱلْمُسْتَغْفِرِينَ بِٱلْأَسْحَارِ ۝ شَهِدَ ٱللَّهُ أَنَّهُۥ لَآ إِلَٰهَ إِلَّا هُوَ وَٱلْمَلَٰٓئِكَةُ وَأُوْلُواْ ٱلْعِلْمِ قَآئِمًۢا بِٱلْقِسْطِ ۚ لَآ إِلَٰهَ

إِلَّا هُوَ ٱلْعَزِيزُ ٱلْحَكِيمُ ۝ إِنَّ ٱلدِّينَ عِندَ ٱللَّهِ ٱلْإِسْلَمُ ۗ وَمَا ٱخْتَلَفَ ٱلَّذِينَ أُوتُوا۟ ٱلْكِتَبَ إِلَّا مِنۢ بَعْدِ مَا جَآءَهُمُ ٱلْعِلْمُ بَغْيًۢا بَيْنَهُمْ ۗ وَمَن يَكْفُرْ بِـَٔايَتِ ٱللَّهِ فَإِنَّ ٱللَّهَ سَرِيعُ ٱلْحِسَابِ ۝ فَإِنْ حَآجُّوكَ فَقُلْ أَسْلَمْتُ وَجْهِىَ لِلَّهِ وَمَنِ ٱتَّبَعَنِ ۗ وَقُل لِّلَّذِينَ أُوتُوا۟ ٱلْكِتَبَ وَٱلْأُمِّيِّـۧنَ ءَأَسْلَمْتُمْ ۚ فَإِنْ أَسْلَمُوا۟ فَقَدِ ٱهْتَدَوا۟ ۖ وَّإِن تَوَلَّوْا۟ فَإِنَّمَا عَلَيْكَ ٱلْبَلَغُ ۗ وَٱللَّهُ بَصِيرٌۢ بِٱلْعِبَادِ ۝ إِنَّ ٱلَّذِينَ يَكْفُرُونَ بِـَٔايَتِ ٱللَّهِ وَيَقْتُلُونَ ٱلنَّبِيِّـۧنَ بِغَيْرِ حَقٍّ وَيَقْتُلُونَ ٱلَّذِينَ يَأْمُرُونَ بِٱلْقِسْطِ مِنَ ٱلنَّاسِ فَبَشِّرْهُم بِعَذَابٍ أَلِيمٍ ۝ أُو۟لَٰٓئِكَ ٱلَّذِينَ حَبِطَتْ أَعْمَلُهُمْ فِى ٱلدُّنْيَا وَٱلْـَٔاخِرَةِ وَمَا لَهُم مِّن نَّصِرِينَ ۝ أَلَمْ تَرَ إِلَى ٱلَّذِينَ أُوتُوا۟ نَصِيبًا مِّنَ ٱلْكِتَبِ يُدْعَوْنَ إِلَىٰ كِتَبِ ٱللَّهِ لِيَحْكُمَ بَيْنَهُمْ ثُمَّ يَتَوَلَّىٰ فَرِيقٌ مِّنْهُمْ وَهُم مُّعْرِضُونَ ۝ ذَٰلِكَ بِأَنَّهُمْ قَالُوا۟ لَن تَمَسَّنَا ٱلنَّارُ إِلَّآ أَيَّامًا مَّعْدُودَٰتٍ ۖ وَغَرَّهُمْ فِى دِينِهِم مَّا كَانُوا۟ يَفْتَرُونَ ۝ فَكَيْفَ إِذَا جَمَعْنَهُمْ لِيَوْمٍ لَّا رَيْبَ فِيهِ وَوُفِّيَتْ كُلُّ نَفْسٍ مَّا كَسَبَتْ وَهُمْ لَا يُظْلَمُونَ ۝ قُلِ ٱللَّهُمَّ مَلِكَ ٱلْمُلْكِ تُؤْتِى ٱلْمُلْكَ مَن تَشَآءُ وَتَنزِعُ ٱلْمُلْكَ مِمَّن تَشَآءُ وَتُعِزُّ مَن تَشَآءُ وَتُذِلُّ مَن تَشَآءُ ۖ بِيَدِكَ ٱلْخَيْرُ ۖ إِنَّكَ عَلَىٰ كُلِّ شَىْءٍ قَدِيرٌ ۝ تُولِجُ ٱلَّيْلَ فِى ٱلنَّهَارِ وَتُولِجُ ٱلنَّهَارَ فِى ٱلَّيْلِ ۖ وَتُخْرِجُ ٱلْحَىَّ مِنَ ٱلْمَيِّتِ وَتُخْرِجُ ٱلْمَيِّتَ مِنَ ٱلْحَىِّ ۖ وَتَرْزُقُ مَن تَشَآءُ بِغَيْرِ حِسَابٍ ۝ لَّا يَتَّخِذِ ٱلْمُؤْمِنُونَ ٱلْكَفِرِينَ أَوْلِيَآءَ مِن دُونِ ٱلْمُؤْمِنِينَ ۖ وَمَن يَفْعَلْ ذَٰلِكَ فَلَيْسَ مِنَ ٱللَّهِ فِى شَىْءٍ إِلَّآ أَن تَتَّقُوا۟ مِنْهُمْ تُقَىٰةً ۗ وَيُحَذِّرُكُمُ ٱللَّهُ نَفْسَهُۥ ۗ وَإِلَى ٱللَّهِ ٱلْمَصِيرُ ۝ قُلْ إِن تُخْفُوا۟ مَا فِى صُدُورِكُمْ أَوْ تُبْدُوهُ يَعْلَمْهُ ٱللَّهُ ۗ وَيَعْلَمُ مَا فِى ٱلسَّمَوَٰتِ وَمَا فِى ٱلْأَرْضِ ۗ وَٱللَّهُ عَلَىٰ كُلِّ شَىْءٍ قَدِيرٌ ۝ يَوْمَ تَجِدُ كُلُّ نَفْسٍ مَّا عَمِلَتْ مِنْ خَيْرٍ مُّحْضَرًا وَمَا عَمِلَتْ مِن سُوٓءٍ تَوَدُّ لَوْ أَنَّ

بَيْنَهَا وَبَيْنَهُ أَمَدًۢا بَعِيدًا ۗ وَيُحَذِّرُكُمُ ٱللَّهُ نَفْسَهُۥ ۗ وَٱللَّهُ رَءُوفٌۢ بِٱلْعِبَادِ ۝ قُلْ إِن كُنتُمْ تُحِبُّونَ ٱللَّهَ فَٱتَّبِعُونِى يُحْبِبْكُمُ ٱللَّهُ وَيَغْفِرْ لَكُمْ ذُنُوبَكُمْ ۗ وَٱللَّهُ غَفُورٌ رَّحِيمٌ ۝ قُلْ أَطِيعُوا۟ ٱللَّهَ وَٱلرَّسُولَ ۖ فَإِن تَوَلَّوْا۟ فَإِنَّ ٱللَّهَ لَا يُحِبُّ ٱلْكَـٰفِرِينَ ۝ ۞ إِنَّ ٱللَّهَ ٱصْطَفَىٰٓ ءَادَمَ وَنُوحًا وَءَالَ إِبْرَٰهِيمَ وَءَالَ عِمْرَٰنَ عَلَى ٱلْعَـٰلَمِينَ ۝ ذُرِّيَّةًۢ بَعْضُهَا مِنۢ بَعْضٍ ۗ وَٱللَّهُ سَمِيعٌ عَلِيمٌ ۝ إِذْ قَالَتِ ٱمْرَأَتُ عِمْرَٰنَ رَبِّ إِنِّى نَذَرْتُ لَكَ مَا فِى بَطْنِى مُحَرَّرًا فَتَقَبَّلْ مِنِّىٓ ۖ إِنَّكَ أَنتَ ٱلسَّمِيعُ ٱلْعَلِيمُ ۝ فَلَمَّا وَضَعَتْهَا قَالَتْ رَبِّ إِنِّى وَضَعْتُهَآ أُنثَىٰ وَٱللَّهُ أَعْلَمُ بِمَا وَضَعَتْ وَلَيْسَ ٱلذَّكَرُ كَٱلْأُنثَىٰ ۖ وَإِنِّى سَمَّيْتُهَا مَرْيَمَ وَإِنِّىٓ أُعِيذُهَا بِكَ وَذُرِّيَّتَهَا مِنَ ٱلشَّيْطَـٰنِ ٱلرَّجِيمِ ۝ فَتَقَبَّلَهَا رَبُّهَا بِقَبُولٍ حَسَنٍ وَأَنۢبَتَهَا نَبَاتًا حَسَنًا وَكَفَّلَهَا زَكَرِيَّا ۖ كُلَّمَا دَخَلَ عَلَيْهَا زَكَرِيَّا ٱلْمِحْرَابَ وَجَدَ عِندَهَا رِزْقًا ۖ قَالَ يَـٰمَرْيَمُ أَنَّىٰ لَكِ هَـٰذَا ۖ قَالَتْ هُوَ مِنْ عِندِ ٱللَّهِ ۖ إِنَّ ٱللَّهَ يَرْزُقُ مَن يَشَآءُ بِغَيْرِ حِسَابٍ ۝ هُنَالِكَ دَعَا زَكَرِيَّا رَبَّهُۥ ۖ قَالَ رَبِّ هَبْ لِى مِن لَّدُنكَ ذُرِّيَّةً طَيِّبَةً ۖ إِنَّكَ سَمِيعُ ٱلدُّعَآءِ ۝ فَنَادَتْهُ ٱلْمَلَـٰٓئِكَةُ وَهُوَ قَآئِمٌ يُصَلِّى فِى ٱلْمِحْرَابِ أَنَّ ٱللَّهَ يُبَشِّرُكَ بِيَحْيَىٰ مُصَدِّقًۢا بِكَلِمَةٍ مِّنَ ٱللَّهِ وَسَيِّدًا وَحَصُورًا وَنَبِيًّا مِّنَ ٱلصَّـٰلِحِينَ ۝ قَالَ رَبِّ أَنَّىٰ يَكُونُ لِى غُلَـٰمٌ وَقَدْ بَلَغَنِىَ ٱلْكِبَرُ وَٱمْرَأَتِى عَاقِرٌ ۖ قَالَ كَذَٰلِكَ ٱللَّهُ يَفْعَلُ مَا يَشَآءُ ۝ قَالَ رَبِّ ٱجْعَل لِّىٓ ءَايَةً ۖ قَالَ ءَايَتُكَ أَلَّا تُكَلِّمَ ٱلنَّاسَ ثَلَـٰثَةَ أَيَّامٍ إِلَّا رَمْزًا ۗ وَٱذْكُر رَّبَّكَ كَثِيرًا وَسَبِّحْ بِٱلْعَشِىِّ وَٱلْإِبْكَـٰرِ ۝ وَإِذْ قَالَتِ ٱلْمَلَـٰٓئِكَةُ يَـٰمَرْيَمُ إِنَّ ٱللَّهَ ٱصْطَفَىٰكِ وَطَهَّرَكِ وَٱصْطَفَىٰكِ عَلَىٰ نِسَآءِ ٱلْعَـٰلَمِينَ ۝ يَـٰمَرْيَمُ ٱقْنُتِى لِرَبِّكِ وَٱسْجُدِى وَٱرْكَعِى مَعَ ٱلرَّٰكِعِينَ ۝ ذَٰلِكَ مِنْ أَنۢبَآءِ ٱلْغَيْبِ نُوحِيهِ إِلَيْكَ ۚ وَمَا كُنتَ لَدَيْهِمْ إِذْ يُلْقُونَ أَقْلَـٰمَهُمْ أَيُّهُمْ يَكْفُلُ مَرْيَمَ وَمَا كُنتَ لَدَيْهِمْ إِذْ يَخْتَصِمُونَ ۝ إِذْ قَالَتِ ٱلْمَلَـٰٓئِكَةُ يَـٰمَرْيَمُ إِنَّ ٱللَّهَ يُبَشِّرُكِ بِكَلِمَةٍ

مِنْهُ ٱسْمُهُ ٱلْمَسِيحُ عِيسَى ٱبْنُ مَرْيَمَ وَجِيهًا فِى ٱلدُّنْيَا وَٱلْآخِرَةِ وَمِنَ ٱلْمُقَرَّبِينَ ۝ وَيُكَلِّمُ ٱلنَّاسَ فِى ٱلْمَهْدِ وَكَهْلًا وَمِنَ ٱلصَّالِحِينَ ۝ قَالَتْ رَبِّ أَنَّىٰ يَكُونُ لِى وَلَدٌ وَلَمْ يَمْسَسْنِى بَشَرٌ ۖ قَالَ كَذَٰلِكِ ٱللَّهُ يَخْلُقُ مَا يَشَآءُ ۚ إِذَا قَضَىٰ أَمْرًا فَإِنَّمَا يَقُولُ لَهُۥ كُن فَيَكُونُ ۝ وَيُعَلِّمُهُ ٱلْكِتَٰبَ وَٱلْحِكْمَةَ وَٱلتَّوْرَىٰةَ وَٱلْإِنجِيلَ ۝ وَرَسُولًا إِلَىٰ بَنِىٓ إِسْرَٰٓءِيلَ أَنِّى قَدْ جِئْتُكُم بِـَٔايَةٍ مِّن رَّبِّكُمْ ۖ أَنِّىٓ أَخْلُقُ لَكُم مِّنَ ٱلطِّينِ كَهَيْـَٔةِ ٱلطَّيْرِ فَأَنفُخُ فِيهِ فَيَكُونُ طَيْرًۢا بِإِذْنِ ٱللَّهِ ۖ وَأُبْرِئُ ٱلْأَكْمَهَ وَٱلْأَبْرَصَ وَأُحْىِ ٱلْمَوْتَىٰ بِإِذْنِ ٱللَّهِ ۖ وَأُنَبِّئُكُم بِمَا تَأْكُلُونَ وَمَا تَدَّخِرُونَ فِى بُيُوتِكُمْ ۚ إِنَّ فِى ذَٰلِكَ لَـَٔايَةً لَّكُمْ إِن كُنتُم مُّؤْمِنِينَ ۝ وَمُصَدِّقًا لِّمَا بَيْنَ يَدَىَّ مِنَ ٱلتَّوْرَىٰةِ وَلِأُحِلَّ لَكُم بَعْضَ ٱلَّذِى حُرِّمَ عَلَيْكُمْ ۚ وَجِئْتُكُم بِـَٔايَةٍ مِّن رَّبِّكُمْ فَٱتَّقُوا۟ ٱللَّهَ وَأَطِيعُونِ ۝ إِنَّ ٱللَّهَ رَبِّى وَرَبُّكُمْ فَٱعْبُدُوهُ ۚ هَـٰذَا صِرَٰطٌ مُّسْتَقِيمٌ ۝ ۞ فَلَمَّآ أَحَسَّ عِيسَىٰ مِنْهُمُ ٱلْكُفْرَ قَالَ مَنْ أَنصَارِىٓ إِلَى ٱللَّهِ ۖ قَالَ ٱلْحَوَارِيُّونَ نَحْنُ أَنصَارُ ٱللَّهِ ءَامَنَّا بِٱللَّهِ وَٱشْهَدْ بِأَنَّا مُسْلِمُونَ ۝ رَبَّنَآ ءَامَنَّا بِمَآ أَنزَلْتَ وَٱتَّبَعْنَا ٱلرَّسُولَ فَٱكْتُبْنَا مَعَ ٱلشَّـٰهِدِينَ ۝ وَمَكَرُوا۟ وَمَكَرَ ٱللَّهُ ۖ وَٱللَّهُ خَيْرُ ٱلْمَـٰكِرِينَ ۝ إِذْ قَالَ ٱللَّهُ يَـٰعِيسَىٰٓ إِنِّى مُتَوَفِّيكَ وَرَافِعُكَ إِلَىَّ وَمُطَهِّرُكَ مِنَ ٱلَّذِينَ كَفَرُوا۟ وَجَاعِلُ ٱلَّذِينَ ٱتَّبَعُوكَ فَوْقَ ٱلَّذِينَ كَفَرُوٓا۟ إِلَىٰ يَوْمِ ٱلْقِيَـٰمَةِ ۖ ثُمَّ إِلَىَّ مَرْجِعُكُمْ فَأَحْكُمُ بَيْنَكُمْ فِيمَا كُنتُمْ فِيهِ تَخْتَلِفُونَ ۝ فَأَمَّا ٱلَّذِينَ كَفَرُوا۟ فَأُعَذِّبُهُمْ عَذَابًا شَدِيدًا فِى ٱلدُّنْيَا وَٱلْآخِرَةِ وَمَا لَهُم مِّن نَّـٰصِرِينَ ۝ وَأَمَّا ٱلَّذِينَ ءَامَنُوا۟ وَعَمِلُوا۟ ٱلصَّـٰلِحَـٰتِ فَيُوَفِّيهِمْ أُجُورَهُمْ ۗ وَٱللَّهُ لَا يُحِبُّ ٱلظَّـٰلِمِينَ ۝ ذَٰلِكَ نَتْلُوهُ عَلَيْكَ مِنَ ٱلْـَٔايَـٰتِ وَٱلذِّكْرِ ٱلْحَكِيمِ ۝ إِنَّ مَثَلَ عِيسَىٰ عِندَ ٱللَّهِ كَمَثَلِ ءَادَمَ ۖ خَلَقَهُۥ مِن تُرَابٍ ثُمَّ قَالَ لَهُۥ كُن فَيَكُونُ ۝

ٱلْحَقُّ مِن رَّبِّكَ فَلَا تَكُن مِّنَ ٱلْمُمْتَرِينَ ۝ فَمَنْ حَآجَّكَ فِيهِ مِنۢ بَعْدِ مَا جَآءَكَ مِنَ ٱلْعِلْمِ فَقُلْ تَعَالَوْا۟ نَدْعُ أَبْنَآءَنَا وَأَبْنَآءَكُمْ وَنِسَآءَنَا وَنِسَآءَكُمْ وَأَنفُسَنَا وَأَنفُسَكُمْ ثُمَّ نَبْتَهِلْ فَنَجْعَل لَّعْنَتَ ٱللَّهِ عَلَى ٱلْكَٰذِبِينَ ۝ إِنَّ هَٰذَا لَهُوَ ٱلْقَصَصُ ٱلْحَقُّ ۚ وَمَا مِنْ إِلَٰهٍ إِلَّا ٱللَّهُ ۚ وَإِنَّ ٱللَّهَ لَهُوَ ٱلْعَزِيزُ ٱلْحَكِيمُ ۝ فَإِن تَوَلَّوْا۟ فَإِنَّ ٱللَّهَ عَلِيمٌۢ بِٱلْمُفْسِدِينَ ۝ قُلْ يَٰٓأَهْلَ ٱلْكِتَٰبِ تَعَالَوْا۟ إِلَىٰ كَلِمَةٍ سَوَآءٍۭ بَيْنَنَا وَبَيْنَكُمْ أَلَّا نَعْبُدَ إِلَّا ٱللَّهَ وَلَا نُشْرِكَ بِهِۦ شَيْـًٔا وَلَا يَتَّخِذَ بَعْضُنَا بَعْضًا أَرْبَابًا مِّن دُونِ ٱللَّهِ ۚ فَإِن تَوَلَّوْا۟ فَقُولُوا۟ ٱشْهَدُوا۟ بِأَنَّا مُسْلِمُونَ ۝ يَٰٓأَهْلَ ٱلْكِتَٰبِ لِمَ تُحَآجُّونَ فِىٓ إِبْرَٰهِيمَ وَمَآ أُنزِلَتِ ٱلتَّوْرَىٰةُ وَٱلْإِنجِيلُ إِلَّا مِنۢ بَعْدِهِۦٓ ۚ أَفَلَا تَعْقِلُونَ ۝ هَٰٓأَنتُمْ هَٰٓؤُلَآءِ حَٰجَجْتُمْ فِيمَا لَكُم بِهِۦ عِلْمٌ فَلِمَ تُحَآجُّونَ فِيمَا لَيْسَ لَكُم بِهِۦ عِلْمٌ ۚ وَٱللَّهُ يَعْلَمُ وَأَنتُمْ لَا تَعْلَمُونَ ۝ مَا كَانَ إِبْرَٰهِيمُ يَهُودِيًّا وَلَا نَصْرَانِيًّا وَلَٰكِن كَانَ حَنِيفًا مُّسْلِمًا وَمَا كَانَ مِنَ ٱلْمُشْرِكِينَ ۝ إِنَّ أَوْلَى ٱلنَّاسِ بِإِبْرَٰهِيمَ لَلَّذِينَ ٱتَّبَعُوهُ وَهَٰذَا ٱلنَّبِىُّ وَٱلَّذِينَ ءَامَنُوا۟ ۗ وَٱللَّهُ وَلِىُّ ٱلْمُؤْمِنِينَ ۝ وَدَّت طَّآئِفَةٌ مِّنْ أَهْلِ ٱلْكِتَٰبِ لَوْ يُضِلُّونَكُمْ وَمَا يُضِلُّونَ إِلَّآ أَنفُسَهُمْ وَمَا يَشْعُرُونَ ۝ يَٰٓأَهْلَ ٱلْكِتَٰبِ لِمَ تَكْفُرُونَ بِـَٔايَٰتِ ٱللَّهِ وَأَنتُمْ تَشْهَدُونَ ۝ يَٰٓأَهْلَ ٱلْكِتَٰبِ لِمَ تَلْبِسُونَ ٱلْحَقَّ بِٱلْبَٰطِلِ وَتَكْتُمُونَ ٱلْحَقَّ وَأَنتُمْ تَعْلَمُونَ ۝ وَقَالَت طَّآئِفَةٌ مِّنْ أَهْلِ ٱلْكِتَٰبِ ءَامِنُوا۟ بِٱلَّذِىٓ أُنزِلَ عَلَى ٱلَّذِينَ ءَامَنُوا۟ وَجْهَ ٱلنَّهَارِ وَٱكْفُرُوٓا۟ ءَاخِرَهُۥ لَعَلَّهُمْ يَرْجِعُونَ ۝ وَلَا تُؤْمِنُوٓا۟ إِلَّا لِمَن تَبِعَ دِينَكُمْ قُلْ إِنَّ ٱلْهُدَىٰ هُدَى ٱللَّهِ أَن يُؤْتَىٰٓ أَحَدٌ مِّثْلَ مَآ أُوتِيتُمْ أَوْ يُحَآجُّوكُمْ عِندَ رَبِّكُمْ ۗ قُلْ إِنَّ ٱلْفَضْلَ بِيَدِ ٱللَّهِ يُؤْتِيهِ مَن يَشَآءُ ۗ وَٱللَّهُ وَٰسِعٌ عَلِيمٌ ۝ يَخْتَصُّ بِرَحْمَتِهِۦ مَن يَشَآءُ ۗ وَٱللَّهُ ذُو ٱلْفَضْلِ ٱلْعَظِيمِ ۝ ۞ وَمِنْ أَهْلِ ٱلْكِتَٰبِ مَنْ إِن تَأْمَنْهُ بِقِنطَارٍ يُؤَدِّهِۦٓ إِلَيْكَ

وَمِنْهُم مَّنْ إِن تَأْمَنْهُ بِدِينَارٍ لَّا يُؤَدِّهِۦٓ إِلَيْكَ إِلَّا مَا دُمْتَ عَلَيْهِ قَآئِمًا ۗ ذَٰلِكَ بِأَنَّهُمْ قَالُوا۟ لَيْسَ عَلَيْنَا فِى ٱلْأُمِّيِّـۧنَ سَبِيلٌ وَيَقُولُونَ عَلَى ٱللَّهِ ٱلْكَذِبَ وَهُمْ يَعْلَمُونَ ۝ بَلَىٰ مَنْ أَوْفَىٰ بِعَهْدِهِۦ وَٱتَّقَىٰ فَإِنَّ ٱللَّهَ يُحِبُّ ٱلْمُتَّقِينَ ۝ إِنَّ ٱلَّذِينَ يَشْتَرُونَ بِعَهْدِ ٱللَّهِ وَأَيْمَٰنِهِمْ ثَمَنًا قَلِيلًا أُو۟لَٰٓئِكَ لَا خَلَٰقَ لَهُمْ فِى ٱلْءَاخِرَةِ وَلَا يُكَلِّمُهُمُ ٱللَّهُ وَلَا يَنظُرُ إِلَيْهِمْ يَوْمَ ٱلْقِيَٰمَةِ وَلَا يُزَكِّيهِمْ وَلَهُمْ عَذَابٌ أَلِيمٌ ۝ وَإِنَّ مِنْهُمْ لَفَرِيقًا يَلْوُۥنَ أَلْسِنَتَهُم بِٱلْكِتَٰبِ لِتَحْسَبُوهُ مِنَ ٱلْكِتَٰبِ وَمَا هُوَ مِنَ ٱلْكِتَٰبِ وَيَقُولُونَ هُوَ مِنْ عِندِ ٱللَّهِ وَمَا هُوَ مِنْ عِندِ ٱللَّهِ وَيَقُولُونَ عَلَى ٱللَّهِ ٱلْكَذِبَ وَهُمْ يَعْلَمُونَ ۝ مَا كَانَ لِبَشَرٍ أَن يُؤْتِيَهُ ٱللَّهُ ٱلْكِتَٰبَ وَٱلْحُكْمَ وَٱلنُّبُوَّةَ ثُمَّ يَقُولَ لِلنَّاسِ كُونُوا۟ عِبَادًا لِّى مِن دُونِ ٱللَّهِ وَلَٰكِن كُونُوا۟ رَبَّٰنِيِّـۧنَ بِمَا كُنتُمْ تُعَلِّمُونَ ٱلْكِتَٰبَ وَبِمَا كُنتُمْ تَدْرُسُونَ ۝ وَلَا يَأْمُرَكُمْ أَن تَتَّخِذُوا۟ ٱلْمَلَٰٓئِكَةَ وَٱلنَّبِيِّـۧنَ أَرْبَابًا ۗ أَيَأْمُرُكُم بِٱلْكُفْرِ بَعْدَ إِذْ أَنتُم مُّسْلِمُونَ ۝ وَإِذْ أَخَذَ ٱللَّهُ مِيثَٰقَ ٱلنَّبِيِّـۧنَ لَمَآ ءَاتَيْتُكُم مِّن كِتَٰبٍ وَحِكْمَةٍ ثُمَّ جَآءَكُمْ رَسُولٌ مُّصَدِّقٌ لِّمَا مَعَكُمْ لَتُؤْمِنُنَّ بِهِۦ وَلَتَنصُرُنَّهُۥ ۚ قَالَ ءَأَقْرَرْتُمْ وَأَخَذْتُمْ عَلَىٰ ذَٰلِكُمْ إِصْرِى ۖ قَالُوٓا۟ أَقْرَرْنَا ۚ قَالَ فَٱشْهَدُوا۟ وَأَنَا۠ مَعَكُم مِّنَ ٱلشَّٰهِدِينَ ۝ فَمَن تَوَلَّىٰ بَعْدَ ذَٰلِكَ فَأُو۟لَٰٓئِكَ هُمُ ٱلْفَٰسِقُونَ ۝ أَفَغَيْرَ دِينِ ٱللَّهِ يَبْغُونَ وَلَهُۥٓ أَسْلَمَ مَن فِى ٱلسَّمَٰوَٰتِ وَٱلْأَرْضِ طَوْعًا وَكَرْهًا وَإِلَيْهِ يُرْجَعُونَ ۝ قُلْ ءَامَنَّا بِٱللَّهِ وَمَآ أُنزِلَ عَلَيْنَا وَمَآ أُنزِلَ عَلَىٰٓ إِبْرَٰهِيمَ وَإِسْمَٰعِيلَ وَإِسْحَٰقَ وَيَعْقُوبَ وَٱلْأَسْبَاطِ وَمَآ أُوتِىَ مُوسَىٰ وَعِيسَىٰ وَٱلنَّبِيُّونَ مِن رَّبِّهِمْ لَا نُفَرِّقُ بَيْنَ أَحَدٍ مِّنْهُمْ وَنَحْنُ لَهُۥ مُسْلِمُونَ ۝ وَمَن يَبْتَغِ غَيْرَ ٱلْإِسْلَٰمِ دِينًا فَلَن يُقْبَلَ مِنْهُ وَهُوَ فِى ٱلْءَاخِرَةِ مِنَ ٱلْخَٰسِرِينَ ۝ كَيْفَ يَهْدِى ٱللَّهُ قَوْمًا كَفَرُوا۟ بَعْدَ إِيمَٰنِهِمْ وَشَهِدُوٓا۟ أَنَّ ٱلرَّسُولَ حَقٌّ وَجَآءَهُمُ ٱلْبَيِّنَٰتُ ۚ

$$\text{وَٱللَّهُ لَا يَهْدِى ٱلْقَوْمَ ٱلظَّٰلِمِينَ ۝ أُو۟لَٰٓئِكَ جَزَآؤُهُمْ أَنَّ عَلَيْهِمْ لَعْنَةَ ٱللَّهِ وَٱلْمَلَٰٓئِكَةِ وَٱلنَّاسِ أَجْمَعِينَ ۝ خَٰلِدِينَ فِيهَا لَا يُخَفَّفُ عَنْهُمُ ٱلْعَذَابُ وَلَا هُمْ يُنظَرُونَ ۝ إِلَّا ٱلَّذِينَ تَابُوا۟ مِنۢ بَعْدِ ذَٰلِكَ وَأَصْلَحُوا۟ فَإِنَّ ٱللَّهَ غَفُورٌ رَّحِيمٌ ۝ إِنَّ ٱلَّذِينَ كَفَرُوا۟ بَعْدَ إِيمَٰنِهِمْ ثُمَّ ٱزْدَادُوا۟ كُفْرًا لَّن تُقْبَلَ تَوْبَتُهُمْ وَأُو۟لَٰٓئِكَ هُمُ ٱلضَّآلُّونَ ۝ إِنَّ ٱلَّذِينَ كَفَرُوا۟ وَمَاتُوا۟ وَهُمْ كُفَّارٌ فَلَن يُقْبَلَ مِنْ أَحَدِهِم مِّلْءُ ٱلْأَرْضِ ذَهَبًا وَلَوِ ٱفْتَدَىٰ بِهِۦٓ ۗ أُو۟لَٰٓئِكَ لَهُمْ عَذَابٌ أَلِيمٌ وَمَا لَهُم مِّن نَّٰصِرِينَ ۝ لَن تَنَالُوا۟ ٱلْبِرَّ حَتَّىٰ تُنفِقُوا۟ مِمَّا تُحِبُّونَ ۚ وَمَا تُنفِقُوا۟ مِن شَىْءٍ فَإِنَّ ٱللَّهَ بِهِۦ عَلِيمٌ ۝}$$

(Al-i-'Imran 001-092)

INTRODUCTION TO CHAPTER (SURAH) 2: AL-BAQARAH (THE COW)

Ibn Kathir's Introduction

The Virtues of Surat Al-Baqarah

The Virtues of Surat Al-Baqarah

In Musnad Ahmad, Sahih Muslim, At-Tirmidhi and An-Nasa'i, it is recorded that Abu Hurayrah said that the Prophet said,

«لَا تَجْعَلُوا بُيُوتَكُمْ قُبُورًا فَإِنَّ الْبَيْتَ الَّذِي تُقْرَأُ فِيهِ سُورَةُ الْبَقَرَةِ لَا يَدْخُلُهُ الشَّيْطَان»

(Do not turn your houses into graves. Verily, Shaytan does not enter the house where Surat Al-Baqarah is recited.) At-Tirmidhi said, "Hasan Sahih.

Also, `Abdullah bin Mas`ud said, "Shaytan flees from the house where Surat Al-Baqarah is heard." This Hadith was collected by An-Nasa'i in Al-Yawm wal-Laylah, and Al-Hakim recorded it in his Mustadrak, and then said that its chain of narration is authentic, although the Two Sahihs did not collect it. In his Musnad, Ad-Darimi recorded that Ibn Mas`ud said, "Shaytan departs the house where Surat Al-Baqarah is being recited, and as he leaves, he passes gas." Ad-Darimi also recorded that Ash-Sha`bi said that `Abdullah bin Mas`ud said, "Whoever recites ten Ayat from Surat Al-

Baqarah in a night, then Shaytan will not enter his house that night. (These ten Ayat are) four from the beginning, Ayat Al-Kursi (255), the following two Ayat (256-257) and the last three Ayat." In another narration, Ibn Mas`ud said, "Then Shaytan will not come near him or his family, nor will he be touched by anything that he dislikes. Also, if these Ayat were to be recited over a senile person, they would wake him up."

Further, Sahl bin Sa`d said that the Messenger of Allah said,

«إِنَّ لِكُلِّ شَيْءٍ سَنَامًا، وَإِنَّ سَنَامَ الْقُرْآنِ الْبَقَرَةُ، وَإِنَّ مَنْ قَرَأَهَا فِي بَيْتِهِ لَيْلَةً لَمْ يَدْخُلْهُ الشَّيْطَانُ ثَلَاثَ لَيَالٍ، وَمَنْ قَرَأَهَا فِي بَيْتِهِ نَهَارًا لَمْ يَدْخُلْهُ الشَّيْطَانُ ثَلَاثَةَ أَيَّامٍ»

(Everything has a hump (or, high peek), and Al-Baqarah is the high peek of the Qur'an. Whoever recites Al-Baqarah at night in his house, then Shaytan will not enter that house for three nights. Whoever recites it during a day in his house, then Shaytan will not enter that house for three days.) This Hadith was collected by Abu Al-Qasim At-Tabarani, Abu Hatim Ibn Hibban in his Sahih and Ibn Marduwyah.

At-Tirmidhi, An-Nasa'i and Ibn Majah recorded that Abu Hurayrah said, "The Messenger of Allah sent an expedition force comprising of many men and asked each about what they memorized of the Qur'an. The Prophet came to one of the youngest men among them and asked him, `What have you memorized (of the Qur'an) young man' He said, `I memorized such and such Surahs and also Al-Baqarah.' The Prophet said, `You memorized Surat Al-Baqarah' He said, `Yes.' The Prophet said, `Then you are their commander.' One of the noted men (or chiefs) commented, `By Allah! I did not learn Surat Al-Baqarah, for fear that I would not be able to implement it. The Messenger of Allah said,

«تَعَلَّمُوا الْقُرْآنَ وَاقْرَءُوهُ، فَإِنَّ مَثَلَ الْقُرْآنِ لِمَنْ تَعَلَّمَهُ فَقَرَأَ وَقَامَ بِهِ كَمَثَلِ جِرَابٍ مَحْشُوٍّ مِسْكًا يَفُوحُ رِيحُهُ فِي كُلِّ مَكَانٍ، وَمَثَلُ مَنْ تَعَلَّمَهُ فَيَرْقُدُ وَهُوَ فِي جَوْفِهِ كَمَثَلِ جِرَابٍ أُوكِيَ عَلَى مِسْكٍ»

(Learn Al-Qur'an and recite it, for the example of whoever learns the Qur'an, recites it and adheres to it, is the example of a bag that is full of musk whose scent fills the air. The example of whoever learns the Qur'an and then sleeps (i.e. lazy) while the Qur'an is in his memory, is the example of a bag that has musk, but is closed tight.)

This is the wording collected by At-Tirmidhi, who said that this Hadith is Hasan. In another narration, At-Tirmidhi recorded this same Hadith in a Mursal manner, so Allah knows best.

Also, Al-Bukhari recorded that Usayd bin Hudayr said that he was once reciting Surat Al-Baqarah while his horse was tied next to him. The horse started to make some noise. When Usayd stopped reciting, the horse stopped moving about. When he resumed reading, the horse started moving about again. When he stopped reciting, the horse stopped moving, and when he resumed reading, the horse started to move again. Meanwhile, his son Yahya was close to the horse, and he feared that the horse might step on him. When he moved his son back, he looked up to the sky and saw a cloud radiating with light that looked like lamps. In the morning, he went to the Prophet and told him what had happened and then said, "O Messenger of Allah! My son Yahya was close to the horse and I feared that she might step on him. When I attended to him and raised my head to the sky, I saw a cloud with lights like lamps. So I went, but I couldn't see it." The Prophet said, "Do you know what that was" He said, "No." The Prophet said,

«تِلْكَ الْمَلَائِكَةُ دَنَتْ لِصَوْتِكَ وَلَو قَرَأْتَ لَأَصْبَحْتَ يَنْظُرُ النَّاسُ إِلَيْهَا، لَا تَتَوَارَى مِنْهُم»

(They were the angels, they came close hearing your voice (reciting Surat Al-Baqarah), and if you had kept reading, the people would have been able to see the angels when the morning came, and the angels would not be hidden from their eyes.)

This is the narration reported by Imam Abu Ubayd Al-Qasim bin Salam in his book Fada'il Al-Qur'an.

Virtues of Surat Al-Baqarah and Surat Al `Imran

Imam Ahmad said that Abu Nu`aym narrated to them that Bishr bin Muhajir said that `Abdullah bin Buraydah narrated to him from his father, "I was sitting with the Prophet and I heard him say,

«تَعَلَّمُوا سُورَةَ الْبَقَرَةِ فَإِنَّ أَخْذَهَا بَرَكَةٌ، وَتَرْكَهَا حَسْرَةٌ، وَلَا تَسْتَطِيعُهَا الْبَطَلَةُ»

(Learn Surat Al-Baqarah, because in learning it there is blessing, in ignoring it there is sorrow, and the sorceresses cannot memorize it.)

He kept silent for a while and then said,

«تَعَلَّمُوا سُورَةَ الْبَقَرَةِ وَآلَ عِمْرَانَ فَإِنَّهُمَا الزَّهْرَاوَانِ، يُظِلَّانِ صَاحِبَهُمَا يَوْمَ الْقِيَامَةِ كَأَنَّهُمَا غَمَامَتَانِ أَوْ غَيَايَتَانِ أَوْ فِرْقَانِ مِنْ طَيْرٍ صَوَافَّ، وَإِنَّ الْقُرْآنَ يَلْقَى صَاحِبَهُ يَوْمَ الْقِيَامَةِ حِينَ يَنْشَقُّ عَنْهُ قَبْرُهُ كَالرَّجُلِ الشَّاحِبِ فَيَقُولُ لَهُ:»

Chapter 2: Al-Baqarah (The Cow), Verses 253-286

هَلْ تَعْرِفُنِي؟ فَيَقُولُ: مَا أَعْرِفُكَ. فَيَقُولُ: أَنَا صَاحِبُكَ الْقُرْآنُ الَّذِي أَظْمَأْتُكَ فِي الْهَوَاجِرِ وَأَسْهَرْتُ لَيْلَكَ وَإِنَّ كُلَّ تَاجِرٍ مِنْ وَرَاءِ تِجَارَتِهِ، وَإِنَّكَ الْيَوْمَ مِنْ وَرَاءِ كُلِّ تِجَارَةٍ فَيُعْطَى الْمُلْكَ بِيَمِينِهِ وَالْخُلْدَ بِشِمَالِهِ وَيُوضَعُ عَلَى رَأْسِهِ تَاجُ الْوَقَارِ، وَيُكْسَى وَالِدَاهُ حُلَّتَانِ لَا يَقُومُ لَهُمَا أَهْلُ الدُّنْيَا، فَيَقُولَانِ: بِمَا كُسِينَا هَذَا؟ فَيُقَالُ: بِأَخْذِ وَلَدِكُمَا الْقُرْآنَ ثُمَّ يُقَالُ: اقْرَأْ وَاصْعَدْ فِي دَرَجِ الْجَنَّةِ وَغُرَفِهَا، فَهُوَ فِي صُعُودٍ مَا دَامَ يَقْرَأُ هَذًّا كَانَ أَوْ تَرْتِيلًا»

(Learn Surat Al-Baqarah and Al `Imran because they are two lights and they shade their people on the Day of Resurrection, just as two clouds, two spaces of shade or two lines of (flying) birds. The Qur'an will meet its companion in the shape of a pale-faced man on the Day of Resurrection when his grave is opened. The Qur'an will ask him, 'Do you know me' The man will say, 'I do not know you.' The Qur'an will say, 'I am your companion, the Qur'an, which has brought you thirst during the heat and made you stay up during the night. Every merchant has his certain trade. But, this Day, you are behind all types of trade.' Kingship will then be given to him in his right hand, eternal life in his left hand and the crown of grace will be placed on his head. His parents will also be granted two garments that the people of this life could never afford. They will say, 'Why were we granted these garments' It will be said, 'Because your son was carrying the Qur'an.' It will be said (to the reader of the Qur'an), 'Read and ascend through the levels of Paradise.' He will go on ascending as long as he recites, whether reciting slowly or quickly.)''

Ibn Majah also recorded part of this Hadith from Bishr bin Al-Muhajir, and this chain of narrators is Hasan, according to the criteria of Imam Muslim.

A part of this Hadith is also supported by other Hadiths. For instance, Imam Ahmad recorded that Abu Umamah Al-Bahili said that he heard the Messenger of Allah say,

«اقْرَأُوا الْقُرْآنَ فَإِنَّهُ شَافِعٌ لِأَهْلِهِ يَوْمَ الْقِيَامَةِ اقْرَأُوا الزَّهْرَاوَيْنِ، الْبَقَرَةَ وَآلَ عِمْرَانَ، فَإِنَّهُمَا يَأْتِيَانِ يَوْمَ الْقِيَامَةِ كَأَنَّهُمَا غَمَامَتَانِ، أَوْ كَأَنَّهُمَا غَيَايَتَانِ أَوْ كَأَنَّهُمَا فِرْقَانِ مِنْ طَيْرٍ صَوَافَّ، يُحَاجَّانِ عَنْ أَهْلِهِمَا يَوْمَ الْقِيَامَةِ»

(Read the Qur'an, because it will intercede on behalf of its people on the Day of Resurrection. Read the two lights, Al-Baqarah and Al `Imran, because they will come in the shape of two clouds, two shades or two lines of birds on the Day of Resurrection and will argue on behalf of their people on that Day.)

The Prophet then said,

«اقْرَأُوا الْبَقَرَةَ فَإِنَّ أَخْذَهَا بَرَكَةٌ وَتَرْكَهَا حَسْرَةٌ وَلَا تَسْتَطِيعُهَا الْبَطَلَةُ»

(Read Al-Baqarah, because in having it there is blessing, and in ignoring there is a sorrow and the sorceresses cannot memorize it.)

Also, Imam Muslim narrated this Hadith in the Book of Prayer

Imam Ahmad narrated that An-Nawwas bin Sam`an said that the Prophet said,

«يُؤْتَى بِالْقُرْآنِ يَوْمَ الْقِيَامَةِ وَأَهْلِهِ الَّذِينَ كَانُوا يَعْمَلُونَ بِهِ تَقْدَمُهُمْ سُورَةُ الْبَقَرَةِ وَآلُ عِمْرَانَ»

(On the Day of Resurrection the Qur'an and its people who used to implement it will be brought forth, preceded by Surat Al-Baqarah and Al `Imran.)

An-Nawwas said, "The Prophet set three examples for these two Surahs and I did not forget these examples ever since. He said,

«كَأَنَّهُمَا غَمَامَتَانِ، أَوْ ظُلَّتَانِ سَودَاوَانِ بَيْنَهُمَا شَرْقٌ، أَوْ كَأَنَّهُمَا فِرْقَانِ مِنْ طَيْرٍ صَوَافَّ، يُحَاجَّانِ عَنْ صَاحِبِهِمَا»

(They will come like two clouds, two dark shades or two lines of birds arguing on behalf of their people.)

It was also recorded in Sahih Muslim and At-Tirmidhi narrated this Hadith, which he rendered Hasan Gharib.

Surat Al-Baqarah was revealed in Al-Madinah

There is no disagreement over the view that Surat Al-Baqarah was revealed in its entirety in Al-Madinah. Moreover, Al-Baqarah was one of the first Surahs to be revealed in Al-Madinah, while, Allah's statement,

(And be afraid of the Day when you shall be brought back to Allah.) (2:281) was the last Ayah to be revealed from the Qur'an. Also, the Ayat about usury were among the last Ayat to be revealed. Khalid bin Ma`dan used to call Al-Baqarah the Fustat (tent) of the Qur'an. Some of the scholars said that it contains a thousand news incidents, a thousand commands and a thousand prohibitions. Those who count said that the number of Al-Baqarah's Ayat is two hundred and eighty-seven, and its words are six thousand two hundred and twenty-one words. Further, its letters are twenty-five thousand five hundred. Allah knows best.

Ibn Jurayj narrated that `Ata' said that Ibn `Abbas said, "Surat Al-Baqarah was revealed in Al-Madinah." Also, Khasif said from Mujahid that `Abdullah bin Az-Zubayr said; "Surat Al-Baqarah was revealed in Al-Madinah." Several Imams and scholars of Tafsir issued similar statements, and there is no difference of opinion over this as we have stated.

The Two Sahihs recorded that Ibn Mas`ud kept the Ka`bah on his left side and Mina on his right side and threw seven pebbles (at the Jamrah) and said, "The one to whom Surat Al-Baqarah was revealed (i.e. the Prophet) performed Rami (the Hajj rite of throwing pebbles) similarly." The Two Sahihs recorded this Hadith.

Further, Ibn Marduwyah reported a Hadith of Shu`bah from `Aqil bin Talhah from `Utbah bin Marthad; "The Prophet saw that his Companions were not in the first lines and he said,

«يَا أَصْحَابَ سُورَةِ الْبَقَرَةِ»

(O Companions of Surat Al-Baqarah.) I Think that this incident occurred during the battle of Hunayn when the Companions retreated. Then, the Prophet commanded Al-`Abbas (his uncle) to yell out,

«يَا أَصْحَابَ الشَّجَرَةِ»

(O Companions of the tree!) meaning the Companions who participated in the pledge of Ar-Ridwan (under the tree). In another narration, Al-`Abbas cried, "O Companions of Surat Al-Baqarah!" encouraging them to come back, so they returned from every direction. Also, during the battle of Al-Yamamah, against the army of Musaylimah the Liar, the Companions first retreated because of the huge number of soldiers in Musaylimah's army. The Muhajirun and the Ansar called out for each other, saying; "O people of Surat Al-Baqarah!" Allah then gave them victory over their enemy, may Allah be pleased with all of the companions of all the Messengers of Allah.

CHAPTER (SURAH) 2: AL-BAQARAH (THE COW), VERSES 253-286

Surah: 2 Ayah: 253

﴿ تِلْكَ ٱلرُّسُلُ فَضَّلْنَا بَعْضَهُمْ عَلَىٰ بَعْضٍ مِّنْهُم مَّن كَلَّمَ ٱللَّهُ وَرَفَعَ بَعْضَهُمْ دَرَجَـٰتٍ وَءَاتَيْنَا عِيسَى ٱبْنَ مَرْيَمَ ٱلْبَيِّنَـٰتِ وَأَيَّدْنَـٰهُ بِرُوحِ ٱلْقُدُسِ وَلَوْ شَآءَ ٱللَّهُ مَا

$$\text{ٱقْتَتَلَ ٱلَّذِينَ مِنْ بَعْدِهِم مِّنْ بَعْدِ مَا جَآءَتْهُمُ ٱلْبَيِّنَـٰتُ وَلَـٰكِنِ ٱخْتَلَفُواْ فَمِنْهُم مَّنْ ءَامَنَ وَمِنْهُم مَّن كَفَرَ وَلَوْ شَآءَ ٱللَّهُ مَا ٱقْتَتَلُواْ وَلَـٰكِنَّ ٱللَّهَ يَفْعَلُ مَا يُرِيدُ ﴿٢٥٣﴾}$$

253. Those Messengers! We preferred some to others; to some of them Allâh spoke (directly); others He raised to degrees (of honor); and to 'Isâ (Jesus), the son of Maryam (Mary), We gave clear proofs and evidences, and supported him with Rûh-ul-Qudus (Jibrael (Gabriel)) If Allâh had willed, succeeding generations would not have fought against each other, after clear Verses of Allâh had come to them, but they differed - some of them believed and others disbelieved. If Allâh had willed, they would not have fought against one another, but Allâh does what He likes.

Transliteration

253. Tilka alrrusulu faddalna baAAdahum AAala baAAdin minhum man kallama Allahu warafaAAa baAAdahum darajatin waatayna AAeesa ibna maryama albayyinati waayyadnahu biroohi alqudusi walaw shaa Allahu ma iqtatala allatheena min baAAdihim min baAAdi ma jaat-humu albayyinatu walakini ikhtalafoo faminhum man amana waminhum man kafara walaw shaa Allahu ma iqtataloo walakinna Allaha yafAAalu ma yureedu

Tafsir Ibn Kathir

Allah Honored Some Prophets Above Others

Allah states that He has honored some Prophets to others. For instance, Allah said,

(And indeed, We have preferred some of the Prophets above others, and to Dawud We gave the Zabur (Psalms)) (17:55).

In the Ayah above, Allah said,

(Those Messengers! We preferred some of them to others; to some of them Allah spoke (directly)) meaning, Musa and Muhammad , and also Adam according to a Hadith recorded in Sahih Ibn Hibban from Abu Dharr.

(Others He raised to degrees (of honor)) as is evident in the Hadith about the Isra' journey, when the Messenger of Allah saw the Prophets in the various heavens according to their rank with Allah.

If somebody asks about the collective meaning of this Ayah and the Hadith that the Two Sahihs collected from Abu Hurayrah which states, "Once, a Muslim man and a Jew had an argument and the Jew said, `No, by Him Who gave Musa superiority over all human beings!' Hearing him, the Muslim man raised his hand and slapped the Jew on his face and said, `Over Muhammad too, O evil one!' The Jew went to the Prophet and complained to him and the Prophet said,

$$\text{«لَا تُفَضِّلُونِي عَلَى الْأَنْبِيَاءِ، فَإِنَّ النَّاسَ يَصْعَقُونَ يَوْمَ الْقِيَامَةِ فَأَكُونُ أَوَّلَ مَنْ}$$

$$\text{يُفِيقُ، فَأَجِدُ مُوسَى بَاطِشًا بِقَائِمَةِ الْعَرْشِ، فَلَا أَدْرِي أَفَاقَ قَبْلِي أَمْ جُوزِيَ بِصَعْقَةِ الطُّورِ؟ فَلَا تُفَضِّلُونِي عَلَى الْأَنْبِيَاءِ»}$$

(Don't give me superiority above the Prophets, for the people will become unconscious on the Day of Resurrection, and I will be the first to be resurrected to see Musa holding on to the pillar of Allah's Throne. I will not know whether the unconsciousness Musa suffered on the Day of the Trumpet sufficed for him, or if he got up before me. So, do not give me superiority above the Prophets.) In another narration, the Prophet said, (Do not give superiority to some Prophets above others.)

The answer to this question is that this Hadith prohibits preferring some Prophets above others in cases of dispute and argument, such as the incident mentioned in the Hadith. The Hadith indicates that it is not up to creation to decide which Prophet is better, for this is Allah's decision. The creation is only required to submit to, obey and believe in Allah's decision.

Allah's statement,

(And We gave `Isa, the son of Maryam, clear signs) refers to the proofs and unequivocal evidences that testify to the truth that `Isa delivered to the Children of Israel, thus testifying that he was Allah's servant and His Messenger to them.

(And supported him with Ruh-il-Qudus) meaning Allah aided `Isa with Jibil, peace be upon him. Allah then said,

(If Allah had willed, succeeding generations would not have fought against each other, after clear Verses of Allah had come to them, but they differed - some of them believed and others disbelieved. If Allah had willed, they would not have fought against one another.) meaning all this happened by Allah's decree, and this is why He said next,

(But Allah does what He wills.)

Surah: 2 Ayah: 254

$$\text{﴿ يَٰٓأَيُّهَا ٱلَّذِينَ ءَامَنُوٓاْ أَنفِقُواْ مِمَّا رَزَقۡنَٰكُم مِّن قَبۡلِ أَن يَأۡتِيَ يَوۡمٌ لَّا بَيۡعٌ فِيهِ وَلَا خُلَّةٌ وَلَا شَفَٰعَةٌۗ وَٱلۡكَٰفِرُونَ هُمُ ٱلظَّٰلِمُونَ ﴾}$$

254. O you who believe! Spend of that with which We have provided for you, before a Day comes when there will be no bargaining, nor friendship, nor intercession. And it is the disbelievers who are the Zâlimûn (wrongdoers).

Transliteration

254. Ya ayyuha allatheena amanoo anfiqoo mimma razaqnakum min qabli an ya/tiya yawmun la bayAAun feehi wala khullatun wala shafaAAatun waalkafiroona humu alththalimoona

Tafsir Ibn Kathir

Allah commands His servants to spend for His sake, in the path of righteousness, from what He has granted them, so that they acquire and keep the reward of this righteous deed with their Lord and King. Let them rush to perform this deed in this life,

(before a Day comes) meaning, the Day of Resurrection,

(when there will be no bargaining, nor friendship, nor intercession.)

This Ayah indicates that on that Day, no one will be able to bargain on behalf of himself or ransom himself with any amount, even if it was the earth's fill of gold; nor will his friendship or relation to anyone benefit him. Similarly, Allah said,

(Then, when the Trumpet is blown, there will be no kinship among them that Day, nor will they ask of one another) (23:101).

(Nor intercession) meaning, they will not benefit by the intercession of anyone.

Allah's statement,

(and it is the disbelievers who are the wrongdoers) indicates that no injustice is worse than meeting Allah on that Day while a disbeliever. Ibn Abi Hatim recorded that `Ata' bin Dinar said, "All thanks are due to Allah Who said,

(and it is the disbelievers who are the wrongdoers) but did not say, `And it is the wrongdoers who are the disbelievers.'"

Surah: 2 Ayah: 255

﴿ ٱللَّهُ لَآ إِلَٰهَ إِلَّا هُوَ ٱلۡحَىُّ ٱلۡقَيُّومُ لَا تَأۡخُذُهُۥ سِنَةٞ وَلَا نَوۡمٞ لَّهُۥ مَا فِى ٱلسَّمَٰوَٰتِ وَمَا فِى ٱلۡأَرۡضِ مَن ذَا ٱلَّذِى يَشۡفَعُ عِندَهُۥٓ إِلَّا بِإِذۡنِهِۦ يَعۡلَمُ مَا بَيۡنَ أَيۡدِيهِمۡ وَمَا خَلۡفَهُمۡ وَلَا يُحِيطُونَ بِشَىۡءٖ مِّنۡ عِلۡمِهِۦٓ إِلَّا بِمَا شَآءَ وَسِعَ كُرۡسِيُّهُ ٱلسَّمَٰوَٰتِ وَٱلۡأَرۡضَ وَلَا يَـُٔودُهُۥ حِفۡظُهُمَا وَهُوَ ٱلۡعَلِىُّ ٱلۡعَظِيمُ ﴾

255. Allâh! Lâ ilâha illa Huwa (none has the right to be worshipped but He), the Ever Living, the One Who sustains and protects all that exists. Neither slumber, nor sleep overtake Him. To Him belongs whatever is in the heavens and whatever is on earth. Who is he that can intercede with Him except with His Permission? He knows what happens to them (His creatures) in this world, and what will happen to them in the Hereafter. And they will never compass anything of His Knowledge

except that which He wills. His Kursî extends over the heavens and the earth, and He feels no fatigue in guarding and preserving them. And He is the Most High, the Most Great. (This Verse 2:255 is called Ayat-ul-Kursî.)

Transliteration

255. Allahu la ilaha illa huwa alhayyu alqayyoomu la ta/khuthuhu sinatun wala nawmun lahu ma fee alssamawati wama fee al-ardi man tha allathee yashfaAAu AAindahu illa bi-ithnihi yaAAlamu ma bayna aydeehim wama khalfahum wala yuheetoona bishay-in min AAilmihi illa bima shaa wasiAAa kursiyyuhu alssamawati waal-arda wala yaooduhu hif*th*uhuma wahuwa alAAaliyyu alAAa*th*eemu

Tafsir Ibn Kathir

The Virtue of Ayat Al-Kursi

This is Ayat Al-Kursi and tremendous virtues have been associated with it, for the authentic Hadith describes it as `the greatest Ayah in the Book of Allah.' Imam Ahmad recorded that `Ubayy bin Ka`b said that the Prophet asked him about the greatest Ayah in the Book of Allah, and `Ubayy answered, "Allah and His Messenger know better." When the Prophet repeated his question several times, `Ubayy said, "Ayat Al-Kursi." The Prophet commented,

»لِيَهْنِكَ الْعِلْمُ أَبَا الْمُنْذِرِ، وَالَّذِي نَفْسِي بِيَدِهِ، إِنَّ لَهَا لِسَانًا وَشَفَتَيْنِ، تُقَدِّسُ الْمَلِكَ عِنْدَ سَاقِ الْعَرْشِ«

(Congratulations for having knowledge, O Abu Al-Mundhir! By He in Whose Hand is my soul! This Ayah has a tongue and two lips with which she praises the King (Allah) next to the leg of the Throne.)

This Hadith was also collected by Muslim, but he did not include the part that starts with, "By He in Whose Hand..."

Imam Ahmad recorded that Abu Ayyub said that he had some dates and a Ghoul used to take some, and he complained to the Prophet. The Prophet said to him, "When you see her, say, `In the Name of Allah, answer to the Messenger of Allah'." Abu Ayyub said that when she came again, he said these words and he was able to grab her. She begged, "I will not come again," so Abu Ayyub released her. Abu Ayyub went to the Prophet and the Prophet asked him, "What did your prisoner do" Abu Ayyub said, "I grabbed her and she said twice, `I will not come again,' and I released her." The Prophet said, "She will come back." Abu Ayyub said, "So I grabbed her twice or three times, yet each time (I would release her when) she vowed not to come back. I would go to the Prophet who would ask me, `What is the news of your prisoner' I would say, `I grabbed her, then released her when she said that she would not return.' The Prophet would say that she would return. Once, I grabbed her and she said, `Release me and I will teach you something to recite so that no harm touches you, that is, Ayat Al-Kursi.' Abu Ayyub went to the Prophet and told him, and the Prophet said, "She is liar, but she told the truth." At-Tirmidhi recorded this Hadith in the chapter of the virtues of the Qur'an and said, "Hasan Gharib." In Arabic, `Ghoul' refers to the Jinn when they appear at night.

Al-Bukhari recorded a similar story in his Sahih from Abu Hurayrah, in the chapters on the virtues of the Qur'an and the description of Shaytan. In this narration, Abu Hurayrah said,

"Allah's Messenger assigned me to keep watch over the Sadaqah (charity) of Ramadan. A person snuck in and started taking handfuls of foodstuff. I caught him and said, `By Allah, I will take you to Allah's Messenger.' He said, `Release me, for I am meek and have many dependents and am in great need.' I released him, and in the morning Allah's Messenger asked me, `What did your prisoner do yesterday, O Abu Hurayrah' I said, `O Allah's Messenger! He complained of being needy and of having many dependents, so I pitied him and let him go.' Allah's Messenger said, `Indeed, he told you a lie and will be coming again.' I believed that he would show up again, for Allah's Messenger had told me that he would return. So, I watched for him. When he (showed up and) started stealing handfuls of foodstuff, I caught hold of him again and said, `I will definitely take you to Allah's Messenger.' He said, `Leave me, for I am very needy and have many dependents. I promise I will not come back again.' I pitied him and let him go. In the morning Allah's Messenger asked me, `What did your prisoner do last night, O Abu Hurayrah!' I replied, `O Allah's Messenger! He complained of his great need and of too many dependents, so I took pity on him and set him free.' Allah's Messenger said, `Verily, he told you a lie; he will return.' I waited for him attentively for the third time, and when he (came and) started stealing handfuls of the foodstuff, I caught hold of him and said, `I will surely take you to Allah's Messenger as it is the third time you promised not to return, yet you returned.' He said, `Let me teach you some words which Allah will give you benefit from.' I asked, `What are they' He replied, `Whenever you go to bed, recite Ayat Al-Kursi- Allahu la ilaha illa Huwal-Hayyul-Qayyum, till you finish the whole verse. (If you do so), Allah will appoint a guard for you who will stay with you, and no Shaytan will come near you until morning.' So, I released him. In the morning, Allah's Messenger asked, `What did your prisoner do yesterday' I replied, `O Allah's Messenger! He claimed that he would teach me some words by which Allah will grant me some benefit, so I let him go.' Allah's Messenger asked, `What are they' I replied, `He said to me: Whenever you go to bed, recite Ayat Al-Kursi from the beginning to the end, Allahu la ilaha illa Huwal-Hayyul-Qayyum. He further said to me: (If you do so), Allah will appoint a guard for you who will stay with you, and no Shaytan will come near you until morning.' (One of the narrators) then commented that they (the Companions) were very keen to do good deeds. The Prophet said, `He spoke the truth, although he is a liar. Do you know whom you were talking to, these three nights, O Abu Hurayrah' Abu Hurayrah said, `No.' He said, `It was Shaytan.'" An-Nasa'i also recorded this Hadith in Al-Yawm wa Al-Laylah.

Allah's Greatest Name is in Ayat Al-Kursi

Imam Ahmad recorded that Asma' bint Yazid bin As-Sakan said, "I heard the Messenger of Allah say about these two Ayat,

(Allah! None has the right to be worshipped but He, the Ever Living, the One Who sustains and protects all that exists) (2:255), and,

(Alif-Lam-Mim. Allah! None has the right to be worshipped but He, the Ever Living, the One Who sustains and protects all that exists) (3:1-2),

«إِنَّ فِيهِمَا اسْمَ اللهِ الْأَعْظَمِ»

(They contain Allah's Greatest Name.)

This is also the narration collected by Abu Dawud, At-Tirmidhi and Ibn Majah, and At-Tirmidhi said, "Hasan Sahih".

Further, Ibn Marduwyah recorded that Abu Umamah reported that the Prophet said,

«اسْمُ اللهِ الْأَعْظَمُ، الَّذِي إِذَا دُعِيَ بِهِ أَجَابَ، فِي ثَلَاثٍ: سُورَةِ الْبَقَرَةِ وَآلِ عِمْرَانَ وَطه»

(Allah's Greatest Name, if He was supplicated with it, He answers the supplication, is in three Surahs - Al-Baqarah, Al `Imran and Ta-Ha.)

Hisham bin `Ammar, the Khatib (orator) of Damascus (one of the narrators in the above narration), said, "As for Al-Baqarah, it is in,

(Allah! None has the right to be worshipped but He, the Ever Living, the One Who sustains and protects all that exists) (2:255); in Al `Imran, it is in,

(Alif-Lam-Mim. Allah! None has the right to be worshipped but He, the Ever Living, the One Who sustains and protects all that exists) (3:1-2), while in Ta-Ha, it is in,

(And (all) faces shall be humbled before (Allah), the Ever Living, the One Who sustains and protects all that exists) (20:111)."

Ayat Al-Kursi has Ten Complete Arabic Sentences

Allah's statement,

(Allah! None has the right to be worshipped but He) mentions that Allah is the One and Only Lord of all creation.

Allah's statement,

(Al-Hayyul-Qayyum) testifies that Allah is the Ever Living, Who never dies, Who sustains everyone and everything. All creation stands in need of Allah and totally relies on Him, while He is the Most Rich, Who stands in need of nothing created. Similarly, Allah said,

(And among His signs is that the heaven and the earth stand by His command) (30:25).

Allah's statement,

(Neither slumber nor sleep overtakes Him) means, no shortcoming, unawareness or ignorance ever touches Allah. Rather, He is aware of, and controls what every soul earns, has perfect watch over everything, nothing escapes His knowledge, and no secret matter is secret to Him. Among His perfect attributes, is the fact that He is never effected by slumber or sleep. Therefore, Allah's statement,

(Neither slumber overtakes Him) indicates that no unawareness due to slumber ever overtakes Allah. Allah said afterwards,

(nor sleep), which is stronger than slumber. It is recorded in the Sahih that Abu Musa said, "The Messenger of Allah delivered a speech regarding four words:

«إِنَّ اللهَللهَلا يَنَامُ، وَلَا يَنْبَغِي لَهُ أَنْ يَنَامَ، يَخْفِضُ الْقِسْطَ وَيَرْفَعُهُ، يُرْفَعُ إِلَيْهِ عَمَلُ النَّهَارِ قَبْلَ عَمَلِ اللَّيْلِ، وَعَمَلُ اللَّيْلِ قَبْلَ عَمَلِ النَّهَارِ، حِجَابُهُ النُّورُ أَوِ النَّارُ لَوْ كَشَفَهُ لَأَحْرَقَتْ سُبُحَاتُ وَجْهِهِ مَا انْتَهَى إِلَيْهِ بَصَرُهُ مِنْ خَلْقِهِ»

(Allah does not sleep, and it does not befit His majesty that He sleeps. He lowers the scales and raises them. The deeds of the day are resurrected in front of Him before the deeds of the night, and the deeds of the night before the deeds of the day. His Veil is light, or fire, and if He removes it, the rays from His Face would burn whatever His sight reaches of His creation.)

Allah's statement,

(To Him belongs whatever is in the heavens and whatever is on the earth) indicates that everyone is a servant for Allah, a part of His kingdom and under His power and authority. Similarly, Allah said,

(There is none in the heavens and the earth but comes unto the Most Gracious (Allah) as a servant. Verily, He knows each one of them, and has counted them a full counting. And everyone of them will come to Him alone on the Day of Resurrection (without any helper, or protector or defender)) (19:93-95).

Allah's statement,

(Who is he that can intercede with Him except with His permission) is similar to His statements,

(And there are many angels in the heavens, whose intercession will avail nothing except after Allah has given leave for whom He wills and is pleased with) (53:26), and,

(They cannot intercede except for him with whom He is pleased) (21:28).

These Ayat assert Allah's greatness, pride, and grace, and that no one dares to intercede with Him on behalf of anyone else, except by His permission. Indeed, the Hadith about the intercession, states that the Prophet said,

«آتِي تَحْتَ الْعَرْشِ فَأَخِرُّ سَاجِدًا، فَيَدَعُنِي مَا شَاءَ اللهُ أَنْ يَدَعَنِي. ثُمَّ يُقَالُ: ارْفَعْ رَأْسَكَ، وَقُلْ تُسْمَعْ، وَاشْفَعْ تُشَفَّعْ قَالَ: فَيَحُدُّ لِي حَدًّا فَأُدْخِلُهُمُ الْجَنَّةَ»

(I will stand under the Throne and fall in prostration, and Allah will allow me to remain in that position as much as He wills. I will thereafter be told, "Raise your head, speak and you will be heard, intercede and your intercession will be accepted". The Prophet then said, "He will allow me a proportion whom I will enter into Paradise.")

Allah's statement,

(He knows what happens to them (His creatures) in this world, and what will happen to them in the Hereafter) this refers to His perfect knowledge of all creation; its past, present and future. Similarly, Allah said that the angels proclaimed;

(And we (angels) descend not except by the command of your Lord (O Muhammad). To Him belongs what is before us and what is behind us, and what is between those two; and your Lord is never forgetful) (19:64).

Allah's statement,

(And they will never compass anything of His Knowledge except that which He wills), asserts the fact that no one attains any part of Allah's knowledge except what Allah conveys and allows. This part of the Ayah indicates that no one ever acquires knowledge of Allah and in His Attributes, except what He conveys to them. For instance, Allah said,

(But they will never compass anything of His knowledge) (20: 110).

Allah said,

(His Kursi extends over the heavens and the earth.)

Waki` narrated in his Tafsir that Ibn `Abbas said, "Kursi is the footstool, and no one is able to give due consideration to (Allah's) Throne." Al-Hakim recorded this Hadith in his Mustadrak from Ibn `Abbas, who did not relate it to the Prophet . Al-Hakim said, "It is Sahih according to the criteria of the Two Sahihs, and they (Al-Bukhari and Muslim) did not record it." In addition, Ad-Dahhak said that Ibn `Abbas said, "If the seven heavens and the seven earths were flattened and laid side by side, they would add up to the size of a ring in a desert, compared to the Kursi."

Allah said,

(And He feels no fatigue in guarding and preserving them) meaning, it does not burden or cause Him fatigue to protect the heavens and earth and all that is in between them. Rather, this is an easy matter for Him. Further, Allah sustains everything, has perfect watch over everything, nothing ever escapes His knowledge and no matter is ever a secret to Him. All matters are insignificant, modest and humble before Him. He is the Most Rich, worthy of all praise. He does what He wills, and no one can ask Him about what He does, while they will be asked. He has supreme power over all things and perfect alertness concerning everything. He is the Most High, the Greatest, there is no deity worthy of worship except Him, and no Lord other than Him.

10. Allah's statement,

(And He is the Most High, the Most Great) is similar to His statement,

(the Most Great, the Most High) (13:9).

These and similar Ayat and authentic Hadiths about Allah's Attributes must be treated the way the Salaf (righteous ancestors) treated them by accepting their apparent meanings without equating them (with the attributes of the creation) or altering their apparent meanings.

﴿ لَآ إِكۡرَاهَ فِى ٱلدِّينِ ۖ قَد تَّبَيَّنَ ٱلرُّشۡدُ مِنَ ٱلۡغَىِّ ۚ فَمَن يَكۡفُرۡ بِٱلطَّٰغُوتِ وَيُؤۡمِنۢ بِٱللَّهِ فَقَدِ ٱسۡتَمۡسَكَ بِٱلۡعُرۡوَةِ ٱلۡوُثۡقَىٰ لَا ٱنفِصَامَ لَهَا ۗ وَٱللَّهُ سَمِيعٌ عَلِيمٌ ﴾

256. There is no compulsion in religion. Verily, the Right Path has become distinct from the wrong path. Whoever disbelieves in Tâghût and believes in Allâh, then he has grasped the most trustworthy handhold that will never break. And Allâh is All-Hearer, All-Knower.

Transliteration

256. La ikraha fee alddeeni qad tabayyana alrrushdu mina alghayyi faman yakfur bialttaghooti wayu/min biAllahi faqadi istamsaka bialAAurwati alwuthqa la infisama laha waAllahu sameeAAun AAaleemun

Tafsir Ibn Kathir

No Compulsion in Religion

Allah said,

(There is no compulsion in religion), meaning, "Do not force anyone to become Muslim, for Islam is plain and clear, and its proofs and evidence are plain and clear. Therefore, there is no need to force anyone to embrace Islam. Rather, whoever Allah directs to Islam, opens his heart for it and enlightens his mind, will embrace Islam with certainty. Whoever Allah blinds his heart and seals his hearing and sight, then he will not benefit from being forced to embrace Islam."

It was reported that the Ansar were the reason behind revealing this Ayah, although its indication is general in meaning. Ibn Jarir recorded that Ibn `Abbas said (that before Islam), "When (an Ansar) woman would not bear children who would live, she would vow that if she gives birth to a child who remains alive, she would raise him as a Jew. When Banu An-Nadir (the Jewish tribe) were evacuated (from Al-Madinah), some of the children of the Ansar were being raised among them, and the Ansar said, `We will not abandon our children.' Allah revealed,

(There is no compulsion in religion. Verily, the right path has become distinct from the wrong path.)"

Abu Dawud and An-Nasa'i also recorded this Hadith. As for the Hadith that Imam Ahmad recorded, in which Anas said that the Messenger of Allah said to a man,

«أَسْلِمْ»

(Embrace Islam.) The man said, "I dislike it." The Prophet said,

«وَإِنْ كُنْتَ كَارِهًا»

(Even if you dislike it.)

First, this is an authentic Hadith, with only three narrators between Imam Ahmad and the Prophet . However, it is not relevant to the subject under discussion, for the Prophet did not force that man to become Muslim. The Prophet merely invited this man to become Muslim, and he replied that he does not find himself eager to become Muslim. The Prophet said to the man that even though he dislikes embracing Islam, he should still embrace it, `for Allah will grant you sincerity and true intent.'

Tawhid is the Most Trustworthy Handhold

Allah's statement,

(Whoever disbelieves in Taghut and believes in Allah, then he has grasped the most trustworthy handhold that will never break. And Allah is All-Hearer, All-Knower) is in reference to, "Whoever shuns the rivals of Allah, the idols, and those that Shaytan calls to be worshipped besides Allah, whoever believes in Allah's Oneness, worships Him alone and testifies that there is no deity worthy of worship except Him, then

(then he has grasped the most trustworthy handhold.)

Therefore, this person will have acquired firmness (in the religion) and proceeded on the correct way and the straight path. Abu Al-Qasim Al-Baghawi recorded that `Umar said, "Jibt means magic, and Taghut means Shaytan. Verily, courage and cowardice are two instincts that appear in men, the courageous fights for those whom he does not know and the coward runs away from defending his own mother. Man's honor resides with his religion and his status is based upon his character, even if he was Persian or Nabatian." `Umar's statement that Taghut is Shaytan is very sound, for this meaning includes every type of evil that the ignorant people of Jahiliyyah (pre Islamic era of ignorace) fell into, such as worshipping idols, referring to them for judgement, and invoking them for victory.

Allah's statement,

(then he has grasped the most trustworthy handhold that will never break) means, "He will have hold of the true religion with the strongest grasp." Allah equated this adherence to the firm handhold that never breaks because it is built solid and because its handle is firmly connected. This is why Allah said here,

(then he has grasped the most trustworthy handhold that will never break.)

Mujahid said, "The most trustworthy handhold is Iman (faith)." As-Suddi said that it refers to Islam. Imam Ahmad recorded that Qays bin `Abbad said, "I was in the Masjid when a man whose face showed signs of humbleness came and prayed two Rak`ahs that were modest in length. The people said, `This is a man from among the people of Paradise.' When he left, I followed him until he entered his house, and I entered it after him and spoke with him. When he felt at ease, I said to him, `When you entered the Masjid, the people said such and such things.' He said, `All praise is due to Allah! No one should say what he has no knowledge of. I will tell you why they said that. I saw a vision during the time of the Messenger of Allah, and I narrated it to him. I saw that I was in a green garden, ' and he described the garden's plants and spaciousness, `and there was an iron pole in the middle of the garden affixed in the earth and its tip reached the sky. On its tip, there was a handle, and I was told to ascend the pole. I said, `I cannot.' Then a helper came and raised my robe from behind and said to me, `Ascend.' I ascended until I grasped the handle and he said to me, `Hold on to the handle.' I awoke from that dream with the handle in my hand. I went to the Messenger of Allah and told him about the vision and he said,

»أَمَّا الرَّوْضَةُ فَرَوْضَةُ الْإِسْلَامِ، وَأَمَّا الْعَمُودُ فَعَمُودُ الْإِسْلَامِ، وَأَمَّا الْعُرْوَةُ فَهِيَ الْعُرْوَةُ الْوُثْقَى، أَنْتَ عَلَى الْإِسْلَامِ حَتَّى تَمُوت«

(As for the garden, it represents Islam; as for the pole, it represents the pillar of Islam; and the handle represents the most trustworthy handhold. You shall remain Muslim until you die.)

This Companion was `Abdullah bin Salam."

This Hadith was also collected in the Two Sahihs; and Al-Bukhari also recorded it with another chain of narration.

Surah: 2 Ayah: 257

﴿ ٱللَّهُ وَلِيُّ ٱلَّذِينَ ءَامَنُوا۟ يُخْرِجُهُم مِّنَ ٱلظُّلُمَـٰتِ إِلَى ٱلنُّورِ ۖ وَٱلَّذِينَ كَفَرُوٓا۟ أَوْلِيَآؤُهُمُ ٱلطَّـٰغُوتُ يُخْرِجُونَهُم مِّنَ ٱلنُّورِ إِلَى ٱلظُّلُمَـٰتِ ۗ أُو۟لَـٰٓئِكَ أَصْحَـٰبُ ٱلنَّارِ ۖ هُمْ فِيهَا خَـٰلِدُونَ ﴾ ۝

257. Allâh is the Walî (Protector or Guardian) of those who believe. He brings them out from darkness into light. But as for those who disbelieve, their Auliyâ (supporters and helpers) are Tâghût (false deities and false leaders), they bring them out from light into darkness. Those are the dwellers of the Fire, and they will abide therein forever. (See V.2:81,82)

Transliteration

257. Allahu waliyyu allatheena amanoo yukhrijuhum mina al*thth*ulumati ila alnnoori waallatheena kafaroo awliyaohumu alttaghootu yukhrijoonahum mina alnnoori ila al*thth*ulumati ola-ika as-habu alnnari hum feeha khalidoona

Tafsir Ibn Kathir

Allah stated that whoever follows what pleases Him, He will guide him to the paths of peace, that is Islam, or Paradise. Verily, Allah delivers His believing servants from the darkness of disbelief, doubt and hesitation, to the light of the plain, clear, explained, easy and unequivocal truth. He also stated that Shaytan is the supporter of the disbelievers who beautifies the paths of ignorance and misguidance that they follow, thus causing them to deviate from the true path into disbelief and wickedness.

(Those are the dwellers of the Fire, and they will abide therein forever.)

This is why Allah mentioned the light in the singular while mentioned the darkness in the plural, because truth is one, while disbelief comes as several types, all of which are false. Similarly, Allah said,

(And verily, this is my straight path, so follow it, and follow not (other) paths, for they will separate you away from His path. This He has ordained for you that you may have Taqwa) (6:153),

(And originated the darknesses and the light) (6:1), and,

(to the right and to the lefts) (16: 48).

There are many other Ayat on the subject that mention the truth in the singular and falsehood in the plural, because of falsehood's many divisions and branches.

Surah: 2 Ayah: 258

﴿ أَلَمْ تَرَ إِلَى ٱلَّذِى حَآجَّ إِبْرَٰهِـۧمَ فِى رَبِّهِۦٓ أَنْ ءَاتَىٰهُ ٱللَّهُ ٱلْمُلْكَ إِذْ قَالَ إِبْرَٰهِـۧمُ رَبِّىَ ٱلَّذِى يُحْىِۦ وَيُمِيتُ قَالَ أَنَا۠ أُحْىِۦ وَأُمِيتُ ۖ قَالَ إِبْرَٰهِـۧمُ فَإِنَّ ٱللَّهَ يَأْتِى بِٱلشَّمْسِ مِنَ ٱلْمَشْرِقِ فَأْتِ بِهَا مِنَ ٱلْمَغْرِبِ فَبُهِتَ ٱلَّذِى كَفَرَ ۗ وَٱللَّهُ لَا يَهْدِى ٱلْقَوْمَ ٱلظَّٰلِمِينَ ۝ ﴾

258. Have you not looked at him who disputed with Ibrâhîm (Abraham) about his Lord (Allâh), because Allâh had given him the kingdom? When Ibrâhîm (Abraham) said (to him): "My Lord (Allâh) is He Who gives life and causes death." He said, "I give life and cause death." Ibrâhîm (Abraham) said, "Verily! Allâh causes the sun to rise from the east; then cause it you to rise from the west." So the disbeliever was utterly defeated. And Allâh guides not the people, who are Zâlimûn (wrongdoers.).

Transliteration

258. Alam tara ila allathee hajja ibraheema fee rabbihi an atahu Allahu almulka ith qala ibraheemu rabbiya allathee yuhyee wayumeetu qala ana ohyee waomeetu qala ibraheemu fa-inna Allaha ya/tee bialshshamsi mina almashriqi fa/ti biha mina almaghribi fabuhita allathee kafara waAllahu la yahdee alqawma alththalimeena

Tafsir Ibn Kathir

The Debate Between Ibrahim Al-Khalil and King Nimrod

The king who disputed with Ibrahim was King Nimrod, son of Canaan, son of Kush, son of Sam, son of Noah, as Mujahid stated. It was also said that he was Nimrod, son of Falikh, son of `Abir, son of Shalikh, son of Arfakhshand, son of Sam, son of Noah. Mujahid said, "The kings who ruled the eastern and western parts of the world are four, two believers and two disbelievers. As for the two believing kings, they were Sulayman bin Dawud and Dhul-Qarnayn. As for the two disbelieving kings, they were Nimrod and Nebuchadnezzar." Allah knows best.

Allah said,

(Have you not looked) meaning, "With your heart, O Muhammad!"

(at him who disputed with Ibrahim about his Lord) meaning, about the existence of Allah. Nimrod denied the existence of a god other than himself, as he claimed, just as Fir`awn said later to his people,

(I know not that you have a god other than me) (28:38).

What made Nimrod commit this transgression, utter disbelief and arrogant rebellion was his tyranny and the fact that he ruled for a long time. This is why the Ayah continued,

(Because Allah had given him the kingdom.)

It appears that Nimrod asked Ibrahim to produce proof that Allah exists. Ibrahim replied,

(My Lord is He Who gives life and causes death) meaning, "The proof of Allah's existence is the creations that exist after they were nothing and perish after they had existed. This only proves the existence of the Creator, Who does what He wills, for these things could not have occurred on their own without a Creator who created them, and He is the Lord that I call to for worship, Alone without a partner."

This is when Nimrod said,

(I give life and cause death.)

Qatadah, Muhammad bin Ishaq and As-Suddi said that he meant, "Two men who deserved execution were to be brought before me, and I would command that one of them be killed, and he would be killed. I would command that the second man be pardoned, and he would be pardoned. This is how I bring life and death." However, it appears that since Nimrod did not deny the existence of a Creator, his statement did not mean what Qatadah said it meant. This explanation does not provide an answer to what Ibrahim said. Nimrod arrogantly and defiantly claimed that he was the creator and pretended that it was he who brings life and death. Later on, Fir`awn imitated him and announced,

(I know not that you have a god other than me) (28: 38).

This is why Ibrahim said to Nimrod,

(Verily, Allah brings the sun from the east; then bring it you from the west.)

This Ayah means, "You claim that it is you who brings life and death. He who brings life and death controls the existence and creates whatever is in it, including controlling its planets and their movements. For instance, the sun rises everyday from the east. Therefore, if you were god, as you claimed, bringing life and death, then bring the sun from the west." Since the king was aware of his weakness, inadequacy and that he was not able to reply to Ibrahim's request, he was idle, silent and unable to comment. Therefore, the proof was established against him. Allah said,

(And Allah guides not the people, who are wrongdoers) meaning, Allah deprives the unjust people of any valid proof or argument. Furthermore, their false proof and arguments are annulled by their Lord, and they have earned His anger and will suffer severe torment.

The meaning that we provided is better than the meaning that some philosophers offered, claiming that Ibrahim used the second argument because it was clearer than the first one. Rather, our explanation asserts that Ibrahim refuted both claims of Nimrod, all praise is due to Allah.

As-Suddi stated that the debate between Ibrahim and Nimrod occurred after Ibrahim was thrown in the fire, for Ibrahim did not meet the king before that day.

Surah: 2 Ayah: 259

﴿ أَوْ كَالَّذِى مَرَّ عَلَىٰ قَرْيَةٍ وَهِىَ خَاوِيَةٌ عَلَىٰ عُرُوشِهَا قَالَ أَنَّىٰ يُحْىِۦ هَـٰذِهِ ٱللَّهُ بَعْدَ مَوْتِهَا ۖ فَأَمَاتَهُ ٱللَّهُ مِاْئَةَ عَامٍ ثُمَّ بَعَثَهُۥ ۖ قَالَ كَمْ لَبِثْتَ ۖ قَالَ لَبِثْتُ يَوْمًا أَوْ بَعْضَ يَوْمٍ ۖ قَالَ بَل لَّبِثْتَ مِاْئَةَ عَامٍ فَٱنظُرْ إِلَىٰ طَعَامِكَ وَشَرَابِكَ لَمْ يَتَسَنَّهْ ۖ وَٱنظُرْ إِلَىٰ حِمَارِكَ وَلِنَجْعَلَكَ ءَايَةً لِّلنَّاسِ ۖ وَٱنظُرْ إِلَى ٱلْعِظَامِ كَيْفَ نُنشِزُهَا ثُمَّ نَكْسُوهَا لَحْمًا ۚ فَلَمَّا تَبَيَّنَ لَهُۥ قَالَ أَعْلَمُ أَنَّ ٱللَّهَ عَلَىٰ كُلِّ شَىْءٍ قَدِيرٌ ﴾

259. Or like the one who passed by a town and it had tumbled over its roofs. He said: "Oh! How will Allâh ever bring it to life after its death?" So Allâh caused him to die for a hundred years, then raised him up (again). He said: "How long did you remain (dead)?" He (the man) said: "(Perhaps) I remained (dead) a day or part of a day". He said: "Nay, you have remained (dead) for a hundred years, look at your food and your drink, they show no change; and look at your donkey! And thus We have made of you a sign for the people. Look at the bones, how We bring them together and clothe them with flesh". When this was clearly shown to him, he said, "I know (now) that Allâh is Able to do all things."

Transliteration

259. Aw kaallathee marra AAala qaryatin wahiya khawiyatun AAala AAurooshiha qala anna yuhyee hathihi Allahu baAAda mawtiha faamatahu Allahu mi-ata AAamin thumma baAAathahu qala kam labithta qala labithtu yawman aw baAAda yawmin qala bal labithta mi-ata AAamin faon*th*ur ila taAAamika washarabika lam yatasannah waon*th*ur ila himarika walinajAAalaka ayatan lilnnasi waon*th*ur ila alAAi*th*ami kayfa nunshizuha thumma naksooha lahman falamma tabayyana lahu qala aAAlamu anna Allaha AAala kulli shay-in qadeerun

Tafsir Ibn Kathir

The Story of `Uzayr

Allah's statement,

(Have you not looked at him who disputed with Ibrahim about his Lord) means, "Have you seen anyone like the person who disputed with Ibrahim about his Lord" Then, Allah connected the Ayah,

(Or like the one who passed by a town in ruin up to its roofs) to the Ayah above by using `or'.

Ibn Abi Hatim recorded that `Ali bin Abi Talib said that the Ayah (2:259) meant `Uzayr. Ibn Jarir also reported it, and this explanation was also reported by Ibn Jarir and Ibn Abi Hatim from Ibn `Abbas, Al-Hasan, Qatadah, As-Suddi and Sulayman bin Buraydah.

Mujahid bin Jabr said that the Ayah refers to a man from the Children of Israel, and the village was Jerusalem, after Nebuchadnezzar destroyed it and killed its people.

(in ruin) means, it became empty of people. Allah's statement,

(up to its roofs) indicates that the roofs and walls (of the village) fell to the ground. `Uzayr stood contemplating about what had happened to that city, after a great civilization used to inhabit it. He said,

(Oh! How will Allah ever bring it to life after its death) because of the utter destruction he saw and the implausibility of its returning to what it used to be. Allah said,

(So Allah caused him to die for a hundred years, then raised him up (again).)

The city was rebuilt seventy years after the man (`Uzayr) died, and its inhabitants increased and the Children of Israel moved back to it. When Allah resurrected `Uzayr after he died, the first organ that He resurrected were his eyes, so that he could witness what Allah does with him, how He brings life back to his body. When his resurrection was complete, Allah said to him, meaning through the angel,

("How long did you remain (dead)" He (the man) said: "(Perhaps) I remained (dead) a day or part of a day.")

The scholars said that since the man died in the early part of the day and Allah resurrected him in the latter part of the day, when he saw that the sun was still apparent, he thought that it was the sun of that very day. He said,

("Or part of a day. " He said: "Nay, you have remained (dead) for a hundred years, look at your food and your drink, they show no change.")

He had grapes, figs and juice, and he found them as he left them; neither did the juice spoil nor the figs become bitter nor the grapes rot.

(And look at your donkey!), "How Allah brings it back to life while you are watching."

(And thus We have made of you a sign for the people) that Resurrection occurs.

(Look at the bones, how We Nunshizuha) meaning, collect them and put them back together. In his Mustadrak, Al-Hakim, recorded that Kharijah bin Zayd bin Thabit said that his father said that the Messenger of Allah read this Ayah,

(how We Nunshizuha.) Al-Hakim said; "Its chain is Sahih and they (Al-Bukhari and Muslim) did not record it." The Ayah was also read,

"Nunshiruha" meaning, bring them back to life, as Mujahid stated.

(And clothe them with flesh.)

As-Suddi said, "`Uzayr observed the bones of his donkey, which were scattered all around him to his right and left, and Allah sent a wind that collected the bones from all over the area. Allah then brought every bone to its place, until they formed a full donkey made of fleshless bones. Allah then covered these bones with flesh, nerves, veins and skin. Allah sent an angel who blew life in the donkeys' nostrils, and the donkey started to bray by Allah's leave." All this occurred while `Uzayr was watching, and this is when he proclaimed,

(He said, "I know (now) that Allah is able to do all things,") meaning, "I know that, and I did witness it with my own eyes. Therefore, I am the most knowledgeable in this matter among the people of my time."

Surah: 2 Ayah: 260

﴿ وَإِذْ قَالَ إِبْرَاهِيمُ رَبِّ أَرِنِى كَيْفَ تُحْىِ ٱلْمَوْتَىٰ قَالَ أَوَلَمْ تُؤْمِن قَالَ بَلَىٰ وَلَـٰكِن لِّيَطْمَئِنَّ قَلْبِى قَالَ فَخُذْ أَرْبَعَةً مِّنَ ٱلطَّيْرِ فَصُرْهُنَّ إِلَيْكَ ثُمَّ ٱجْعَلْ عَلَىٰ كُلِّ جَبَلٍ مِّنْهُنَّ جُزْءًا ثُمَّ ٱدْعُهُنَّ يَأْتِينَكَ سَعْيًا وَٱعْلَمْ أَنَّ ٱللَّهَ عَزِيزٌ حَكِيمٌ ﴾ (٢٦٠)

260. And (remember) when Ibrâhîm (Abraham) said, "My Lord! Show me how You give life to the dead." He (Allâh) said: "Do you not believe?" He (Ibrâhîm (Abraham)) said: "Yes (I believe), but to be stronger in Faith." He said: "Take four birds, then cause them to incline towards you (then slaughter them, cut them into pieces), and then put a portion of them on every hill, and call them, they will come to you in haste. And know that Allâh is All-Mighty, All-Wise."

Transliteration

260. Wa-ith qala ibraheemu rabbi arinee kayfa tuhyee almawta qala awa lam tu/min qala bala walakin liyatma-inna qalbee qala fakhuth arbaAAatan mina alttayri fasurhunna ilayka thumma ijAAal AAala kulli jabalin minhunna juz-an thumma odAAuhunna ya/teenaka saAAyan waiAAlam anna Allaha AAazeezun hakeemun

Tafsir Ibn Kathir

The Khalil Supplicates to Allah to Show Him How He Resurrects the Dead

The scholars said that there are reasons behind this request by Ibrahim. For instance, when Ibrahim said to Nimrod,

e(My Lord (Allah) is He Who gives life and causes death,) he wanted to solidify his knowledge about resurrection by actually witnessing it with his eyes. Prophet Ibrahim said,

("My Lord! Show me how You give life to the dead." He (Allah) said: "Do you not believe" He (Ibrahim) said: "Yes (I believe), but to be stronger in faith.")

Al-Bukhari recorded that Abu Hurayrah said that the Messenger of Allah said,

«نَحْنُ أَحَقُّ بِالشَّكِّ مِنْ إِبْرَاهِيمَ إِذْ قَالَ [رَبِّ أَرِنِي كَيْفَ تُحْيِي الْمَوْتَى قَالَ أَوَلَمْ تُؤْمِن قَالَ بَلَى وَلَكِن لِّيَطْمَئِنَّ قَلْبِي]»

(We are more liable to be in doubt than Ibrahim when he said, "My Lord! Show me how You give life to the dead." Allah said, "Don't you believe" Ibrahim said, "Yes (I believe), but (I ask) in order to be stronger in faith.")

The Prophet's statement in the Hadith means, "We are more liable to seek certainty."

The Answer to Al-Khalil's Request

Allah said,

(He said: "Take four birds, then cause them to incline towards you.")

Scholars of Tafsir disagreed over the type of birds mentioned here, although this matter in not relevant due to the fact that the Qur'an did not mention it. Allah's statement,

(cause them to incline towards you) means, cut them to pieces. This is the explanation of Ibn `Abbas, `Ikrimah, Sa`id bin Jubayr, Abu Malik, Abu Al-Aswad Ad-Dili, Wahb bin Munabbih, Al-Hasan and As-Suddi. Therefore, Ibrahim caught four birds, slaughtered them, removed the feathers, tore the birds to pieces and mixed the pieces together. He then placed parts of these mixed pieces on four or seven hills. Ibn `Abbas said, "Ibrahim kept the heads of these birds in his hand. Next, Allah commanded Ibrahim to call the birds to him, and he did as Allah commanded him. Ibrahim witnessed the feathers, blood and flesh of these birds fly to each other, and the parts flew each to their bodies, until every bird came back to life and came walking at a fast pace towards Ibrahim, so that the example that Ibrahim was witnessing would become more impressive. Each bird came to collect its head from Ibrahim's hand, and if he gave the bird another head the bird refused to accept it. When Ibrahim gave each bird its own head, the head was placed on its body by Allah's leave and power. " This is why Allah said,

(And know that Allah is All-Mighty, All-Wise) and no one can overwhelm or resist Him. Whatever Allah wills, occurs without hindrance, because He is the All-Mighty, Supreme above all things, and He is Wise in His statements, actions, legislation and decrees.

`Abdur-Razzaq recorded that Ma`mar said that Ayyub said that Ibn `Abbas commented on what Ibrahim said, (but to be stronger in Faith), "To me, there is no Ayah in the Qur'an that brings more hope than this Ayah." Ibn Abi Hatim recorded that Muhammad bin Al-Munkadir said that `Abdullah bin `Abbas met `Abdullah bin `Amr bin Al-`As and said to him, "Which Ayah in the Qur'an carries more hope for you" Ibn `Amr said,

(Say: "O `Ibadi (My servants) who have transgressed against themselves (by committing evil deeds and sins)! Despair not.) (39:53).

Ibn `Abbas said, "But I say that it is Allah's statement,

(And (remember) when Ibrahim said, "My Lord! Show me how You give life to the dead." He (Allah) said: "Do you not believe" He (Ibrahim) said: "Yes (I believe)...)

Allah accepted Ibrahim's affirmation when he merely said, `Yes.' This Ayah refers to the doubts that attack the heart and the thoughts that Shaytan inspires." Al-Hakim also recorded this in Al-Mustadrak and said; "Its chain is Sahih but they did not record it."

Surah: 2 Ayah: 261

﴿ مَّثَلُ ٱلَّذِينَ يُنفِقُونَ أَمْوَٰلَهُمْ فِى سَبِيلِ ٱللَّهِ كَمَثَلِ حَبَّةٍ أَنۢبَتَتْ سَبْعَ سَنَابِلَ فِى كُلِّ سُنۢبُلَةٍ مِّا۟ئَةُ حَبَّةٍ ۗ وَٱللَّهُ يُضَٰعِفُ لِمَن يَشَآءُ ۗ وَٱللَّهُ وَٰسِعٌ عَلِيمٌ ﴾

261. The likeness of those who spend their wealth in the Way of Allâh, is as the likeness of a grain (of corn); it grows seven ears, and each ear has a hundred grains. Allâh gives manifold increase to whom He wills. And Allâh is All-Sufficient for His creatures' needs, All-Knower.

Transliteration

261. Mathalu allatheena yunfiqoona amwalahum fee sabeeli Allahi kamathali habbatin anbatat sabAAa sanabila fee kulli sunbulatin mi-atu habbatin waAllahu yudaAAifu liman yashao waAllahu wasiAAun AAaleemun

Tafsir Ibn Kathir

Rewards of Spending in Allah's Cause

This is a parable that Allah made of the multiplication of rewards for those who spend in His cause, seeking His pleasure. Allah multiplies the good deed ten to seven hundred times. Allah said,

(The parable of those who spend their wealth in the way of Allah...)

Sa`id bin Jubayr commented, "Meaning spending in Allah's obedience." Makhul said that the Ayah means, "Spending on Jihad, on horse stalls, weapons and so forth." The parable in the Ayah is more impressive on the heart than merely mentioning the number seven hundred. This Ayah indicates that Allah `grows' the good deeds for its doers, just as He grows the plant for whoever sows it in fertile land. The Sunnah also mentions that the deeds are multiplied up to seven hundred folds. For instance, Imam

Ahmad recorded that Abu Mas`ud said that a man once gave away a camel, with its bridle on, in the cause of Allah and the Messenger of Allah said,

«لَتَأْتِيَنَّ يَوْمَ الْقِيَامَةِ بِسَبْعِمِائَةِ نَاقَةٍ مَخْطُومَة»

(On the Day of Resurrection, you will have seven hundred camels with their bridles.)

Muslim and An-Nasa'i also recorded this Hadith, and Muslim's narration reads, "A man brought a camel with its bridle on and said, `O Messenger of Allah! This is in the sake of Allah.' The Messenger said,

«لَكَ بِهَا يَوْمَ الْقِيَامَةِ سَبْعُمِائَةِ نَاقَة»

(You will earn seven hundred camels as reward for it on the Day of Resurrection.)

Another Hadith: Ahmad recorded that Abu Hurayrah said that the Messenger of Allah said,

«كُلُّ عَمَلِ ابْنِ آدَمَ يُضَاعَفُ، الْحَسَنَةُ بِعَشَرِ أَمْثَالِهَا، إِلَى سَبْعِمِائَةِ ضِعْفٍ، إِلَى مَا شَاءَ اللهُ، يَقُولُ اللهُ: إِلَّا الصَّوْمَ فَإِنَّهُ لِي، وَأَنَا أَجْزِي بِهِ، يَدَعُ طَعَامَهُ وَشَهْوَتَهُ مِنْ أَجْلِي، وَلِلصَّائِمِ فَرْحَتَانِ: فَرْحَةٌ عِنْدَ فِطْرِهِ وَفَرْحَةٌ عِنْدَ لِقَاءِ رَبِّهِ، وَلَخُلُوفُ فَمِ الصَّائِمِ أَطْيَبُ عِنْدَ اللهِ مِنْ رِيحِ الْمِسْكِ، الصَّوْمُ جُنَّةٌ، الصَّوْمُ جُنَّة»

(Every good deed that the son of Adam performs will be multiplied ten folds, to seven hundred folds, to many other folds, to as much as Allah wills. Allah said, "Except the fast, for it is for Me and I will reward for it. One abandons his food and desire in My sake." The fasting person has two times of happiness: when he breaks his fast and when he meets his Lord. Verily, the odor that comes from the mouth of whoever fasts is more pure to Allah than the scent of musk. Fasting is a shield (against sinning), fasting is a shield.) Muslim recorded this Hadith.

Allah's statement,

(Allah gives manifold increase to whom He wills) is according to the person's sincerity in his deeds.

(And Allah is All-Sufficient for His creatures' needs, All-Knower) meaning, His Favor is so wide that it encompasses much more than His creation, and He has full knowledge in whoever deserves it, or does not deserve it. All the praise and thanks are due to Allah.

Surah: 2 Ayah: 262, Surah: 2 Ayah: 263 & Surah: 2 Ayah: 264

﴿ ٱلَّذِينَ يُنفِقُونَ أَمْوَٰلَهُمْ فِى سَبِيلِ ٱللَّهِ ثُمَّ لَا يُتْبِعُونَ مَآ أَنفَقُواْ مَنًّا وَلَآ أَذًى هُمْ أَجْرُهُمْ عِندَ رَبِّهِمْ وَلَا خَوْفٌ عَلَيْهِمْ وَلَا هُمْ يَحْزَنُونَ ﴾

262. Those who spend their wealth in the Cause of Allâh, and do not follow up their gifts with reminders of their generosity or with injury, their reward is with their Lord. On them shall be no fear, nor shall they grieve.

﴿ ۞ قَوْلٌ مَّعْرُوفٌ وَمَغْفِرَةٌ خَيْرٌ مِّن صَدَقَةٍ يَتْبَعُهَآ أَذًى وَٱللَّهُ غَنِىٌّ حَلِيمٌ ﴾

263. Kind words and forgiving of faults are better than Sadaqah (charity) followed by injury. And Allâh is Rich (Free of all needs) and He is Most-Forbearing.

﴿ يَٰٓأَيُّهَا ٱلَّذِينَ ءَامَنُواْ لَا تُبْطِلُواْ صَدَقَٰتِكُم بِٱلْمَنِّ وَٱلْأَذَىٰ كَٱلَّذِى يُنفِقُ مَالَهُۥ رِئَآءَ ٱلنَّاسِ وَلَا يُؤْمِنُ بِٱللَّهِ وَٱلْيَوْمِ ٱلْءَاخِرِ فَمَثَلُهُۥ كَمَثَلِ صَفْوَانٍ عَلَيْهِ تُرَابٌ فَأَصَابَهُۥ وَابِلٌ فَتَرَكَهُۥ صَلْدًا لَّا يَقْدِرُونَ عَلَىٰ شَىْءٍ مِّمَّا كَسَبُواْ وَٱللَّهُ لَا يَهْدِى ٱلْقَوْمَ ٱلْكَٰفِرِينَ ﴾

264. O you who believe! Do not render in vain your Sadaqah (charity) by reminders of your generosity or by injury, like him who spends his wealth to be seen of men, and he does not believe in Allâh, nor in the Last Day. His likeness is the likeness of a smooth rock on which is a little dust; on it falls heavy rain which leaves it bare. They are not able to do anything with what they have earned. And Allâh does not guide the disbelieving people.

Transliteration

262. Allatheena yunfiqoona amwalahum fee sabeeli Allahi thumma la yutbiAAoona ma anfaqoo mannan wala athan lahum ajruhum AAinda rabbihim wala khawfun AAalayhim wala hum yahzanoona 263. Qawlun maAAroofun wamaghfiratun khayrun min sadaqatin yatbaAAuha athan waAllahu ghaniyyun haleemun 264. Ya ayyuha allatheena amanoo la tubtiloo sadaqatikum bialmanni waal-atha kaallathee yunfiqu malahu ri-aa alnnasi wala yu/minu biAllahi waalyawmi al-akhiri famathaluhu kamathali safwanin AAalayhi turabun faasabahu wabilun fatarakahu saldan la yaqdiroona AAala shay-in mimma kasaboo waAllahu la yahdee alqawma alkafireena

Tafsir Ibn Kathir

To Remind About Charity Given is Forbidden

Allah praises those who spend from their money in His cause, and then refrain from reminding those who received the charity of that fact, whether these hints take the form of words or actions.

Allah's statement,

(or with injury), indicates that they do not cause harm to those whom they gave the charity to, for this harm will only annul the charity. Allah next promised them the best rewards for this good deed,

(their reward is with their Lord), indicating that Allah Himself will reward them for these righteous actions. Further,

(On them shall be no fear) regarding the horrors of the Day of Resurrection,

(nor shall they grieve) regarding the offspring that they leave behind and the adornment and delights of this world. They will not feel sorry for this, because they will acquire what is far better for them.

Allah then said,

(Kind words) meaning, compassionate words and a supplication for Muslims,

(and forgiving) meaning, forgiving an injustice that took the form of actions or words,

(are better than Sadaqah (charity) followed by injury.)

(And Allah is Rich) not needing His creation,

(Most Forbearing) forgives, releases and pardons them.

There are several Hadiths that prohibit reminding people of acts of charity. For instance, Muslim recorded that Abu Dharr said that the Messenger of Allah said,

«ثَلَاثَةٌ لَا يُكَلِّمُهُمُ اللهُ يَوْمَ الْقِيَامَةِ، وَلَا يَنْظُرُ إِلَيْهِم، وَلَا يُزَكِّيهِمْ، وَلَهُمْ عَذَابٌ أَلِيمٌ: الْمَنَّانُ بِمَا أَعْطَى، وَالْمُسْبِلُ إِزَارَهُ، وَالْمُنَفِّقُ سِلْعَتَهُ بِالْحَلِفِ الْكَاذِبِ»

(Three persons whom Allah shall neither speak to on the Day of Resurrection nor look at nor purify, and they shall receive a painful torment: he who reminds (the people) of what he gives away, he who lengthens his clothes below the ankles and he who swears an oath while lying, to sell his merchandise.)

This is why Allah said,

(O you who believe! Do not render in vain your Sadaqah (charity) by reminders of your generosity or by injury) stating that the charity will be rendered in vain if it is followed by harm or reminders. In this case, the reward of giving away charity is not sufficient enough to nullify the harm and reminders. Allah then said,

(like him who spends his wealth to be seen of men) meaning, "Do not nullify your acts of charity by following them with reminders and harm, just like the charity of those who give it to show off to people." The boasting person pretends to give away charity for Allah's sake, but in reality seeks to gain people's praise and the reputation of being kind or generous, or other material gains of this life. All the while, he does not think about Allah or gaining His pleasure and generous rewards, and this is why Allah said,

(and he does not believe in Allah, nor in the Last Day.)

Allah next set the example of whoever gives charity to show off. Ad-Dahhak commented that the example fits one who follows his acts of charity with reminders or harm. Allah said,

(His likeness is the likeness of Safwan) where Safwan, from is Safwanah, meaning `the smooth rocks,'

(on which is little dust; on it falls a Wabil) meaning, heavy rain,

(which leaves it bare.) This Ayah means that heavy rain left the Safwan completely barren of dust. Such is the case with Allah's action regarding the work of those who show off, as their deeds are bound to vanish and disappear, even though people think that these deeds are as plentiful as specks of dust. So Allah said,

(They are not able to do anything with what they have earned. And Allah does not guide the disbelieving people.)

Surah: 2 Ayah: 265

﴿ وَمَثَلُ ٱلَّذِينَ يُنفِقُونَ أَمْوَٰلَهُمُ ٱبْتِغَآءَ مَرْضَاتِ ٱللَّهِ وَتَثْبِيتًا مِّنْ أَنفُسِهِمْ كَمَثَلِ جَنَّةٍ بِرَبْوَةٍ أَصَابَهَا وَابِلٌ فَـَٔاتَتْ أُكُلَهَا ضِعْفَيْنِ فَإِن لَّمْ يُصِبْهَا وَابِلٌ فَطَلٌّ وَٱللَّهُ بِمَا تَعْمَلُونَ بَصِيرٌ ﴾

265. And the likeness of those who spend their wealth seeking Allâh's Pleasure while they in their own selves are sure and certain that Allâh will reward them (for their spending in His Cause), is the likeness of a garden on a height; heavy rain falls on it and it doubles its yield of harvest. And if it does not receive heavy rain, light rain suffices it. And Allâh is All-Seer (knows well) of what you do.

Transliteration

265. Wamathalu allatheena yunfiqoona amwalahumu ibtighaa mardati Allahi watathbeetan min anfusihim kamathali jannatin birabwatin asabaha wabilun faatat

okulaha diAAfayni fa-in lam yusibha wabilun fatallun waAllahu bima taAAmaloona baseerun

Tafsir Ibn Kathir

This is the example of the believers who give away charity seeking only Allah's pleasure,

(while they in their own selves are sure and certain) meaning, they are certain that Allah shall reward them for these righteous acts with the best rewards. Similarly, in a Hadith collected by Al-Bukhari and Muslim, the Messenger of Allah said,

«مَنْ صَامَ رَمَضَانَ إِيمَانًا وَاحْتِسَابًا»

(Whoever fasts Ramadan with faith and expectation...) meaning, believing that Allah commanded the fast, all the while awaiting His reward for fasting it.

Allah's statement,

(is that of a garden on a Rabwah) means, the example of a garden on `a height above the ground', as the majority of scholars have stated. Ibn `Abbas and Ad-Dahhak added that it also has flowing rivers.

Allah's statement,

(Wabil falls on it) means, heavy rain as we stated, So it produces its,

(yield of harvest) meaning, fruits or produce,

(doubles), as compared to other gardens.

(And if it does not receive Wabil, a Tall suffices it.)

Ad-Dahhak said that the `Tall' is light rain. The Ayah indicates that the garden on the Rabwah is always fertile, for if heavy rain does not fall on it, light rain will suffice for it. Such is the case regarding the believer's good deeds, for they never become barren. Rather, Allah accepts the believer's righteous deeds and increases them, each according to his deeds. This is why Allah said next,

(And Allah is All-Seer of what you do) meaning, none of His servants' deeds ever escapes His perfect watch.

Surah: 2 Ayah: 266

﴿ أَيَوَدُّ أَحَدُكُمْ أَن تَكُونَ لَهُ جَنَّةٌ مِّن نَّخِيلٍ وَأَعْنَابٍ تَجْرِى مِن تَحْتِهَا ٱلْأَنْهَـٰرُ لَهُ فِيهَا مِن كُلِّ ٱلثَّمَرَٰتِ وَأَصَابَهُ ٱلْكِبَرُ وَلَهُ ذُرِّيَّةٌ ضُعَفَآءُ فَأَصَابَهَا

$$\text{إِعْصَارٌ فِيهِ نَارٌ فَٱحْتَرَقَتْ ۗ كَذَٰلِكَ يُبَيِّنُ ٱللَّهُ لَكُمُ ٱلْآيَاتِ لَعَلَّكُمْ تَتَفَكَّرُونَ ﴿٢٦٦﴾}$$

266. Would any of you wish to have a garden with date-palms and vines, with rivers flowing underneath, and all kinds of fruits for him therein, while he is stricken with old age, and his children are weak (not able to look after themselves), then it is struck with a fiery whirlwind, so that it is burnt? Thus does Allâh make clear His Ayât (proofs, evidences, verses) to you that you may give thought.

Transliteration

266. Ayawaddu ahadukum an takoona lahu jannatun min nakheelin waaAAnabin tajree min tahtiha alanharu lahu feeha min kulli alththamarati waasabahu alkibaru walahu thurriyyatun duAAafao faasabaha iAAsarun feehi narun faihtaraqat kathalika yubayyinu Allahu lakumu al-ayati laAAallakum tatafakkaroona

Tafsir Ibn Kathir

The Example of Evil Deeds Nullifying Good Deeds

Al-Bukhari recorded that Ibn `Abbas and `Ubayd bin `Umayr said that `Umar bin Al-Khattab asked the Companions of the Messenger of Allah, "According to your opinion, about whom was this Ayah revealed,

(Would any of you wish to have a garden with date palms and vines...)."

They said, "Allah knows best." `Umar became angry and said, "Say we know or we do not know." Ibn `Abbas said, "O Leader of the Faithful! I have an opinion about it." `Umar said, "O my nephew! Say your opinion and do not belittle yourself." Ibn `Abbas said, "This is an example set for a deed." `Umar said, "What type of deed" Ibn `Abbas said, "For a wealthy man who works in Allah's pleasure and then Allah sends Shaytan to him, and he works in disobedience, until he annuls his good works."

This Hadith suffices as an explanation for the Ayah, for it explains the example it sets by a person who does good first and then follows it with evil, may Allah save us from this end. So, this man annulled his previous good works with his latter evil works. When he desperately needed the deeds of the former type, there were none. This is why Allah said,

(while he is striken with old age, and his children are weak (not able to look after themselves), then it is struck with a whirlwind) with heavy wind,

(that is fiery, so that it is burnt) meaning, its fruits were burnt and its trees were destroyed. Therefore, what will his condition be like

Ibn Abi Hatim recorded that Al-`Awfi said that Ibn `Abbas said, "Allah has set a good parable, and all His parables are good. He said,

(Would any of you wish to have a garden with date palms and vines, with rivers flowing underneath, and all kinds of fruits for him therein.)

But he lost all this in his old age,

(while he is striken with old age) while his offspring and children are weak just before the end of his life. Then a lightning storm came and destroyed his garden. Then he did not have the strength to grow another garden, nor did his offspring offer enough help. This is the condition of the disbeliever on the Day of Resurrection when he returns to Allah, for he will not have any good deeds to provide an excuse - or refuge - for him, just as the man in the parable had no strength to replant the garden. The disbeliever will not find anything to resort to for help, just as the offspring of the man in the parable did not provide him with help. So he will be deprived of his reward when he most needs it, just as the man in the parable was deprived of Allah's garden when he most needed it, when he became old and his offspring weak."

In his Mustadrak, Al-Hakim recorded that the Messenger of Allah used to say in his supplication,

«اللَّهُمَّ اجْعَلْ أَوْسَعَ رِزْقِكَ عَلَيَّ عِنْدَ كِبَرِ سِنِّي وَانْقِضَاءِ عُمُرِي»

(O Allah! Make Your biggest provision for me when I am old in age and at the time my life ends.)

This is why Allah said, (Thus Allah makes clear to you His Laws in order that you may give thought) meaning, comprehend and understand the parables and their intended implications. Similarly, Allah said,

(And these similitudes We put forward for mankind; but none will understand them except those who have knowledge (of Allah and His signs)) (29:43).

Surah: 2 Ayah: 267, Ayah: 268 & Ayah: 269

﴿ يَٰٓأَيُّهَا ٱلَّذِينَ ءَامَنُوٓاْ أَنفِقُواْ مِن طَيِّبَٰتِ مَا كَسَبۡتُمۡ وَمِمَّآ أَخۡرَجۡنَا لَكُم مِّنَ ٱلۡأَرۡضِۖ وَلَا تَيَمَّمُواْ ٱلۡخَبِيثَ مِنۡهُ تُنفِقُونَ وَلَسۡتُم بِـَٔاخِذِيهِ إِلَّآ أَن تُغۡمِضُواْ فِيهِۚ وَٱعۡلَمُوٓاْ أَنَّ ٱللَّهَ غَنِيٌّ حَمِيدٌ ﴾

267. O you who believe! Spend of the good things which you have (legally) earned, and of that which We have produced from the earth for you, and do not aim at that which is bad to spend from it, (though) you would not accept it save if you close your eyes and tolerate therein. And know that Allâh is Rich (Free of all needs), and Worthy of all praise.

﴿ ٱلشَّيْطَـٰنُ يَعِدُكُمُ ٱلْفَقْرَ وَيَأْمُرُكُم بِٱلْفَحْشَآءِ ۖ وَٱللَّهُ يَعِدُكُم مَّغْفِرَةً مِّنْهُ وَفَضْلًا ۗ وَٱللَّهُ وَٰسِعٌ عَلِيمٌ ﴿٢٦٨﴾

268. Shaitân (Satan) threatens you with poverty and orders you to commit Fahshâ (evil deeds, illegal sexual intercourse, sins); whereas Allâh promises you Forgiveness from Himself and Bounty, and Allâh is All-Sufficient for His creatures' needs, All-Knower.

﴿ يُؤْتِى ٱلْحِكْمَةَ مَن يَشَآءُ ۚ وَمَن يُؤْتَ ٱلْحِكْمَةَ فَقَدْ أُوتِىَ خَيْرًا كَثِيرًا ۗ وَمَا يَذَّكَّرُ إِلَّآ أُوْلُواْ ٱلْأَلْبَـٰبِ ﴿٢٦٩﴾

269. He grants Hikmah to whom He pleases, and he, to whom Hikmah is granted, is indeed granted abundant good. But none remember (will receive admonition) except men of understanding.

Transliteration

267. Ya ayyuha allatheena amanoo anfiqoo min tayyibati ma kasabtum wamimma akhrajna lakum mina al-ardi wala tayammamoo alkhabeetha minhu tunfiqoona walastum bi-akhitheehi illa an tughmidoo feehi waiAAlamoo anna Allaha ghaniyyun hameedun 268. Alshshaytanu yaAAidukumu alfaqra waya/murukum bialfahsha-i waAllahu yaAAidukum maghfiratan minhu wafadlan waAllahu wasiAAun AAaleemun 269. Yu/tee alhikmata man yashao waman yu/ta alhikmata faqad ootiya khayran katheeran wama yaththakkaru illa oloo al-albabi

Tafsir Ibn Kathir

The Encouragement to Spend Honest Money for Allah's Sake

Allah commands His believing servants to spend in charity, as Ibn `Abbas stated, from the pure, honest money that they earned and from the fruits and vegetables that He has grown for them in the land. Ibn `Abbas said, "Allah commanded them to spend from the purest, finest and best types of their money and prohibited spending from evil and dishonest money, because Allah is pure and good and only accepts that which is pure and good." This is why Allah said,

(and do not aim at that which is bad) meaning, filthy (impure) money,

(to spend from it, (though) you would not accept it) meaning, "If you were given this type, you would not take it, except if you tolerate the deficiency in it. Verily, Allah is far Richer than you, He is in no need of this money, so do not give, for His sake, what you would dislike for yourselves." It was reported that,

(and do not aim at that which is bad to spend from it) means, "Do not spend from the dishonest, impure money instead of the honest, pure money."

Ibn Jarir recorded that Al-Bara' bin `Azib commented on Allah's statement,

(O you who believe! Spend of the good things which you have (legally) earned, and of that which We have produced from the earth for you, and do not aim at that which is bad to spend from it,) that it was revealed about the Ansar. When the season for harvesting date-trees would start, the Ansar would collect ripe-date branches from their gardens and hang them on a rope erected between two pillars in the Masjid of the Messenger of Allah. The poor emigrant Companions would eat from these dates. However, some of them (Ansar) would also add lesser type of dates in between ripe-date branches, thinking they are allowed to do so. Allah revealed this Ayah about those who did this,

(and do not aim at that which is bad to spend from it.)

`Ali bin Abi Talhah said that Ibn `Abbas commented on the Ayah,

(you would not accept it save if you close your eyes and tolerate therein) means, "If you had a right on someone who would pay you less than what you gave them, you would not agree until you require more from them to make up the difference. This is why Allah said,

(save if you close your eyes and tolerate therein) meaning, `How do you agree for Me what you do not agree for yourselves, while I have a right to the best and most precious of your possessions'' Ibn Abi Hatim and Ibn Jarir recorded this Hadith and Ibn Jarir added, "And this is the meaning of Allah's statement,

(By no means shall you attain Al-Birr, unless you spend of that which you love)'' (4:92)

Allah said next,

(And know that Allah is Rich (free of all needs), and worthy of all praise) meaning, "Although Allah commanded you to give away the purest of your money in charity, He is far Richer from needing your charity, but the purpose is that the distance between the rich and the poor becomes less.'' Similarly, Allah said,

(It is neither their meat nor their blood that reaches Allah, but it is piety from you that reaches Him) (22:37).

Allah is Rich and free of needing anything from any of His creatures, while all of His creatures stand in need of Him. Allah's bounty encompassing, and what He has never ends. Therefore, whoever gives away good and pure things in charity, let him know that Allah is the Most Rich, His favor is enormous and He is Most Generous, Most Compassionate; and He shall reward him for his charity and multiply it many times. So who would lend to He Who is neither poor nor unjust, Who is worthy of all praise in all His actions, statements, and decisions, of Whom there is neither a deity worthy of worship except Him, nor a Lord other than Him

Shaytanic Doubts Concerning Spending in Charity

Allah said,

(Shaytan threatens you with poverty and orders you to commit Fahsha'; whereas Allah promises you forgiveness from Himself and bounty, and Allah is All-Sufficient for His creatures' needs, All-Knower.)

Ibn Abi Hatim recorded that `Abdullah bin Mas`ud said that the Messenger of Allah said,

«إِنَّ لِلشَّيْطَانِ لَمَّةً بِابْنِ آدَمَ، وَلِلْمَلَكِ لَمَّةً، فَأَمَّا لَمَّةُ الشَّيْطَانِ فَإِيعَادٌ بِالشَّرِّ وَتَكْذِيبٌ بِالْحَقِّ، وَ أَمَّا لَمَّةُ الْمَلَكِ فَإِيعَادٌ بِالْخَيْرِ، وَتَصْدِيقٌ بِالْحَقِّ، فَمَنْ وَجَدَ ذَلِكَ فَلْيَعْلَمْ أَنَّهُ مِنَ اللهِ، فَلْيَحْمَدِ اللهَ، وَمَنْ وَجَدَ الْأُخْرَى فَلْيَتَعَوَّذْ مِنَ الشَّيْطَان»

(Shaytan has an effect on the son of Adam, and the angel also has an effect. As for the effect of Shaytan, it is by his threatening with evil repercussions and rejecting the truth. As for the effect of the angel, it is by his promise of a good end and believing in the truth. Whoever finds the latter, let him know that it is coming from Allah and let him thank Allah for it. Whoever finds the former, let him seek refuge - with Allah - from Shaytan.)

The Prophet then recited,

(Shaytan threatens you with poverty and orders you to commit Fahsha'; whereas Allah promises you forgiveness from Himself and bounty)

This is the narration that At-Tirmidhi and An-Nasa'i collected in the book of Tafsir in their Sunan collections. Allah said,

(Shaytan threatens you with poverty), so that you hold on to whatever you have and refrain from spending it in Allah's pleasure.

(And orders you to commit Fahsha'), meaning, "Shaytan forbids you from spending in charity because of the false fear of becoming poor, and he encourages evil deeds, sins, indulging in what is prohibited, and immoral conduct." Allah said,

(Whereas Allah promises you forgiveness from Himself) instead of the evil that Shaytan enjoins on you,

(And Bounty) as opposed to the poverty that Shaytan frightens you with,

(And Allah is All-Sufficient for His creatures' needs, All-Knower.)

The Meaning of Al-Hikmah

Allah said,

(He grants Hikmah to whom He wills.)

`Ali bin Abi Talhah reported that Ibn `Abbas said, "That is knowledge of the Qur'an. For instance, the abrogating and the abrogated, what is plain and clear and what is not as plain and clear, what it allows, and what it does not allow, and its parables." Imam Ahmad recorded that Ibn Mas`ud said that he heard the Messenger of Allah saying,

«لَا حَسَدَ إِلَّا فِي اثْنَتَيْنِ: رَجُلٌ آتَاهُ اللهُ مَالًا فَسَلَّطَهُ عَلَى هَلَكَتِهِ فِي الْحَقِّ، وَرَجُلٌ آتَاهُ اللهُ حِكْمَةً فَهُوَ يَقْضِي بِهَا وَيُعَلِّمُهَا»

(There is no envy except in two instances: a person whom Allah has endowed with wealth and he spends it righteously, and a person whom Allah has given Hikmah and he judges by it and teaches it to others.)

This was also collected by Al-Bukhari, Muslim, An-Nasa'i, Ibn Majah.

Allah's statement,

(But none remember (will receive admonition) except men of understanding.) means, "Those who will benefit from the advice are those who have sound minds and good comprehension with which they understand the words (of advice and reminder) and their implications."

Surah: 2 Ayah: 270 & Ayah: 271

﴿ وَمَا أَنفَقْتُم مِّن نَّفَقَةٍ أَوْ نَذَرْتُم مِّن نَّذْرٍ فَإِنَّ ٱللَّهَ يَعْلَمُهُۥ ۗ وَمَا لِلظَّٰلِمِينَ مِنْ أَنصَارٍ ﴾

270. And whatever you spend for spendings (e.g., in Sadaqah - charity for Allâh's Cause) or whatever vow you make, be sure Allâh knows it all. And for the Zâlimûn (wrong-doers.) there are no helpers.

﴿ إِن تُبْدُواْ ٱلصَّدَقَٰتِ فَنِعِمَّا هِىَ ۖ وَإِن تُخْفُوهَا وَتُؤْتُوهَا ٱلْفُقَرَآءَ فَهُوَ خَيْرٌ لَّكُمْ ۚ وَيُكَفِّرُ عَنكُم مِّن سَيِّـَٔاتِكُمْ ۗ وَٱللَّهُ بِمَا تَعْمَلُونَ خَبِيرٌ ﴾

271. If you disclose your Sadaqât (alms-giving), it is well; but if you conceal them, and give them to the poor, that is better for you. (Allâh) will expiate you some of your sins. And Allâh is Well-Acquainted with what you do.

Transliteration

270. Wama anfaqtum min nafaqatin aw nathartum min nathrin fa-inna Allaha yaAAlamuhu wama lilththalimeena min ansarin   271. In tubdoo alssadaqati

faniAAimma hiya wa-in tukhfooha watu/tooha alfuqaraa fahuwa khayrun lakum wayukaffiru AAankum min sayyi-atikum waAllahu bima taAAmaloona khabeerun

Tafsir Ibn Kathir

Allah states that He has perfect knowledge of the good deeds performed by all of His creation, such as charity and various vows, and He rewards tremendously for these deeds, provided they are performed seeking His Face and His promise. Allah also warns those who do not work in his obedience, but instead disobey His command, reject His revelation and worship others besides Him:

(And for the wrongdoers there are no helpers.) meaning, who will save them from Allah's anger and torment on the Day of Resurrection.

The Virtue of Disclosing or Concealing Charity

Allah said,

(If you disclose your Sadaqat, it is well) meaning, "It is well if you make known the charity that you give away."

Allah's statement,

(But if you conceal them and give them to the poor, that is better for you.) this indicates that concealing charity is better than disclosing it, because it protects one from showing off and boasting. However, if there is an apparent wisdom behind disclosing the charity, such as the people imitating this righteous act, then disclosing it becomes better than concealing it. The Messenger of Allah said,

«الْجَاهِرُ بِالْقُرْآنِ كَالْجَاهِرِ بِالصَّدَقَةِ، وَالْمُسِرُّ بِالْقُرْآنِ كَالْمُسِرِّ بِالصَّدَقَةِ»

(He who utters aloud Qur'anic recitation is just like he who discloses charity acts. He who conceals Qur'anic recitation is just like he who conceals charity acts.)

The Ayah indicates that it is better that acts of charity be concealed, as reiterated by the Hadith that the Two Sahihs recorded from Abu Hurayrah that the Messenger of Allah said,

«سَبْعَةٌ يُظِلُّهُمُ اللهُ فِي ظِلِّهِ يَوْمَ لَا ظِلَّ إِلَّا ظِلُّهُ: إِمَامٌ عَادِلٌ، وَشَابٌّ نَشَأَ فِي عِبَادَةِ اللهِ، وَرَجُلَانِ تَحَابَّا فِي اللهِ، اجْتَمَعَا عَلَيْهِ وَتَفَرَّقَا عَلَيْهِ، وَرَجُلٌ قَلْبُهُ مُعَلَّقٌ بِالْمَسْجِدِ، إِذَا خَرَجَ مِنْهُ حَتَّى يَرْجِعَ إِلَيْهِ، وَرَجُلٌ ذَكَرَ اللهَ خَالِيًا فَفَاضَتْ عَيْنَاهُ، وَرَجُلٌ دَعَتْهُ امْرَأَةٌ ذَاتُ مَنْصِبٍ وَجَمَالٍ، فَقَالَ: إِنِّي أَخَافُ اللهَ رَبَّ

الْعَالَمِينَ، وَرَجُلٌ تَصَدَّقَ بِصَدَقَةٍ فَأَخْفَاهَا، حَتَّى لَا تَعْلَمَ شِمَالُهُ مَا تُنْفِقُ يَمِينُهُ»

(Allah will give shade to seven on the Day when there will be no shade but His. (They are:) a just ruler, a youth who has been brought up in the worship of Allah, two persons who love each other only for Allah's sake who meet and part in Allah's cause only, a man whose heart is attached to the Masjids from the time he departs the Masjid until he returns to it, a person who remembers Allah in seclusion and his eyes are then flooded with tears, a man who refuses the call of a charming woman of noble birth for illicit intercourse with her and says, `I fear Allah, Lord of the worlds', and a man who gives charitable gifts so secretly that his left hand does not know what his right hand has given.)

Allah's statement, ((Allah) will expiate you some of your sins) means, in return for giving away charity, especially if it was concealed. Therefore, you will gain goodness by your rank being raised, and your sins being forgiven.

Allah's statement,

(And Allah is Well-Acquainted with what you do) means, "No good deed that you perform escapes His knowledge, and He shall reward for it."

Surah: 2 Ayah: 272, Ayah: 273 & Ayah: 274

﴿ ۞ لَّيْسَ عَلَيْكَ هُدَاهُمْ وَلَٰكِنَّ ٱللَّهَ يَهْدِى مَن يَشَآءُ ۗ وَمَا تُنفِقُوا۟ مِنْ خَيْرٍ فَلِأَنفُسِكُمْ ۚ وَمَا تُنفِقُونَ إِلَّا ٱبْتِغَآءَ وَجْهِ ٱللَّهِ ۚ وَمَا تُنفِقُوا۟ مِنْ خَيْرٍ يُوَفَّ إِلَيْكُمْ وَأَنتُمْ لَا تُظْلَمُونَ ۝ ﴾

272. Not upon you (Muhammad (peace be upon him)) is their guidance, but Allâh guides whom He wills. And whatever you spend in good, it is for yourselves, when you spend not except seeking Allâh's Countenance. And whatever you spend in good, it will be repaid to you in full, and you shall not be wronged.

﴿ لِلْفُقَرَآءِ ٱلَّذِينَ أُحْصِرُوا۟ فِى سَبِيلِ ٱللَّهِ لَا يَسْتَطِيعُونَ ضَرْبًا فِى ٱلْأَرْضِ يَحْسَبُهُمُ ٱلْجَاهِلُ أَغْنِيَآءَ مِنَ ٱلتَّعَفُّفِ تَعْرِفُهُم بِسِيمَٰهُمْ لَا يَسْـَٔلُونَ ٱلنَّاسَ إِلْحَافًا ۗ وَمَا تُنفِقُوا۟ مِنْ خَيْرٍ فَإِنَّ ٱللَّهَ بِهِۦ عَلِيمٌ ۝ ﴾

273. (Charity is) for Fuqarâ (the poor), who in Allâh's Cause are restricted (from travel), and cannot move about in the land (for trade or work). The one who knows them not, thinks that they are rich because of their modesty. You may

know them by their mark, they do not beg of people at all. And whatever you spend in good, surely Allâh knows it well.

﴿ ٱلَّذِينَ يُنفِقُونَ أَمْوَٰلَهُم بِٱلَّيْلِ وَٱلنَّهَارِ سِرًّا وَعَلَانِيَةً فَلَهُمْ أَجْرُهُمْ عِندَ رَبِّهِمْ وَلَا خَوْفٌ عَلَيْهِمْ وَلَا هُمْ يَحْزَنُونَ ﴾

274. Those who spend their wealth (in Allâh's Cause) by night and day, in secret and in public, they shall have their reward with their Lord. On them shall be no fear, nor shall they grieve.

Transliteration

272. Laysa AAalayka hudahum walakinna Allaha yahdee man yashao wama tunfiqoo min khayrin falianfusikum wama tunfiqoona illa ibtighaa wajhi Allahi wama tunfiqoo min khayrin yuwaffa ilaykum waantum la tu*th*lamoona **273.** Lilfuqara-i allatheena ohsiroo fee sabeeli Allahi la yastateeAAoona darban fee al-ardi yahsabuhumu aljahilu aghniyaa mina alttaAAaffufi taAArifuhum biseemahum la yas-aloona alnnasa ilhafan wama tunfiqoo min khayrin fa-inna Allaha bihi AAaleemun **274.** Allatheena yunfiqoona amwalahum biallayli waalnnahari sirran waAAalaniyatan falahum ajruhum AAinda rabbihim wala khawfun AAalayhim wala hum yahzanoona

Tafsir Ibn Kathir

Giving Charity to Polytheists

Abu `Abdur-Rahman An-Nasa'i recorded that Ibn `Abbas said that they, "Disliked giving charity to their polytheist relatives, but were later on allowed to give it to them when they inquired about this matter, and this Ayah was revealed,

(Not upon you (Muhammad) is their guidance, but Allah guides whom He wills. And whatever you spend in good, it is for yourselves, when you spend not except seeking Allah's Face. And whatever you spend in good, it will be repaid to you in full, and you shall not be wronged.)

Allah's statement,

(And whatever you spend in good, it is for yourselves) is similar to His other statement,

(Whosoever does righteous good deed, it is for (the benefit of) his ownself.)

There are many other similar Ayat in the Qur'an.

Allah said next,

(When you spend not except seeking Allah's Face.)

Al-Hasan Al-Basri commented, "Whenever the believer spends, including what he spends on himself, he seeks Allah's Face with it." `Ata' Al-Khurasani said that the Ayah means, "You give away charity for the sake of Allah. Therefore, you will not be asked about the deeds (or wickedness) of those who receive it." This is a sound meaning indicating that when one spends in charity for Allah's sake, then his reward will be with Allah. He will not be asked if the charity unintentionally reached righteous, evil, deserving or undeserving persons, for he will be rewarded for his good intention. The proof to this statement is the Ayah,

(And whatever you spend in good, it will be repaid to you in full, and you shall not be wronged.)

The Two Sahihs recorded a Hadith by Abu Hurayrah that the Messenger of Allah said,

«قَالَ رَجُلٌ: لَأَتَصَدَّقَنَّ اللَّيْلَةَ بِصَدَقَةٍ، فَخَرَجَ بِصَدَقَتِهِ فَوَضَعَهَا فِي يَدِ زَانِيَةٍ، فَأَصْبَحَ النَّاسُ يَتَحَدَّثُونَ: تُصُدِّقَ عَلَى زَانِيَةٍ، فَقَالَ: اللَّهُمَّ لَكَ الْحَمْدُ عَلَى زَانِيَةٍ، لَأَتَصَدَّقَنَّ اللَّيْلَةَ بِصَدَقَةٍ، فَخَرَجَ بِصَدَقَتِهِ فَوَضَعَهَا فِي يَدِ غَنِيٍّ، فَأَصْبَحُوا يَتَحَدَّثُونَ: تُصُدِّقَ اللَّيْلَةَ عَلَى غَنِيٍّ، قَالَ: اللَّهُمَّ لَكَ الْحَمْدُ عَلَى غَنِيٍّ، لَأَتَصَدَّقَنَّ اللَّيْلَةَ بِصَدَقَةٍ، فَخَرَجَ بِصَدَقَتِهِ فَوَضَعَهَا فِي يَدِ سَارِقٍ، فَأَصْبَحُوا يَتَحَدَّثُونَ: تُصُدِّقَ اللَّيْلَةَ عَلَى سَارِقٍ، فَقَالَ: اللَّهُمَّ لَكَ الْحَمْدُ عَلَى زَانِيَةٍ، وَعَلَى غَنِيٍّ، وَعَلَى سَارِقٍ. فَأُتِيَ فَقِيلَ لَهُ: أَمَّا صَدَقَتُكَ فَقَدْ قُبِلَتْ، وَأَمَّا الزَّانِيَةُ فَلَعَلَّهَا أَنْ تَسْتَعِفَّ بِهَا عَنْ زِنَاهَا، وَلَعَلَّ الْغَنِيَّ يَعْتَبِرُ فَيُنْفِقُ مِمَّا أَعْطَاهُ اللهُ، وَلَعَلَّ السَّارِقَ أَنْ يَسْتَعِفَّ بِهَا عَنْ سَرِقَتِهِ»

(A man said, "Tonight, I shall give charity." He went out with his charity and (unknowingly) gave it to an adulteress. The next morning the people said that alms were given to an adulteress. The man said, "O Allah! All the praises are for You. (I gave my alms) to an adulteress. Tonight, I shall give alms again." He went out with his charity and (unknowingly) gave it to a rich person. The next morning (the people) said, "Last night, a wealthy person was given alms." He said, "O Allah! All the praises are for You. (I gave alms) to a wealthy man. Tonight, I shall again give charity." So he went out with his charity and (unknowingly) gave it to a thief. The next morning (the people) said, "Last night, a thief was given alms." He said, "O Allah! All the praises are for You. (I have given alms) to an adulteress, a wealthy man and a thief." Then, someone came to him and said, "The alms that you gave away were accepted. As for the adulteress, the alms might make her abstain from adultery. As for the wealthy man, it might make him take a lesson and spend his wealth that Allah has given him. As for the thief, it might make him abstain from stealing.")

Who Deserves Charity

Allah said,

((Charity is) for the poor, who in Allah's cause are restricted (from travel)) meaning, the migrants who migrated to Allah and His Messenger, resided in Al-Madinah and did not have resources that sufficiently provided them with their needs,

(And cannot Darban (move about) in the land) meaning, "They cannot travel in the land to seek means of livelihood." Allah said in other instances (using a variation of the word Darban)

(And when you (Muslims) travel in the land, there is no sin on you if you shorten the Salah (the prayer)) (4:101), and,

(He knows that there will be some among you sick, others traveling through the land, seeking of Allah's bounty, yet others fighting in Allah's cause) (73:20).

Allah then said,

(The one who knows them not, thinks that they are rich because of their modesty) meaning, those who do not know their situation think that they are well-off, because they are modest in their clothes and speech. There is a Hadith with this meaning that the Two Sahihs recorded from Abu Hurayrah that the Messenger of Allah said,

«لَيْسَ الْمِسْكِينُ بِهذَا الطَّوَّافِ الَّذِي تَرُدُّهُ التَّمْرَةُ وَالتَّمْرَتَانِ، وَاللُّقْمَةُ وَاللُّقْمَتَانِ، وَالْأُكْلَةُ وَالْأُكْلَتَانِ، وَلكِنِ الْمِسْكِينُ الَّذِي لَا يَجِدُ غِنًى يُغْنِيهِ، وَلَا يُفْطَنُ لَهُ فَيُتَصَدَّقَ عَلَيْهِ، وَلَا يَسْأَلُ النَّاسَ شَيْئًا»

(The Miskin (needy) is not he who wanders about and whose need is sufficed by a date or two, a bite or two or a meal or two. Rather, the Miskin is he who neither has enough resources to sustain him, all the while people are unaware of his need so they do not give to him, nor does he ask people for anything.)

Imam Ahmad also recorded this Hadith from Ibn Mas`ud.

Allah's statement,

(You may know them by their mark) means, "Those who have good minds discover their situation," just as Allah said in other instances,

(The mark of them (i.e. of their faith) is on their faces) (48:29), and,

(But surely, you will know them by the tone of their speech!) (47:30). Allah's statement, (they do not beg of people at all) means, they do not beg and, thus, do not require people to provide them with more than what they actually need. Indeed, those who ask people for help, while having what suffices for their needs, have begged.

Imam Ahmad recorded that Abu Sa`id said, "My mother sent me to the Messenger of Allah to ask him for help, but when I came by him I sat down. The Prophet faced me and said to me,

«مَنِ اسْتَغْنَى أَغْنَاهُ اللهُ، وَمَنِ اسْتَعَفَّ أَعَفَّهُ اللهُ، وَمَنِ اسْتَكَفَّ كَفَاهُ اللهُ، وَمَنْ سَأَلَ وَلَهُ قِيمَةُ أُوقِيَةٍ فَقَدْ أَلْحَفَ»

(Whoever felt satisfied, then Allah will enrich him. Whoever is modest, Allah will make him decent. Whoever is content, then Allah will suffice for him. Whoever asks people, while having a small amout, he will have begged the people.)

Abu Sa`id said, "I said to myself, `I have a camel, Al-Yaqutah, and indeed, it is worth more than a small amount.' And I went back without asking the Prophet for anything." This is the same wording for this Hadith collected by Abu Dawud and An-Nasa'i.

Allah's statement,

(And whatever you spend in good, surely Allah knows it well) indicates that no charity escapes Him, and He will reward it fully and perfectly on the Day of Resurrection, when it is most desperately needed.

Praise for those who Spend in Charity

Allah said,

(Those who spend their wealth (in Allah's cause) by night and day, in secret and in public, they shall have their reward with their Lord. On them shall be no fear, nor shall they grieve.)

This Ayah praises those who spend in charity for Allah's sake, seeking His pleasure, day and night, publicly and in secret, including what one spends on his family. The Two Sahihs recorded that the Messenger of Allah said to Sa`d bin Abi Waqqas:

«وَإِنَّكَ لَنْ تُنْفِقَ نَفَقَةً تَبْتَغِي بِهَا وَجْهَ اللهِ إِلَّا ازْدَدْتَ بِهَا دَرَجَةً وَرِفْعَةً، حَتَّى مَا تَجْعَلُ فِي فِي امْرَأَتِك»

(You will not spend charity with which you seek Allah's Face, but you will ascend a higher degree and status because of it, including what you put in your wife's mouth.)

Imam Ahmad recorded that Abu Mas`ud said that the Prophet said,

«إِنَّ الْمُسْلِمَ إِذَا أَنْفَقَ عَلَى أَهْلِهِ نَفَقَةً يَحْتَسِبُهَا، كَانَتْ لَهُ صَدَقَةً»

(When the Muslim spends on his family while awaiting the reward for it from Allah, it will be written as charity for him.)

Al-Bukhari and Muslim also recorded this Hadith.

Allah said,

(shall have their reward with their Lord), on the Day of Resurrection, as reward for what they spent in acts of obedience. We previously explained the Ayah,

(there shall be no fear on them nor shall they grieve.)

Surah: 2 Ayah: 275

﴿ٱلَّذِينَ يَأْكُلُونَ ٱلرِّبَوٰاْ لَا يَقُومُونَ إِلَّا كَمَا يَقُومُ ٱلَّذِى يَتَخَبَّطُهُ ٱلشَّيْطَـٰنُ مِنَ ٱلْمَسِّ ۚ ذَٰلِكَ بِأَنَّهُمْ قَالُوٓاْ إِنَّمَا ٱلْبَيْعُ مِثْلُ ٱلرِّبَوٰاْ ۗ وَأَحَلَّ ٱللَّهُ ٱلْبَيْعَ وَحَرَّمَ ٱلرِّبَوٰاْ ۚ فَمَن جَآءَهُۥ مَوْعِظَةٌ مِّن رَّبِّهِۦ فَٱنتَهَىٰ فَلَهُۥ مَا سَلَفَ وَأَمْرُهُۥٓ إِلَى ٱللَّهِ ۖ وَمَنْ عَادَ فَأُوْلَـٰٓئِكَ أَصْحَـٰبُ ٱلنَّارِ ۖ هُمْ فِيهَا خَـٰلِدُونَ ﴿٢٧٥﴾﴾

275. Those who eat Ribâ (usury) will not stand (on the Day of Resurrection) except like the standing of a person beaten by Shaitân (Satan) leading him to insanity. That is because they say: "Trading is only like Ribâ (usury)," whereas Allâh has permitted trading and forbidden Ribâ (usury). So whosoever receives an admonition from his Lord and stops eating Ribâ (usury) shall not be punished for the past; his case is for Allâh (to judge); but whoever returns (to Ribâ (usury)) such are the dwellers of the Fire - they will abide therein.

Transliteration

275. Allatheena ya/kuloona alrriba la yaqoomoona illa kama yaqoomu allathee yatakhabbatuhu alshshaytanu mina almassi thalika bi-annahum qaloo innama albayAAu mithlu alrriba waahalla Allahu albayAAa waharrama alrriba faman jaahu mawAAithatun min rabbihi faintaha falahu ma salafa waamruhu ila Allahi waman AAada faola-ika as-habu alnnari hum feeha khalidoona

Tafsir Ibn Kathir

The Punishment for Dealing with Riba (Interest and Usury)

After Allah mentioned the righteous believers who give charity, pay Zakah and spend on their relatives and families at various times and conditions, He then mentioned those who deal in usury and illegally acquire people's money, using various evil methods and wicked ways. Allah describes the condition of these people when they are resurrected from their graves and brought back to life on the Day of Resurrection:

(Those who eat Riba will not stand (on the Day of Resurrection) except like the standing of a person beaten by Shaytan leading him to insanity.)

This Ayah means, on the Day of Resurrection, these people will get up from their graves just as the person afflicted by insanity or possessed by a demon would. Ibn `Abbas said, "On the Day of Resurrection, those who consume Riba will be resurrected while insane and suffering from seizures." Ibn Abi Hatim also recorded this and then commented, "This Tafsir was reported from `Awf bin Malik, Sa`id bin Jubayr, As-Suddi, Ar-Rabi` bin Anas, Qatadah and Muqatil bin Hayyan." Al-Bukhari recorded that Samurah bin Jundub said in the long Hadith about the dream that the Prophet had,

«فَأَتَيْنَا عَلَى نَهَرٍ حَسِبْتُ أَنَّهُ كَانَ يَقُولُ: أَحْمَرَ مِثْلَ الدَّمِ، وَإِذَا فِي النَّهَرِ رَجُلٌ سَابِحٌ يَسْبَحُ، وَإِذَا عَلَى شَطِّ النَّهَرِ رَجُلٌ قَدْ جَمَعَ عِنْدَهُ حِجَارَةً كَثِيرَةً، وَإِذَا ذَلِكَ السَّابِحُ يَسْبَحُ مَا يَسْبَحُ، ثُمَّ يَأْتِي ذَلِكَ الَّذِي قَدْ جَمَعَ الْحِجَارَةَ عِنْدَهُ، فَيَفْغَرُ لَهُ فَاهُ فَيُلْقِمُهُ حَجَرًا»

(We reached a river -the narrator said, "I thought he said that the river was as red as blood"- and found that a man was swimming in the river, and on its bank there was another man standing with a large collection of stones next to him. The man in the river would swim, then come to the man who had collected the stones and open his mouth, and the other man would throw a stone in his mouth.)

The explanation of this dream was that the person in the river was one who consumed Riba.

Allah's statement,

(That is because they say: "Trading is only like Riba," whereas Allah has permitted trading and forbidden Riba) indicates that the disbelievers claimed that Riba was allowed due to the fact that they rejected Allah's commandments, not that they equated Riba with regular trade. The disbelievers did not recognize that Allah allowed trade in the Qur'an, for if they did, they would have said, "Riba is trade." Rather, they said,

(Trading is only like Riba) meaning, they are similar, so why did Allah allow this, but did not allow that, they asked in defiance of Allah's commandments.

Allah's statement,

(Whereas Allah has permitted trading and forbidden Riba) might be a continuation of the answer to the disbelievers' claim, who uttered it, although they knew that Allah decided that ruling on trade is different from that of Riba. Indeed, Allah is the Most Knowledgeable, Most Wise, Whose decision is never resisted. Allah is never asked about what He does, while they will be asked. He is knowledgeable of the true reality of all things and the benefits they carry. He knows what benefits His servants, so He allows it for them, and what harms them, so He forbids them from it. He is more merciful with them than the mother with her own infant.

Thereafter, Allah said,

(So whosoever receives an admonition from his Lord and stops eating Riba, shall not be punished for the past; his case is for Allah (to judge),) meaning, those who have knowledge that Allah made usury unlawful, and refrain from indulging in it as soon as they acquire this knowledge, then Allah will forgive their previous dealings in Riba,

(Allah has forgiven what is past.)

On the day Makkah was conquered the Prophet said,

«وَكُلُّ رِبًا فِي الْجَاهِلِيَّةِ مَوْضُوعٌ تَحْتَ قَدَمَيَّ هَاتَيْنِ، وَأَوَّلُ رِبًا أَضَعُ، رِبَا الْعَبَّاسِ»

(All cases of Riba during the time of Jahiliyyah (pre-Islamic period of ignorance) is annulled and under my feet, and the first Riba I annul is the Riba of Al-'Abbas (the Prophet's uncle).)

We should mention that the Prophet did not require the return of the interest that they gained on their Riba during the time of Jahiliyyah. Rather, he pardoned the cases of Riba that occured in the past, just as Allah said,

(shall not be punished for the past; his case is for Allah (to judge).)

Sa`id bin Jubayr and As-Suddi said that,

(shall not be punished for the past) refers to the Riba one consumed before it was prohibited. Allah then said,

(But whoever returns) meaning, deals in Riba after gaining knowledge that Allah prohibited it, then that warrants punishment, and in this case, the proof will have been established against such person. This is why Allah said,

(such are the dwellers of the Fire - they will abide therein forever.)

Abu Dawud recorded that Jabir said, "When

(Those who eat Riba will not stand (on the Day of Resurrection) except like a person beaten by Shaytan leading him to insanity) was revealed, the Messenger of Allah said,

«مَنْ لَمْ يَذَرِ الْمُخَابَرَةَ فَلْيُؤْذِنْ بِحَرْبٍ مِنَ اللهِ وَرَسُولِهِ»

(Whoever does not refrain from Mukhabarah, then let him receive a notice of war from Allah and His Messenger.)"

Al-Hakim also recorded this in his Mustadrak, and he said, "It is Sahih according to the criteria of Muslim, and he did not record it." Mukhabarah (sharecropping), farming land in return for some of its produce, was prohibited. Muzabanah, trading fresh dates still on trees with dried dates already on the ground, was prohibited. Muhaqalah, which refers to trading produce not yet harvested, with crops already harvested, was also prohibited. These were prohibited to eradicate the possibility that Riba might be involved, for the quality and equity of such items are only known after they become dry.

The subject of Riba is a difficult subject for many scholars. We should mention that the Leader of the Faithful, `Umar bin Al-Khattab, said, "I wished that the Messenger of Allah had made three matters clearer for us, so that we could refer to his decision: the grandfather (regarding inheriting from his grandchildren), the Kalalah (those who leave neither descendants nor ascendants as heirs) and some types of Riba." `Umar was referring to the types of transactions where it is not clear whether they involve Riba or not. The Shari`ah supports the rule that for any matter that is unlawful, then the means to it are also unlafwful, because whatever results in the unlawful is unlawful, in the same way that whenever an obligation will not be complete except with something, then that something is itself an obligation.

The Two Sahihs recorded that An-Nu`man bin Bashir said that he heard the Messenger of Allah say,

»إِنَّ الْحَلَالَ بَيِّنٌ وَإِنَّ الْحَرَامَ بَيِّنٌ، وَبَيْنَ ذَلِكَ أُمُورٌ مُشْتَبِهَاتٌ، فَمَنِ اتَّقَى الشُّبُهَاتِ اسْتَبْرَأَ لِدِينِهِ وَعِرْضِهِ، وَمَنْ وَقَعَ فِي الشُّبُهَاتِ وَقَعَ فِي الْحَرَامِ، كَالرَّاعِي يَرْعَى حَوْلَ الْحِمَى يُوشِكُ أَنْ يَرْتَعَ فِيهِ«

(Both lawful and unlawful things are evident, but in between them there are matters that are not clear. So whoever saves himself from these unclear matters, he saves his religion and his honor. And whoever indulges in these unclear matters, he will have fallen into the prohibitions, just like a shepherd who grazes (his animals) near a private pasture, at any moment he is liable to enter it.)

The Sunan records that Al-Hasan bin `Ali said that he heard the Messenger of Allah say,

»دَعْ مَا يَرِيبُكَ إِلَى مَا لَا يَرِيبُكَ«

(Leave that which makes you doubt for that which does not make you doubt.)

Ahmad recorded that Sa`id bin Al-Musayyib said that `Umar said, "The Ayah about Riba was one of the last Ayat to be revealed, and the Messenger of Allah died before he explained it to us. So leave that which makes you doubt for that which does not make you doubt."

Ibn Majah recorded that Abu Hurayrah said that the Messenger of Allah said,

«الرِّبَا سَبْعُونَ حُوبًا، أَيْسَرُهَا أَنْ يَنْكِحَ الرَّجُلُ أُمَّه»

(Riba is seventy types, the least of which is equal to one having sexual intercourse with his mother.)

Continuing on the subject of prohibiting the means that lead to the unlawful, there is a Hadith that Ahmad recorded in which `A'ishah said, "When the Ayat in Surat Al-Baqarah about Riba were revealed, the Messenger of Allah went out to the Masjid and recited them and also prohibited trading in alcohol." The Six collections recorded this Hadith, with the exception of At-Tirmidhi. The Two Sahihs recorded that the Messenger of Allah said,

«لَعَنَ اللهُ الْيَهُودَ، حُرِّمَتْ عَلَيْهِمُ الشُّحُومُ فَجَمَلُوهَا فَبَاعُوهَا، وَأَكَلُوا أَثْمَانَهَا»

(May Allah curse the Jews! Allah forbade them to eat animal fat, but they melted it and sold it, eating its price.)

`Ali and Ibn Mas`ud narrated that the Messenger of Allah said,

«لَعَنَ اللهُ آكِلَ الرِّبَا وَمُوكِلَهُ وَشَاهِدَيْهِ وَكَاتِبَه»

(May Allah curse whoever consumes Riba, whoever pays Riba, the two who are witnesses to it, and the scribe who records it.)

They say they only have witnesses and a scribe to write the Riba contract when they want it to appear to be a legitimate agreement, but it is still invalid because the ruling is applied to the agreement itself, not the form that it appears in. Verily, deeds are judged by their intentions.

Surah: 2 Ayah: 276 & Ayah: 277

﴿يَمْحَقُ ٱللَّهُ ٱلرِّبَوٰاْ وَيُرْبِى ٱلصَّدَقَٰتِ ۗ وَٱللَّهُ لَا يُحِبُّ كُلَّ كَفَّارٍ أَثِيمٍ ۝﴾

276. Allâh will destroy Ribâ (usury) and will give increase for Sadaqât (deeds of charity, alms, etc.) And Allâh likes not the disbelievers, sinners.

﴿ إِنَّ ٱلَّذِينَ ءَامَنُواْ وَعَمِلُواْ ٱلصَّٰلِحَٰتِ وَأَقَامُواْ ٱلصَّلَوٰةَ وَءَاتَوُاْ ٱلزَّكَوٰةَ لَهُمْ أَجْرُهُمْ عِندَ رَبِّهِمْ وَلَا خَوْفٌ عَلَيْهِمْ وَلَا هُمْ يَحْزَنُونَ ۝ ﴾

277. Truly those who believe, and do deeds of righteousness, and perform As-Salât (Iqâmat-as-Salât), and give Zakât, they will have their reward with their Lord. On them shall be no fear, nor shall they grieve.

Transliteration

276. Yamhaqu Allahu alrriba wayurbee alssadaqati waAllahu la yuhibbu kulla kaffarin atheemin 277. Inna allatheena amanoo waAAamiloo alssalihati waaqamoo alssalata waatawoo alzzakata lahum ajruhum AAinda rabbihim wala khawfun AAalayhim wala hum yahzanoona

Tafsir Ibn Kathir

Allah Does Not Bless Riba

Allah states that He destroys Riba, either by removing this money from those who eat it, or by depriving them of the blessing, and thus the benefit of their money. Because of their Riba, Allah will torment them in this life and punish them for it on the Day of Resurrection. Allah said,

(Say: "Not equal are Al-Khabith (evil things) and At-Tayyib (good things), even though the abundance of Al-Khabith may please you") (5:100)

(And put the wicked (disbelievers and doers of evil deeds) one over another, heap them together and cast them into Hell) (8:37), and,

(And that which you give in gift (to others), in order that it may increase (your wealth by expecting to get a better one in return) from other people's property, has no increase with Allah) (30:39).

Ibn Jarir said that Allah's statement,

(Allah will destroy Riba) is similar to the statement reported of `Abdullah bin Mas`ud, "Riba will end up with less, even if it was substantial." Imam Ahmad recorded a similar statement in Al-Musnad.

Allah Increases Charity, Just as One Raises His Animal

Allah's statement,

(And will give increase for Sadaqat) means, Allah makes charity grow, or He increases it. Al-Bukhari recorded that Abu Hurayrah said that the Messenger of Allah said,

«مَنْ تَصَدَّقَ بِعَدْلِ تَمْرَةٍ مِنْ كَسْبٍ طَيِّبٍ، وَلَا يَقْبَلُ اللهُ إِلَّا الطَّيِّبَ، فَإِنَّ اللهَ

$$\text{يَتَقَبَّلُهَا بِيَمِينِهِ، ثُمَّ يُرَبِّيهَا لِصَاحِبِهِ، كَمَا يُرَبِّي أَحَدُكُمْ فَلُوَّهُ حَتَّى تَكُونَ مِثْلَ الْجَبَلِ}}$$

(Whoever gives in charity what equals a date from honest resources, and Allah only accepts that which is good and pure, then Allah accepts it with His right (Hand) and raises it for its giver, just as one of you raises his animal, until it becomes as big as a mountain.)

This was recorded in the book of Zakah.

Allah Does not Like the Disbelieving Sinners

Allah's statement,

(And Allah likes not the disbelievers, sinners) indicates that Allah does not like he who has a disbelieving heart, who is a sinner in tongue and action. There is a connection between the beginning of the Ayah on Riba and what Allah ended it with. Those who consume Riba are not satisfied with the permissible and pure resources that Allah provided them. Instead, they try to illegally acquire people's money by relying on evil methods. This demonstrates their lack of appreciation for the bounty that Allah provides.

Praising Those Who Thank Allah

Allah praised those who believe in His Lordship, obey His commands, thank Him and appreciate Him. They are those who are kind to His creation, establish prayer and give charity due on their money. Allah informed them of the honor that He has prepared for them and that they will be safe from the repercussions of the Day of Resurrection. Allah said,

(Truly, those who believe, and do deeds of righteousness, and perform the Salah and give Zakah, they will have their reward with their Lord. On them shall be no fear, nor shall they grieve.)

Surah: 2 Ayah: 278, Ayah: 279, Ayah: 280 & Ayah: 281

$$\text{﴿ يَا أَيُّهَا الَّذِينَ آمَنُوا اتَّقُوا اللَّهَ وَذَرُوا مَا بَقِيَ مِنَ الرِّبَا إِنْ كُنْتُمْ مُؤْمِنِينَ ۝ ﴾}$$

278. O you who believe! Be afraid of Allâh and give up what remains (due to you) from Ribâ (usury) (from now onward), if you are (really) believers.

$$\text{﴿ فَإِنْ لَمْ تَفْعَلُوا فَأْذَنُوا بِحَرْبٍ مِنَ اللَّهِ وَرَسُولِهِ ۖ وَإِنْ تُبْتُمْ فَلَكُمْ رُءُوسُ أَمْوَالِكُمْ لَا تَظْلِمُونَ وَلَا تُظْلَمُونَ ۝ ﴾}$$

279. And if you do not do it, then take a notice of war from Allâh and His Messenger but if you repent, you shall have your capital sums. Deal not unjustly (by asking more than your capital sums), and you shall not be dealt with unjustly (by receiving less than your capital sums).

﴿ وَإِن كَانَ ذُو عُسْرَةٍ فَنَظِرَةٌ إِلَىٰ مَيْسَرَةٍ ۚ وَأَن تَصَدَّقُوا۟ خَيْرٌ لَّكُمْ ۖ إِن كُنتُمْ تَعْلَمُونَ ﴿٢٨٠﴾ ﴾

280. And if the debtor is in a hard time (has no money), then grant him time till it is easy for him to repay, but if you remit it by way of charity, that is better for you if you did but know.

﴿ وَٱتَّقُوا۟ يَوْمًا تُرْجَعُونَ فِيهِ إِلَى ٱللَّهِ ۖ ثُمَّ تُوَفَّىٰ كُلُّ نَفْسٍ مَّا كَسَبَتْ وَهُمْ لَا يُظْلَمُونَ ﴿٢٨١﴾ ﴾

281. And be afraid of the Day when you shall be brought back to Allâh. Then every person shall be paid what he earned, and they shall not be dealt with unjustly.

Transliteration

278. Ya ayyuha allatheena amanoo ittaqoo Allaha watharoo ma baqiya mina alrriba in kuntum mu/mineena   279. Fa-in lam tafAAaloo fa/thanoo biharbin mina Allahi warasoolihi wa-in tubtum falakum ruoosu amwalikum la ta*th*limoona wala tu*th*lamoona   280. Wa-in kana thoo AAusratin fana*th*iratun ila maysaratin waan tasaddaqoo khayrun lakum in kuntum taAAlamoona   281. Waittaqoo yawman turjaAAoona feehi ila Allahi thumma tuwaffa kullu nafsin ma kasabat wahum la yu*th*lamoona

Tafsir Ibn Kathir

The Necessity of Taqwa and Avoiding Riba

Allah commands His believing servants to fear Him and warns them against what would bring them closer to His anger and drive them away from His pleasure. Allah said,

(O you who believe! Have Taqwa of Allah) meaning, fear Him and remember that He is watching all that you do.

(And give up what remains of Riba) meaning, abandon the Riba that people still owe you upon hearing this warning,

(if you indeed have been believers) believing in the trade that He allowed you and the prohibition of Riba. Zayd bin Aslam, Ibn Jurayj, Muqatil bin Hayyan and As-Suddi said that this Ayah was revealed about Bani `Amr bin `Umayr, a sub-tribe of Thaqif, and Bani Al-Mughirah, from the tribe of Bani Makhzum, between whom were outstanding transactions of Riba leftover from time of Jahiliyyah. When Islam came and both tribes became Muslims, Thaqif required Bani Al-Mughirah to pay the Riba of that transaction, but Bani Al-Mughirah said, "We do not pay Riba in Islam." `Attab bin Usayd, the Prophet's deputy on Makkah, wrote to the Messenger of Allah about this matter. This Ayah was then revealed and the Messenger of Allah conveyed it to `Attab,

(O you who believe! Be afraid of Allah and give up what remains (due to you) from Riba (from now onward), if you are (really) believers. And if you do not do it, then take a notice of war from Allah and His Messenger.)

They said, "We repent to Allah and abandon whatever is left of our Riba", and they all abandoned it This Ayah serves as a stern threat to those who continue to deal in Riba after Allah revealed this warning.

Riba Constitutes War Against Allah and His Messenger

Ibn Jurayj said that Ibn `Abbas said that,

(then take a notice of war) means, "Be sure of a war from Allah and His Messenger." He also said, "On the Day of Resurrection, those who eat Riba will be told, `take up arms for war.'" He then recited,

(And if you do not do it, then take a notice of war from Allah and His Messenger.)

`Ali bin Abi Talhah said that Ibn `Abbas said about,

(And if you do not do it, then take a notice of war from Allah and His Messenger,) "Whoever kept dealing with Riba and did not refrain from it, then the Muslim Leader should require him to repent. If he still did not refrain from Riba, the Muslim Leader should cut off his head."

Allah then said,

(But if you repent, you shall have your capital sums. Deal not unjustly) by taking the Riba,

(And you shall not be dealt with unjustly) meaning, your original capital will not diminish. Rather, you will receive only what you lent without increase or decrease. Ibn Abi Hatim recorded that `Amr bin Al-Ahwas said, "The Messenger of Allah gave a speech during the Farewell Hajj saying;

»أَلَا إِنَّ كُلَّ رِبًا كَانَ فِي الْجَاهِلِيَّةِ، مَوْضُوعٌ عَنْكُمْ كُلُّهُ، لَكُمْ رُؤُوسُ أَمْوَالِكُمْ لَا تَظْلِمُونَ وَلَاتُظْلَمُونَ، وَأَوَّلُ رِبًا مَوْضُوعٍ، رِبَا الْعَبَّاسِ بْنِ عَبْدِالْمُطَّلِبِ مَوْضُوعٌ كُلُّهُ«

Chapter 2: Al-Baqarah (The Cow), Verses 253-286

(Verily, every case of Riba from the Jahiliyyah is completely annulled. You will only take back your capital, without increase or decrease. The first Riba that I annul is the Riba of Al-`Abbas bin `Abdul-Muttalib, all of it is annulled.)

Being Kind to Debtors Who Face Financial Difficulties

Allah said,

(And if the debtor is having a hard time, then grant him time till it is easy for him to repay; but if you remit it by way of charity, that is better for you if you did but know.) Allah commands creditors to be patient with debtors who are having a hard time financially,

(And if the debtor is having a hard time (has no money), then grant him time till it is easy for him to repay.)

During the time of Jahiliyyah, when the debt came to term, the creditor would say to the debtor, "Either pay now or interest will be added to the debt."

Allah encouraged creditors to give debtors respite regarding their debts and promised all that is good, and a great reward from Him for this righteous deed,

(But if you remit it by way of charity, that is better for you if you did but know) meaning, if you forfeit your debts and cancel them completely.

Imam Ahmad recorded that Sulayman bin Buraydah said that his father said, "I heard the Messenger of Allah say,

《مَنْ أَنْظَرَ مُعْسِرًا، فَلَهُ بِكُلِّ يَوْمٍ مِثْلُهُ صَدَقَة》

(Whoever gives time to a debtor facing hard times, will gain charity of equal proportions for each day he gives.)

I also heard the Prophet say,

《مَنْ أَنْظَرَ مُعْسِرًا، فَلَهُ بِكُلِّ يَوْمٍ مِثْلُهُ صَدَقَة》

(Whoever gives time to a debtor facing hard times, will earn charity multiplied two times for each day he gives.) I said, `O Messenger of Allah! I heard you say, `Whoever gives time to a debtor facing hard times, will gain charity of equal proportions for each day he gives.' I also heard you say, `Whoever gives time to a debtor facing hard times, will earn charity multiplied by two times for each day he gives.' He said,

《لَهُ بِكُلِّ يَوْمٍ مِثْلُهُ صَدَقَةٌ قَبْلَ أَنْ يَحِلَّ الدَّيْنُ، فَإِذَا حَلَّ الدَّيْنُ فَأَنْظَرَهُ، فَلَهُ

«بِكُلِّ يَوْمٍ مِثْلَاهُ صَدَقَةً»

(He will earn charity of equal proportions for each day (he gives time) before the term of the debt comes to an end, and when the term comes to an end, he will again acquire charity multiplied by two times for each day if he gives more time.)"

Ahmad recorded that Muhammad bin Ka`b Al-Qurazi said that Abu Qatadah had a debt on a man, who used to hide from Abu Qatadah when he looked for him to pay what he owed him. One day, Abu Qatadah came looking for the debtor and a young boy came out, and he asked him about the debtor and found out that he was in the house eating. Abu Qatadah said in a loud voice, "O Fellow! Come out, for I was told that you are in the house." The man came out and Abu Qatadah asked him, "Why are you hiding from me" The man said, "I am having a hard time financially, and I do not have any money." Abu Qatadah said, "By Allah, are you truly facing a hard time" He said, "Yes." Abu Qatadah cried and said, "I heard the Messenger of Allah say,

«مَنْ نَفَّسَ عَنْ غَرِيمِهِ أَوْ مَحَا عَنْهُ، كَانَ فِي ظِلِّ الْعَرْشِ يَوْمَ الْقِيَامَةِ»

(Whoever gives time to his debtor, or forgives the debt, will be in the shade of the Throne (of Allah) on the Day of Resurrection.)"

Muslim also recorded this Hadith in his Sahih.

Al-Hafiz Abu Ya`la Al-Mawsili recorded that Hudhayfah said that the Messenger of Allah said,

«أُتِيَ اللَّهُ بِعَبْدٍ مِنْ عَبِيدِهِ يَوْمَ الْقِيَامَةِ قَالَ: مَاذَا عَمِلْتَ لِي فِي الدُّنْيَا؟ فَقَالَ: مَا عَمِلْتُ لَكَ يَا رَبِّ مِثْقَالَ ذَرَّةٍ فِي الدُّنْيَا أَرْجُوكَ بِهَا قَالَهَا ثَلَاثَ مَرَّاتٍ قَالَ الْعَبْدُ عِنْدَ آخِرِهَا: يَا رَبِّ إِنَّكَ كُنْتَ أَعْطَيْتَنِي فَضْلَ مَالٍ، وَكُنْتُ رَجُلًا أُبَايِعُ النَّاسَ، وَكَانَ مِنْ خُلُقِي الْجَوَازُ، فَكُنْتُ أُيَسِّرُ عَلَى الْمُوسِرِ وَأُنْظِرُ الْمُعْسِرَ، قَالَ: فَيَقُولُ اللَّهُ عَزَّ وَجَلَّ: أَنَا أَحَقُّ مَنْ يُيَسِّرُ، ادْخُلِ الْجَنَّةَ»

(On the Day of Resurrection, one of Allah's servants will be summoned before Him and He will ask him, "What deeds did you perform for Me in your life" He will say, "O Lord! In my life, I have not performed a deed for Your sake that equals an atom," three times. The third time, the servant will add, "O Lord! You granted me wealth and I used to be a merchant. I used to be lenient, giving easy terms to those well-off and giving time to the debtors who faced hard times." Allah will say, "I Am the Most Worthy of giving easy terms. Therefore, enter Paradise.")

Al-Bukhari, Muslim and Ibn Majah also recorded this Hadith from Hudhayfah, and Muslim recorded a similar wording from `Uqbah bin `Amir and Abu Mas`ud Al-Badri. Allah further advised His servants, by reminding them that this life will soon end and all the wealth in it will vanish. He also reminded them that the Hereafter will surely come, when the Return to Him will occur, and that He will hold His creation accountable for what they did, rewarding them or punishing them accordingly. Allah also warned them against His torment,

(And have Taqwa for the Day when you shall be brought back to Allah. Then every person shall be paid what he earned, and they shall not be dealt with unjustly.)

It was reported that this was the last Ayah revealed from the Glorious Qur'an. An-Nasa'i recorded that Ibn `Abbas said, "The last Ayah to be revealed from the Qur'an was,

(And have Taqwa for the Day when you shall be brought back to Allah. Then every person shall be paid what he earned, and they shall not be dealt with unjustly.")

This is the same narration reported by Ad-Dahhak and Al-`Awfi from Ibn `Abbas.

Surah: 2 Ayah: 282

﴿ يَٰٓأَيُّهَا ٱلَّذِينَ ءَامَنُوٓاْ إِذَا تَدَايَنتُم بِدَيْنٍ إِلَىٰٓ أَجَلٍ مُّسَمًّى فَٱكْتُبُوهُ ۚ وَلْيَكْتُب بَّيْنَكُمْ كَاتِبٌۢ بِٱلْعَدْلِ ۚ وَلَا يَأْبَ كَاتِبٌ أَن يَكْتُبَ كَمَا عَلَّمَهُ ٱللَّهُ ۚ فَلْيَكْتُبْ وَلْيُمْلِلِ ٱلَّذِى عَلَيْهِ ٱلْحَقُّ وَلْيَتَّقِ ٱللَّهَ رَبَّهُۥ وَلَا يَبْخَسْ مِنْهُ شَيْـًٔا ۚ فَإِن كَانَ ٱلَّذِى عَلَيْهِ ٱلْحَقُّ سَفِيهًا أَوْ ضَعِيفًا أَوْ لَا يَسْتَطِيعُ أَن يُمِلَّ هُوَ فَلْيُمْلِلْ وَلِيُّهُۥ بِٱلْعَدْلِ ۚ وَٱسْتَشْهِدُواْ شَهِيدَيْنِ مِن رِّجَالِكُمْ ۖ فَإِن لَّمْ يَكُونَا رَجُلَيْنِ فَرَجُلٌ وَٱمْرَأَتَانِ مِمَّن تَرْضَوْنَ مِنَ ٱلشُّهَدَآءِ أَن تَضِلَّ إِحْدَىٰهُمَا فَتُذَكِّرَ إِحْدَىٰهُمَا ٱلْأُخْرَىٰ ۚ وَلَا يَأْبَ ٱلشُّهَدَآءُ إِذَا مَا دُعُواْ ۚ وَلَا تَسْـَٔمُوٓاْ أَن تَكْتُبُوهُ صَغِيرًا أَوْ كَبِيرًا إِلَىٰٓ أَجَلِهِۦ ۚ ذَٰلِكُمْ أَقْسَطُ عِندَ ٱللَّهِ وَأَقْوَمُ لِلشَّهَٰدَةِ وَأَدْنَىٰٓ أَلَّا تَرْتَابُوٓاْ ۖ إِلَّآ أَن تَكُونَ تِجَٰرَةً حَاضِرَةً تُدِيرُونَهَا بَيْنَكُمْ فَلَيْسَ عَلَيْكُمْ جُنَاحٌ أَلَّا تَكْتُبُوهَا ۗ وَأَشْهِدُوٓاْ إِذَا تَبَايَعْتُمْ ۚ وَلَا يُضَآرَّ كَاتِبٌ وَلَا شَهِيدٌ ۚ وَإِن تَفْعَلُواْ فَإِنَّهُۥ فُسُوقٌۢ بِكُمْ ۗ وَٱتَّقُواْ ٱللَّهَ ۖ وَيُعَلِّمُكُمُ ٱللَّهُ ۗ وَٱللَّهُ بِكُلِّ شَىْءٍ عَلِيمٌ ۝

282. O you who believe! When you contract a debt for a fixed period, write it down. Let a scribe write it down in justice between you. Let not the scribe refuse to write as Allâh has taught him, so let him write. Let him (the debtor) who incurs

the liability dictate, and he must fear Allâh, his Lord, and diminish not anything of what he owes. But if the debtor is of poor understanding, or weak, or is unable to dictate for himself, then let his guardian dictate in justice. And get two witnesses out of your own men. And if there are not two men (available), then a man and two women, such as you agree for witnesses, so that if one of them (two women)errs, the other can remind her. And the witnesses should not refuse when they are called (for evidence). you should not become weary to write it (your contract),whether it be small or big, for its fixed term, that is more just with Allâh; more solid as evidence, and more convenient to prevent doubts among yourselves, save when it is a present trade which you carry out in the spot among yourselves, then there is no sin on you if you do not write it down. But take witnesses whenever you make a commercial contract. Let neither scribe nor witness suffer any harm, but if you do (such harm), it would be wickedness in you. So be afraid of Allâh; and Allâh teaches you. And Allâh is the All-Knower of each and everything.

Transliteration

282. Ya ayyuha allatheena amanoo itha tadayantum bidaynin ila ajalin musamman faoktuboohu walyaktub baynakum katibun bialAAadli wala ya/ba katibun an yaktuba kama AAallamahu Allahu falyaktub walyumlili allathee AAalayhi alhaqqu walyattaqi Allaha rabbahu wala yabkhas minhu shayan fa-in kana allathee AAalayhi alhaqqu safeehan aw daAAeefan aw la yastateeAAu an yumilla huwa falyumlil waliyyuhu bialAAadli waistashhidoo shaheedayni min rijalikum fa-in lam yakoona rajulayni farajulun waimraatani mimman tardawna mina alshshuhada-i an tadilla ihdahuma fatuthakkira ihdahuma al-okhra wala ya/ba alshshuhadao itha ma duAAoo wala tas-amoo an taktuboohu sagheeran aw kabeeran ila ajalihi thalikum aqsatu AAinda Allahi waaqwamu lilshshahadati waadna alla tartaboo illa an takoona tijaratan hadiratan tudeeroonaha baynakum falaysa AAalaykum junahun alla taktubooha waashhidoo itha tabayaAAtum wala yudarra katibun wala shaheedun wa-in tafAAaloo fa-innahu fusooqun bikum waittaqoo Allaha wayuAAallimukumu Allahu waAllahu bikulli shay-in AAaleemun

Tafsir Ibn Kathir

The Necessity of Writing Transactions That Take Effect Later on

This Ayah is the longest in the Glorious Qur'an. Imam Abu Ja`far bin Jarir recorded that Sa`id bin Al-Musayyib said that he was told that the Ayah most recently revealed from above the Throne -- the last Ayah to be revealed in the Qur'an -- was the Ayah about debts.

Allah's statement,

(O you who believe! When you contract a debt for a fixed period, write it down) directs Allah's believing servants to record their business transactions when their term is delayed, to preserve the terms and timing of these transactions, and the memory of witnesses, as mentioned at the end of the Ayah,

Chapter 2: Al-Baqarah (The Cow), Verses 253-286

(that is more just with Allah; more solid as evidence, and more convenient to prevent doubts among yourselves.)

The Two Sahihs recorded that Ibn `Abbas said, "Allah's Messenger came to Al-Madinah, while the people were in the habit of paying in advance for fruits to be delivered within one or two years. The Messenger of Allah said,

«مَنْ أَسْلَفَ، فَلْيُسْلِفْ فِي كَيْلٍ مَعْلُومٍ، وَوَزْنٍ مَعْلُومٍ، إِلَى أَجَلٍ مَعْلُومٍ»

(Whoever pays money in advance (for dates to be delivered later) should pay it for known specified measure and weight (of the dates) for a specified date.)

Allah's statement,

(write it down) is a command from Him to record such transactions to endorse and preserve their terms. Ibn Jurayj said, "Whoever borrowed should write the terms, and whoever bought should have witnesses." Abu Sa`id, Ash-Sha`bi, Ar-Rabi` bin Anas, Al-Hasan, Ibn Jurayj and Ibn Zayd said that recording such transactions was necessary before, but was then abrogated by Allah's statement,

(Then if one of you entrusts the other, let the one who is entrusted discharge his trust (faithfully).)

Allah's statement,

(Let a scribe write it down in justice between you) and in truth. Therefore, the scribe is not allowed to cheat any party of the contract and is to only record what the parties of the contract agreed to, without addition or deletion. Allah's statement,

(Let not the scribe refuse to write, as Allah has taught him, so let him write) means, "Those who know how to write should not refrain from writing transaction contracts when asked to do so." Further, let writing such contracts be a type of charity from the scribe for those who are not lettered, just as Allah taught him what he knew not. Therefore, let him write, just as the Hadith stated,

«إِنَّ مِنَ الصَّدَقَةِ أَنْ تُعِينَ صَانِعًا، أَوْ تَصْنَعَ لِأَخْرَقَ»

(It is a type of charity to help a worker and to do something for a feeble person.)

In another Hadith, the Prophet said,

«مَنْ كَتَمَ عِلْمًا يَعْلَمُهُ، أُلْجِمَ يَوْمَ الْقِيَامَةِ بِلِجَامٍ مِنْ نَارٍ»

(Whoever kept knowledge to himself will be restrained by a bridle made of fire on the Day of Resurrection.) Mujahid and `Ata' said that if asked to do so, "The scribe is required to record."

Allah's statement,

(Let him (the debtor) who incurs the liability dictate, and he must have Taqwa of Allah, his Lord) indicates that the debtor should dictate to the scribe what he owes, so let him fear Allah,

(And diminish not anything of what he owes,) meaning, not hide any portion of what he owes.

(But if the debtor is of poor understanding) and is not allowed to decide on such matters, because he used to waste money, for instance,

(Or weak), such as being too young or insane,

(Or is unable to dictate for himself) because of a disease, or ignorance about such matters,

(then let his guardian dictate in justice.)

Witnesses Should Attend the Dictation of Contracts

Allah said,

(And get two witnesses out of your own men) requiring witnesses to attend the dictation of contracts to further preserve the contents,

(And if there are not two men (available), then a man and two women) this requirement is only for contracts that directly or indirectly involve money. Allah requires that two women take the place of one man as witness, because of the woman's shortcomings, as the Prophet described. Muslim recorded in his Sahih that Abu Hurayrah said that the Messenger of Allah said,

«يَا مَعْشَرَ النِّسَاءِ تَصَدَّقْنَ وَأَكْثِرْنَ الِاسْتِغْفَارَ، فَإِنِّي رَأَيْتُكُنَّ أَكْثَرَ أَهْلِ النَّارِ»

(O women! Give away charity and ask for forgiveness, for I saw that you comprise the majority of the people of the Fire.)

One eloquent woman said, "O Messenger of Allah! Why do we comprise the majority of the people of the Fire" He said,

«تُكْثِرْنَ اللَّعْنَ، وَتَكْفُرْنَ الْعَشِيرَ، وَمَا رَأَيْتُ مِنْ نَاقِصَاتِ عَقْلٍ وَدِينٍ، أَغْلَبَ لِذِي لُبَ مِنْكُنّ»

(You curse a lot and you do not appreciate your mate. I have never seen those who have shortcoming in mind and religion controlling those who have sound minds, other than you.) She said, "O Messenger of Allah! What is this shortcoming in mind and religion" He said,

«أَمَّا نُقْصَانُ عَقْلِهَا، فَشَهَادَةُ امْرَأَتَيْنِ تَعْدِلُ شَهَادَةَ رَجُلٍ، فَهَذَا نُقْصَانُ الْعَقْلِ، وَتَمْكُثُ اللَّيَالِي لَا تُصَلِّي وَتُفْطِرُ فِي رَمَضَانَ، فَهَذَا نُقْصَانُ الدِّين»

(As for the shortcoming in her mind, the testimony of two women equals the testimony of one man, and this is the shortcoming in the mind. As for the shortcoming in the religion, woman remains for nights at a time when she does not pray and breaks the fast in Ramadan)

Allah's statement,

(such as you agree for witnesses) requires competency in the witnesses. Further, Allah's statement,

(so that if one of them errs) refers to the two women witnesses; whenever one of them forgets a part of the testimony,

(the other can remind her) meaning, the other woman's testimony mends the shortcoming of forgetfulness in the first woman.

Allah's statement,

(And the witnesses should not refuse when they are called) means, when people are called to be witnesses, they should agree, as Qatadah and Ar-Rabi` bin Anas stated. Similarly, Allah said,

(Let not the scribe refuse to write as Allah has taught him,

«أَمَّا نُقْصَانُ عَقْلِهَا، فَشَهَادَةُ امْرَأَتَيْنِ تَعْدِلُ شَهَادَةَ رَجُلٍ، فَهَذَا نُقْصَانُ الْعَقْلِ، وَتَمْكُثُ اللَّيَالِي لَا تُصَلِّي وَتُفْطِرُ فِي رَمَضَانَ، فَهَذَا نُقْصَانُ الدِّين»

(As for the shortcoming in her mind, the testimony of two women equals the testimony of one man, and this is the shortcoming in the mind. As for the shortcoming in the religion, woman remains for nights at a time when she does not pray and breaks the fast in Ramadan)

Allah's statement,

(such as you agree for witnesses) requires competency in the witnesses. Further, Allah's statement, (so that if one of them errs) refers to the two women witnesses; whenever one of them forgets a part of the testimony,

(the other can remind her) meaning, the other woman's testimony mends the shortcoming of forgetfulness in the first woman.

Allah's statement,

(And the witnesses should not refuse when they are called) means, when people are called to be witnesses, they should agree, as Qatadah and Ar-Rabi` bin Anas stated. Similarly, Allah said,

(Let not the scribe refuse to write as Allah has taught him, so let him write.)

Some say that this Ayah indicates that agreeing to become a witness is Fard Kifayah (required on at least a part of the Muslim Ummah). However, the majority of the scholars say that the Ayah,

(And the witnesses should not refuse when they are called) is referring to testifying to what the witnesses actually witnessed, thus befitting their description of being `witnesses'. Therefore, when the witness is called to testify to what he witnessed, he is required to give testimony, unless this obligation was already fulfilled, in which case such testimony becomes Fard Kifayah. Mujahid and Abu Mijlaz said, "If you are called to be a witness, then you have the choice to agree. If you witnessed and were called to testify, then come forward." It was reported that Ibn `Abbas and Al-Hasan Al-Basri said that the obligation includes both cases, agreeing to be a witness and testifying to what one witnessed.

Allah's statement,

(You should not become weary to write it (your contract), whether it be small or large, for its fixed term) perfects this direction from Allah by commanding that the debt be written, whether the amount is large or small. Allah said,

(You should not become weary) meaning, do not be discouraged against writing transactions and their terms, whether the amount involved is large or small. Allah's statement,

(that is more just with Allah; more solid as evidence, and more convenient to prevent doubts among yourselves) means, writing transactions that will be fulfillled at a later date is more just with Allah meaning better and more convenient in order to preserve the terms of the contract. Therefore, recording such agreements helps the witnesses, when they see their handwriting - or signatures - later on and thus remember what they witnessed, for it is possible that the witnesses might forget what they witnessed.

(And more convenient to prevent doubts among yourselves) meaning, this helps repel any doubt. Since if you need to refer to the contract that you wrote and the doubt will end.

Allah's statement,

(save when it is a present trade which you carry out on the spot among yourselves, then there is no sin on you if you do not write it down) indicates that if the transaction will be fulfilled immediately, then there is no harm if it is not recorded.

As for requiring witnesses to be present in trading transactions, Allah said,

(But take witnesses whenever you make a commercial contract.)

However, this command was abrogated by,

(Then if one of you entrusts the other, let the one who is entrusted discharge his trust (faithfully).)

Or, it could be that having witnesses in such cases is only recommended and not obligatory, as evident from the Hadith that Khuzaymah bin Thabit Al-Ansari narrated which Imam Ahmad collected. `Umarah bin Khuzaymah Al-Ansari said that his uncle, who was among the Prophet's Companions, told him that the Prophet was making a deal for a horse with a bedouin man. The Prophet asked the bedouin to follow him so that he could pay him the price of the horse. The Prophet went ahead of the bedouin. The bedouin met several men who tried to buy his horse, not knowing if the Prophet was actually determined to buy it. Some people offered more money for the horse than the Prophet had. The bedouin man said to the Prophet , "If you want to buy this horse, then buy it or I will sell it to someone else." When he heard the bedouin man's words, the Prophet stood up and said, "Have I not bought that horse from you" The bedouin said, "By Allah! I have not sold it to you." The Prophet said, "Rather, I did buy it from you." The people gathered around the Prophet and the Bedouin while they were disputing, and the bedouin said, "Bring forth a witness who testifies that I sold you the horse." Meanwhile, the Muslims who came said to the bedouin, "Woe to you! The Prophet only says the truth." When Khuzaymah bin Thabit came and heard the dispute between the Prophet and the bedouin who was saying, "Bring forth a witness who testifies that I sold you the horse, " Khuzaymah said, "I bear witness that you sold him the horse." The Prophet said to Khuzaymah, "What is the basis of your testimony" Khuzaymah said, "That I entrusted you, O Messenger of Allah!" Therefore, the Messenger made Khuzaymah's testimony equal to the testimony of two men. This was also recorded by Abu Dawud and An-Nasa. Allah's statement,

(Let neither scribe nor witness suffer (or cause) any harm) also indicates that the scribe and the witness must not cause any harm, such as, when the scribe writes other than what he is being dictated, or the witness testifies to other than what he heard or conceals his testimony. This is the explanation of Al-Hasan and Qatadah."

Allah's statement,

(But if you do (such harm), it would be wickedness in you) means, "If you defy what you were commanded and commit what you were prohibited, then it is because of the sin that resides and remains with you; sin that you never release or rid yourselves from."

Allah's statement,

(So have Taqwa of Allah) means, fear Him, remember His watch over you, implement His command and avoid what He prohibited,

(And Allah teaches you.) Similarly, Allah said,

(O you who believe! If you have Taqwa of Allah, He will grant you Furqan ((a criterion to judge between right and wrong))) (8:29), and,

(O you who believe! Have Taqwa of Allah, and believe in His Messenger, He will give you a double portion of His mercy, and He will give you a light by which you shall walk (straight)) (57:28).

Allah said;

(And Allah is the All-Knower of everything) stating that Allah has perfect knowledge in all matters and in their benefits or repercussions, and nothing escapes His perfect watch, for His knowledge encompasses everything in existence.

Surah: 2 Ayah: 283

﴿ ۞ وَإِن كُنتُمْ عَلَىٰ سَفَرٍ وَلَمْ تَجِدُوا۟ كَاتِبًا فَرِهَٰنٌ مَّقْبُوضَةٌ ۖ فَإِنْ أَمِنَ بَعْضُكُم بَعْضًا فَلْيُؤَدِّ ٱلَّذِى ٱؤْتُمِنَ أَمَٰنَتَهُۥ وَلْيَتَّقِ ٱللَّهَ رَبَّهُۥ ۗ وَلَا تَكْتُمُوا۟ ٱلشَّهَٰدَةَ ۚ وَمَن يَكْتُمْهَا فَإِنَّهُۥٓ ءَاثِمٌ قَلْبُهُۥ ۗ وَٱللَّهُ بِمَا تَعْمَلُونَ عَلِيمٌ ﴾

283. And if you are on a journey and cannot find a scribe, then let there be a pledge taken (mortgaging); then if one of you entrust the other, let the one who is entrusted discharge his trust (faithfully), and let him be afraid of Allâh, his Lord. And conceal not the evidence for he, who hides it, surely his heart is sinful. And Allâh is All-Knower of what you do.

Transliteration

283. Wa-in kuntum AAala safarin walam tajidoo katiban farihanun maqboodatun fa-in amina baAAdukum baAAdan falyu-addi allathee i/tumina amanatahu walyattaqi Allaha rabbahu wala taktumoo alshshahadata waman yaktumha fa-innahu athimun qalbuhu waAllahu bima taAAmaloona AAaleemun

Tafsir Ibn Kathir

What is the `Mortgaging' Mentioned in the Ayah

Allah said,

(And if you are on a journey) meaning, traveling and some of you borrowed some money to be paid at a later date,

(and cannot find a scribe) who would record the debt for you. Ibn `Abbas said, "And even if they find a scribe, but did not find paper, ink or pen." Then,

Chapter 2: Al-Baqarah (The Cow), Verses 253-286

(let there be a pledge taken (mortgaging)) given to the creditor in lieu of writing the transaction. The Two Sahihs recorded that Anas said that the Messenger of Allah died while his shield was mortgaged with a Jew in return for thirty Wasq (approximately 180 kg) of barley, which the Prophet bought on credit as provisions for his household. In another narration, the Hadith stated that this Jew was among the Jews of Al-Madinah.

Allah said,

(then if one of you entrusts the other, let the one who is entrusted discharge his trust (faithfully).)

Ibn Abi Hatim recorded, with a sound chain of narration, that Abu Sa`id Al-Khudri said, "This Ayah abrogated what came before it (i.e. that which required recording the transaction and having witnesses present)." Ash-Sha`bi said, "If you trust each other, then there is no harm if you do not write the loan or have witnesses present." Allah's statement,

(And let him have Taqwa of Allah) means, the debtor.

Imam Ahmad and the Sunan recorded that Qatadah said that Al-Hasan said that Samurah said that the Messenger of Allah said,

«عَلَى الْيَدِ مَا أَخَذَتْ، حَتَّى تُؤَدِّيَه»

(The hand (of the debtor) will carry the burden of what it took until it gives it back.)

Allah's statement,

(And conceal not the evidence) means, do not hide it or refuse to announce it. Ibn `Abbas and other scholars said, "False testimony is one of the worst of the major sins, and such is the case with hiding the true testimony. This is why Allah said,

(For he who hides it, surely, his heart is sinful).

As-Suddi commented, "Meaning he is a sinner in his heart."

This is similar to Allah's statement,

(We shall not hide testimony of Allah, for then indeed we should be of the sinful) (5:106).

Allah said,

(O you who believe! Stand out firmly for justice, as witnesses to Allah, even though it be against yourselves, or your parents, or your kin, be he rich or poor, Allah is a better Protector to both (than you). So follow not the lusts (of your hearts), lest you avoid justice; and if you distort your witness or refuse to give it, verily, Allah is Ever Well-Acquainted with what you do) (4:135) and in this Ayah (2:283) He said,

(And conceal not the evidence, for he who hides it, surely, his heart is sinful. And Allah is All-Knower of what you do.)

Surah: 2 Ayah: 284

﴿ لِّلَّهِ مَا فِى ٱلسَّمَٰوَٰتِ وَمَا فِى ٱلْأَرْضِ ۗ وَإِن تُبْدُواْ مَا فِىٓ أَنفُسِكُمْ أَوْ تُخْفُوهُ يُحَاسِبْكُم بِهِ ٱللَّهُ ۖ فَيَغْفِرُ لِمَن يَشَآءُ وَيُعَذِّبُ مَن يَشَآءُ ۗ وَٱللَّهُ عَلَىٰ كُلِّ شَىْءٍ قَدِيرٌ ﴾

284. To Allâh belongs all that is in the heavens and all that is on the earth, and whether you disclose what is in your ownselves or conceal it, Allâh will call you to account for it. Then He forgives whom He wills and punishes whom He wills. And Allâh is Able to do all things.

Transliteration

284. Lillahi ma fee alssamawati wama fee al-ardi wa-in tubdoo ma fee anfusikum aw tukhfoohu yuhasibkum bihi Allahu fayaghfiru liman yashao wayuAAaththibu man yashao waAllahu AAala kulli shay-in qadeerun

Tafsir Ibn Kathir

Would the Servants be Accountable for What They Conceal in Their Hearts

Allah states that His is the kingship of the heavens and earth and of what and whoever is on or between them, that He has perfect watch over them. No apparent matter or secret that the heart conceals is ever a secret to Him, however minor it is. Allah also states that He will hold His servants accountable for what they do and what they conceal in their hearts. In similar statements, Allah said,

(Say (O Muhammad): "Whether you hide what is in your breasts or reveal it, Allah knows it, and He knows what is in the heavens and what is in the earth. And Allah is able to do all things) (3:29), and,

(He knows the secret and that which is yet more hidden.)

There are many other Ayat on this subject. In this Ayah (2:284), Allah states that He has knowledge of what the hearts conceal, and consequently, He will hold the creation accountable for whatever is in their hearts. This is why when this Ayah was revealed, it was hard on the Companions, since out of their strong faith and conviction, they were afraid that such reckoning would diminish their good deeds.

Imam Ahmad recorded that Abu Hurayrah said, "When

(To Allah belongs all that is in the heavens and all that is on the earth, and whether you disclose what is in yourselves or conceal it, Allah will call you to account for it. Then He forgives whom He wills and punishes whom He wills. And Allah is able to do all things)

was revealed to the Messenger of Allah , it was very hard for the Companions of the Messenger . The Companions came to the Messenger and fell to their knees saying, `O Messenger of Allah! We were asked to perform what we can bear of deeds: the prayer, the fast, Jihad and charity. However, this Ayah was revealed to you, and we cannot bear it.' The Messenger of Allah said,

«أَتُرِيدُونَ أَنْ تَقُولُوا كَما قَالَ أَهْلُ الْكِتَابَيْنِ مِنْ قَبْلِكُمْ: سَمِعْنَا وَعَصَيْنَا؟ بَلْ قُولُوا: سَمِعْنَا وَأَطَعْنَا غُفْرَانَكَ رَبَّنَا وَإِلَيْكَ الْمَصِيرِ»

(Do you want to repeat what the People of the Two Scriptures before you said, that is, `We hear and we disobey' Rather, say, `We hear and we obey, and we seek Your forgiveness, O our Lord, and the Return is to You.)

When the people accepted this statement and their tongues recited it, Allah sent down afterwards,

(The Messenger believes in what has been sent down to him from his Lord, and (so do)the believers. Each one believes in Allah, His Angels, His Books, and His Messengers. (They say,) "We make no distinction between one another of His Messengers - and they say, "We hear, and we obey. (We seek) Your forgiveness, our Lord, and to You is the return (of all).")

When they did that, Allah abrogated the Ayah (2:284) and sent down the Ayah,

(Allah burdens not a person beyond his scope. He gets reward for that (good) which he has earned, and he is punished for that (evil) which he has earned. "Our Lord! Punish us not if we forget or fall into error.") until the end."

Muslim recorded it with the wording; "When they did that, Allah abrogated it (2:284) and sent down,

(Allah burdens not a person beyond his scope. He gets reward for that (good) which he has earned, and he is punished for that (evil) which he has earned. "Our Lord! Punish us not if we forget or fall into error".)

Allah said, `I shall (accept your supplication),'

("Our Lord! Lay not on us a burden like that which You did lay on those before us (Jews and Christians)")

Allah said, `I shall (accept your supplication),'

("Our Lord! Put not on us a burden greater than we have strength to bear. ")

Allah said, `I shall (accept your supplication),'

("Pardon us and grant us forgiveness. Have mercy on us. You are our Mawla (Supporter and Protector) and give us victory over the disbelieving people.")

Allah said, `I shall.'"

Imam Ahmad recorded that Mujahid said, "I saw Ibn `Abbas and said to him, `O Abu Abbas! I was with Ibn `Umar, and he read this Ayah and cried.' He asked, `Which Ayah' I said,

`(And whether you disclose what is in yourselves or conceal it.)'

Ibn `Abbas said, `When this Ayah was revealed, it was very hard on the Companions of the Messenger of Allah and worried them tremendously. They said: O Messenger of Allah! We know that we would be punished according to our statements and our actions, but as for what occurs in our hearts, we do not control what is in them.' The Messenger of Allah said,

»قُولُوا: سَمِعْنَا وَأَطَعْنَا«

(Say, `We hear and we obey.') They said, `We hear and we obey.' Thereafter, this Ayah abrogated the previous Ayah,

(The Messenger believes in what has been sent down to him from his Lord, and (so do) the believers. Each one believes in Allah), until,

(Allah burdens not a person beyond his scope. He gets reward for that (good) which he has earned, and he is punished for that (evil) which he has earned.)

Therefore, they were pardoned what happens in their hearts, and were held accountable only for their actions.'"

The Group recorded that Abu Hurayrah said that the Messenger of Allah said,

»إِنَّ اللهَ تَجَاوَزَ لِي عَنْ أُمَّتِي مَا حَدَّثَتْ بِهِ أَنْفُسَهَا مَا لَمْ تَكَلَّمْ أَوْ تَعْمَل«

(Allah has pardoned my Ummah for what they say to themselves, as long as they do not utter it or act on it.)

The Two Sahihs recorded that Abu Hurayrah said that the Messenger of Allah said,

»قَالَ اللهُ: إِذَا هَمَّ عَبْدِي بِسَيِّئَةٍ فَلَا تَكْتُبُوهَا عَلَيْهِ، فَإِنْ عَمِلَهَا فَاكْتُبُوهَا سَيِّئَةً، وَإِذَا هَمَّ بِحَسَنَةٍ فَلَمْ يَعْمَلْهَا فَاكْتُبُوهَا حَسَنَةً، فَإِنْ عَمِلَهَا فَاكْتُبُوهَا عَشْرًا«

(Allah said (to His angels), "If My servant intends to commit an evil deed, do not record it as such for him, and if he commits it, write it for him as one evil deed. If he intends to perform a good deed, but did not perform it, then write it for him as one good deed, and if he performs it, write it for him as ten good deeds.")

Surah: 2 Ayah: 285 & Ayah: 286

﴿ ءَامَنَ ٱلرَّسُولُ بِمَآ أُنزِلَ إِلَيْهِ مِن رَّبِّهِۦ وَٱلْمُؤْمِنُونَ ۚ كُلٌّ ءَامَنَ بِٱللَّهِ وَمَلَـٰٓئِكَتِهِۦ وَكُتُبِهِۦ وَرُسُلِهِۦ لَا نُفَرِّقُ بَيْنَ أَحَدٍ مِّن رُّسُلِهِۦ ۚ وَقَالُوا۟ سَمِعْنَا وَأَطَعْنَا ۖ غُفْرَانَكَ رَبَّنَا وَإِلَيْكَ ٱلْمَصِيرُ ﴾ ٢٨٥

285. The Messenger (Muhammad (peace be upon him)) believes in what has been sent down to him from his Lord, and (so do) the believers. Each one believes in Allâh, His Angels, His Books, and His Messengers. They say, "We make no distinction between one another of His Messengers" - and they say, "We hear, and we obey. (We seek) Your Forgiveness, our Lord, and to You is the return (of all)."

﴿ لَا يُكَلِّفُ ٱللَّهُ نَفْسًا إِلَّا وُسْعَهَا ۚ لَهَا مَا كَسَبَتْ وَعَلَيْهَا مَا ٱكْتَسَبَتْ ۗ رَبَّنَا لَا تُؤَاخِذْنَآ إِن نَّسِينَآ أَوْ أَخْطَأْنَا ۚ رَبَّنَا وَلَا تَحْمِلْ عَلَيْنَآ إِصْرًا كَمَا حَمَلْتَهُۥ عَلَى ٱلَّذِينَ مِن قَبْلِنَا ۚ رَبَّنَا وَلَا تُحَمِّلْنَا مَا لَا طَاقَةَ لَنَا بِهِۦ ۖ وَٱعْفُ عَنَّا وَٱغْفِرْ لَنَا وَٱرْحَمْنَآ ۚ أَنتَ مَوْلَىٰنَا فَٱنصُرْنَا عَلَى ٱلْقَوْمِ ٱلْكَـٰفِرِينَ ﴾ ٢٨٦

286. Allâh burdens not a person beyond his scope. He gets reward for that (good) which he has earned, and he is punished for that (evil) which he has earned. "Our Lord! Punish us not if we forget or fall into error, our Lord! Lay not on us a burden like that which You did lay on those before us (Jews and Christians); our Lord! Put not on us a burden greater than we have strength to bear. Pardon us and grant us Forgiveness. Have mercy on us. You are our Maulâ (Patron, Supporter and Protector, etc.) and give us victory over the disbelieving people."

Transliteration

285. Amana alrrasoolu bima onzila ilayhi min rabbihi waalmu/minoona kullun amana biAllahi wamalaikatihi wakutubihi warusulihi la nufarriqu bayna ahadin min rusulihi waqaloo samiAAna waataAAna ghufranaka rabbana wa-ilayka almaseeru   286. La yukallifu Allahu nafsan illa wusAAaha laha ma kasabat waAAalayha ma iktasabat rabbana la tu-akhithna in naseena aw akhta/na rabbana wala tahmil AAalayna isran kama hamaltahu AAala allatheena min qablina rabbana wala tuhammilna ma la taqata lana bihi waoAAfu AAanna waighfir lana wairhamna anta mawlana faonsurna AAala alqawmi alkafireena

Tafsir Ibn Kathir

The Hadiths on the Virtue of These Two Ayat, May Allah Benefit Us by Them Al-Bukhari recorded that Abu Mas`ud said that the Messenger of Allah said,

«مَنْ قَرَأَ بِالْآيَتَيْنِ مِنْ آخِرِ سُورَةِ الْبَقَرَةِ فِي لَيْلَةٍ، كَفَتَاه»

(Whoever recites the last two Ayat in Surat Al-Baqarah at night, they will suffice for him.)

The rest of the six also recorded similar wording for this Hadith. The Two Sahihs recorded this Hadith using various chains of narration, and Imam Ahmad also recorded it.

Muslim recorded that `Abdullah said, "When the Messenger of Allah went on the Isra journey, he ascended to the Sidrat Al-Muntaha in the sixth heaven, where whatever ascends from the earth ends at, and whatever descends from above it ends at.

(When that covered the lote tree which did cover it!) (53:16) meaning, a mat made of gold.

The Messenger of Allah was then given three things: the five prayers, the last Ayat in Surat Al-Baqarah and forgiveness for whoever did not associate anything or anyone with Allah from his Ummah."

Earlier we mentioned the Hadith regarding the virtues of Surat Al-Fatihah from Ibn `Abbas which stated, "While the Messenger of Allah was with Jibil, he heard a noise from above. Jibil lifted his sight to the sky and said, `This is a door that was opened just now in heaven, and it was never opened before.' An angel came down through the door to the Prophet and said, `Receive the good news of two lights that you have been given and which no Prophet before you was given: the Opener of the Book (Al-Fatihah) and the last Ayat in Surat Al-Baqarah. You will not read a letter of them, but you will be granted its benefit.'" This Hadith was collected by Muslim and An-Nasa'i, and this is the wording collected by An-Nasa'i.

The Tafsir of the Last Two Ayat of Surat Al-Baqarah

Allah said,

(Each one believes in Allah, His Angels, His Books, and His Messengers. (They say,) "We make no distinction between one another of His Messengers.")

Therefore, each of the believers believes that Allah is the One and Only and the Sustainer, there is no deity worthy of worship except Him and there is no Lord except Him. The believers also believe in all Allah's Prophets and Messengers, in the Books that were revealed from heaven to the Messengers and Prophets, who are indeed the servants of Allah. Further, the believers do not differentiate between any of the Prophets, such as, believing in some of them and rejecting others. Rather, all of Allah's Prophets and Messengers are, to the believers, truthful, righteous, and they were each guided to the path of righteousness, even when some of them bring what abrogates the Law of some others by Allah's leave. Later on, the Law of Muhammad, the Final Prophet and Messenger from Allah, abrogated all the laws of the Prophets before him. So the Last Hour will commence while Muhammad's Law remains the only valid Law, and all the while a group of his Ummah will always be on the path of truth, apparent and dominant. Allah's statement,

(And they say, "We hear, and we obey") means, we heard Your statement, O our Lord, comprehended and implemented it, and adhered to its implications.

((We seek) Your forgiveness, our Lord) contains a plea and supplication for Allah's forgiveness, mercy and kindness.

Allah's statement,

(Allah burdens not a person beyond his scope) means, Allah does not ask a soul what is beyond its ability. This only demonstrates Allah's kindness, compassion and generosity towards His creation. This Ayah is the Ayah that abrogated the Ayah that worried the Companions, that is, Allah's statement,

(And whether you disclose what is in yourselves or conceal it, Allah will call you to account for it.)

This indicates that although Allah will question His servants and judge them, He will only punish for what one is able to protect himself from. As for what one cannot protect himself from, such as what one says to himself - or passing thoughts - they will not be punished for that. We should state here that to dislike the evil thoughts that cross one's mind is a part of faith. Allah said next,

(He gets reward for that which he has earned) of good,

(And he is punished for that which he has earned) of evil, that is, concerning the acts that one is responsible for.

Allah then said, (mentioning what the believers said) while directing His servants to supplicate to Him, all the while promising them that He will answer their supplication:

("Our Lord! Push us not if we forget or fall into error,") meaning, "If we forgot an obligation or fell into a prohibition, or made an error while ignorant of its ruling." We mentioned the Hadith by Abu Hurayrah, that Muslim collected, wherein Allah said, "I shall (accept your supplication)." There is also the Hadith by Ibn `Abbas that Allah said, "I did (accept your supplication)."

(Our Lord! Lay not on us a burden like that which You did lay on those before us (Jews and Christians),) means, "Even if we were able to perform them, do not require us to perform the difficult deeds as You required the previous nations before us, such as the burdens that were placed on them. You sent Your Prophet Muhammad , the Prophet of mercy, to abrogate these burdens through the Law that You revealed to him, the Hanifi (Islamic Monotheism), easy religion." Muslim recorded that Abu Hurayrah said that the Messenger of Allah said that Allah said, "I shall (accept your supplication)." Ibn `Abbas narrated that the Messenger of Allah said that Allah said, "I did (accept your supplication)." There is the Hadith recorded through various chains of narration that the Messenger of Allah said,

$$«بُعِثْتُ بِالْحَنِيفِيَّةِ السَّمْحَة»$$

(I was sent with the easy Hanifiyyah way.)

(Our Lord! Put not on us a burden greater than we have strength to bear) of obligations, hardships and afflictions, do not make us bear what we cannot bear of this.

(Our Lord! Put not on us a burden greater than we have strength to bear.)

We mentioned that Allah said, "I shall (accept your supplication)" in one narration, and, "I did (accept your supplication)," in another narration.

(Pardon us) meaning, between us and You regarding what You know of our shortcomings and errors.

(And grant us forgiveness) concerning what is between us and Your servants. So do not expose our errors and evil deeds to them.

(Have mercy on us) in what will come thereafter. Therefore, do not allow us to fall into another error. They say that those who commit error need three things: Allah's forgiveness for what is between Him and them, that He conceals these errors from His other servants, and thus does not expose them before the servants, and that He grants them immunity from further error." We mentioned before that Allah answered these pleas, "I shall," in one narration and, "I did," in another narration.

(You are our Mawla) meaning, You are our supporter and helper, our trust is in You, You are sought for each and every type of help and our total reliance is on You. There is no power or strength except from You.

(And give us victory over the disbelieving people) those who rejected Your religion, denied Your Oneness, refused the Message of Your Prophet , worshipped other than You and associated others in Your worship. Give us victory and make us prevail above them in this and the Hereafter. Allah said, "I shall," in one narration, and, "I did," in the Hadith that Muslim collected from Ibn `Abbas.

Further, Ibn Jarir recorded that Abu Ishaq said that whenever Mu`adh would finish reciting this Surah,

(And give us victory over the disbelieving people), he would say "Amin."

CHAPTER (SURAH) 3: AL-I-'IMRAN (THE FAMILY OF 'IMRAN), VERSES 001-092

In the Name of Allâh, the Most Gracious, the Most Merciful.

Surah: 3 Ayah: 1, Ayah: 2, Ayah: 3 & Ayah: 4

﴿ الٓمٓ ﴾

1. Alif-Lâm-Mîm. (These letters are one of the miracles of the Qur'ân, and none but Allâh (Alone) knows their meanings).

﴿ ٱللَّهُ لَآ إِلَٰهَ إِلَّا هُوَ ٱلۡحَیُّ ٱلۡقَیُّومُ ﴾

2. Allâh! Lâ ilahâ illa Huwa (none has the right to be worshipped but He), the Ever Living, the One Who sustains and protects all that exists.

﴿ نَزَّلَ عَلَیۡكَ ٱلۡكِتَٰبَ بِٱلۡحَقِّ مُصَدِّقࣰا لِّمَا بَیۡنَ یَدَیۡهِ وَأَنزَلَ ٱلتَّوۡرَىٰةَ وَٱلۡإِنجِیلَ ﴾

3. It is He Who has sent down the Book (the Qur'ân) to you (Muhammad (peace be upon him)) with truth, confirming what came before it. And he sent down the Taurât (Torah) and the Injeel (Gospel).

﴿ مِن قَبۡلُ هُدࣰى لِّلنَّاسِ وَأَنزَلَ ٱلۡفُرۡقَانَۗ إِنَّ ٱلَّذِینَ كَفَرُواْ بِـَٔایَٰتِ ٱللَّهِ لَهُمۡ عَذَابࣱ شَدِیدࣱۗ وَٱللَّهُ عَزِیزࣱ ذُو ٱنتِقَامࣲ ﴾

4. Aforetime, as a guidance to mankind. And He sent down the criterion (of judgement between right and wrong (this Qur'ân)) Truly, those who disbelieve in the Ayât (proofs, evidences, verses, lessons, signs, revelations, etc.) of Allâh, for them there is a severe torment; and Allâh is All-Mighty, All-Able of Retribution.

Transliteration

1. Alif-lam-meem 2. Allahu la ilaha illa huwa alhayyu alqayyoomu 3. Nazzala AAalayka alkitaba bialhaqqi musaddiqan lima bayna yadayhi waanzala alttawrata waalinjeela 4. Min qablu hudan lilnnasi waanzala alfurqana inna allatheena kafaroo bi-ayati Allahi lahum AAathabun shadeedun waAllahu AAazeezun thoo intiqamin

Tafsir Ibn Kathir

We mentioned the Hadith in the Tafsir of Ayat Al-Kursi (2:255) that mentions that Allah's Greatest Name is contained in these two Ayat,

(Allah! None has the right to be worshipped but He, the Ever Living, the One Who sustains and protects all that exists) and,

(Alif-Lam-Mim. Allah! None has the right to be worshipped but He, the Ever Living, the One Who sustains and protects all that exists.)

We also explained the Tafsir of,

(Alif-Lam-Mim) in the beginning of Surat Al-Baqarah, and the meaning of,

(Allah! La ilaha illa Huwa, Al-Hayyul-Qayyum) in the Tafsir of Ayat Al-Kursi. Allah's statement,

(It is He Who has sent down the Book to you with truth,) means, revealed the Qur'an to you, O Muhammad, in truth, meaning there is no doubt or suspicion that it is revealed from Allah. Verily, Allah revealed the Qur'an with His knowledge, and the angels testify to this fact, Allah is sufficient as a Witness. Allah's statement,

(Confirming what came before it) means, from the previous divinely revealed Books, sent to the servants and Prophets of Allah. These Books testify to the truth of the Qur'an, and the Qur'an also testifies to the truth these Books contained, including the news and glad tidings of Muhammad's prophethood and the revelation of the Glorious Qur'an.

Allah said,

(And He sent down the Tawrah) to Musa (Musa) son of `Imran,

(And the Injil), to `Isa, son of Mary,

(Aforetime) meaning, before the Qur'an was revealed,

(As a guidance to mankind) in their time.

(And He sent down the criterion) which is the distinction between misguidance, falsehood and deviation on one hand, and guidance, truth and piety on the other hand. This is because of the indications, signs, plain evidences and clear proofs that it contains, and because of its explanations, clarifications, etc.

Allah's statement,

(Truly, those who disbelieve in the Ayat of Allah) means they denied, refused and unjustly rejected them,

(For them there is a severe torment) on the Day of Resurrection,

(And Allah is All-Mighty) meaning, His grandeur is invincible and His sovereignty is infinite,

(All-Able of Retribution.) from those who reject His Ayat and defy His honorable Messengers and great Prophets.

Surah: 3 Ayah: 5 & Ayah: 6

﴿ إِنَّ ٱللَّهَ لَا يَخْفَىٰ عَلَيْهِ شَىْءٌ فِى ٱلْأَرْضِ وَلَا فِى ٱلسَّمَآءِ ۞ ﴾

5. Truly, nothing is hidden from Allâh, in the earth or in the heavens.

﴿ هُوَ ٱلَّذِى يُصَوِّرُكُمْ فِى ٱلْأَرْحَامِ كَيْفَ يَشَآءُ ۚ لَآ إِلَٰهَ إِلَّا هُوَ ٱلْعَزِيزُ ٱلْحَكِيمُ ۞ ﴾

6. He it is Who shapes you in the wombs as He wills. Lâ ilâha illa Huwa (none has the right to be worshipped but He), the All-Mighty, the All-Wise.

Transliteration

5. Inna Allaha la yakhfa AAalayhi shay-on fee al-ardi wala fee alssama/-I 6. Huwa allathee yusawwirukum fee al-arhami kayfa yashao la ilaha illa huwa alAAazeezu alhakeemu

Tafsir Ibn Kathir

Allah states that He has perfect knowledge in the heavens and earth and that nothing in them is hidden from His watch.

(He it is Who shapes you in the wombs as He wills.) meaning, He creates you in the wombs as He wills, whether male or female, handsome or otherwise, happy or miserable.

(La ilaha illa Huwa (none has the right to be worshipped but He), the Almighty, the All-Wise.) meaning, He is the Creator and thus is the only deity worthy of worship, without partners, and His is the perfect might, wisdom and decision. This Ayah refers to the fact that `Isa, son of Mary, is a created servant, just as Allah created the rest of mankind. Allah created `Isa in the womb (of his mother) and shaped him as He willed. Therefore, how could `Isa be divine, as the Christians, may Allah's curses descend on them, claim `Isa was created in the womb and his creation changed from stage to stage, just as Allah said,

(He creates you in the wombs of your mothers, creation after creation in three veils of darkness.) (39:6).

Surah: 3 Ayah: 7, Ayah: 8 & Ayah: 9

﴿ هُوَ ٱلَّذِىٓ أَنزَلَ عَلَيْكَ ٱلْكِتَٰبَ مِنْهُ ءَايَٰتٌ مُّحْكَمَٰتٌ هُنَّ أُمُّ ٱلْكِتَٰبِ وَأُخَرُ مُتَشَٰبِهَٰتٌ ۖ فَأَمَّا ٱلَّذِينَ فِى قُلُوبِهِمْ زَيْغٌ فَيَتَّبِعُونَ مَا تَشَٰبَهَ مِنْهُ ٱبْتِغَآءَ ٱلْفِتْنَةِ

$$\text{وَٱبْتِغَآءَ تَأْوِيلِهِۦ ۗ وَمَا يَعْلَمُ تَأْوِيلَهُۥٓ إِلَّا ٱللَّهُ ۗ وَٱلرَّٰسِخُونَ فِى ٱلْعِلْمِ يَقُولُونَ ءَامَنَّا بِهِۦ كُلٌّ مِّنْ عِندِ رَبِّنَا ۗ وَمَا يَذَّكَّرُ إِلَّآ أُو۟لُوا۟ ٱلْأَلْبَٰبِ ۝}$$

7. It is He Who has sent down to you (Muhammad (peace be upon him)) the Book (this Qur'ân). In it are Verses that are entirely clear, they are the foundations of the Book

$$\text{رَبَّنَا لَا تُزِغْ قُلُوبَنَا بَعْدَ إِذْ هَدَيْتَنَا وَهَبْ لَنَا مِن لَّدُنكَ رَحْمَةً ۚ إِنَّكَ أَنتَ ٱلْوَهَّابُ ۝}$$

8. (They say): "Our Lord! Let not our hearts deviate (from the truth) after You have guided us, and grant us mercy from You. Truly, You are the Bestower."

$$\text{رَبَّنَآ إِنَّكَ جَامِعُ ٱلنَّاسِ لِيَوْمٍ لَّا رَيْبَ فِيهِ ۚ إِنَّ ٱللَّهَ لَا يُخْلِفُ ٱلْمِيعَادَ ۝}$$

9. Our Lord! Verily, it is You Who will gather mankind together on the Day about which there is no doubt. Verily, Allâh never breaks His Promise".

Transliteration

7. Huwa allathee anzala AAalayka alkitaba minhu ayatun muhkamatun hunna ommu alkitabi waokharu mutashabihatun faamma allatheena fee quloobihim zayghun fayattabiAAoona ma tashabaha minhu ibtighaa alfitnati waibtighaa ta/weelihi wama yaAAlamu ta/weelahu illa Allahu waalrrasikhoona fee alAAilmi yaqooloona amanna bihi kullun min AAindi rabbina wama yaththakkaru illa oloo al-albabi 8. Rabbana la tuzigh quloobana baAAda ith hadaytana wahab lana min ladunka rahmatan innaka anta alwahhabu 9. Rabbana innaka jamiAAu alnnasi liyawmin la rayba feehi inna Allaha la yukhlifu almeeAAada

Tafsir Ibn Kathir

The Mutashabihat and Muhkamat Ayat

Allah states that in the Qur'an, there are Ayat that are Muhkamat, entirely clear and plain, and these are the foundations of the Book which are plain for everyone. And there are Ayat in the Qur'an that are Mutashabihat not entirely clear for many, or some people. So those who refer to the Muhkam Ayat to understand the Mutashabih Ayat, will have acquired the correct guidance, and vice versa. This is why Allah said,

(They are the foundations of the Book), meaning, they are the basis of the Qur'an, and should be referred to for clarification, when warranted,

(And others not entirely clear) as they have several meanings, some that agree with the Muhkam and some that carry other literal indications, although these meaning might not be desired.

The Muhkamat are the Ayat that explain the abrogating rulings, the allowed, prohibited, laws, limits, obligations and rulings that should be believed in and implemented. As for the Mutashabihat Ayat, they include the abrogated Ayat, parables, oaths, and what should be believed in, but not implemented.

Muhammad bin Ishaq bin Yasar commented on,

(In it are verses that are entirely clear) as "Containing proof of the Lord, immunity for the servants and a refutation of opponents and of falsehood. They cannot be changed or altered from what they were meant for." He also said, "As for the unclear Ayat, they can (but must not) be altered and changed, and this is a test from Allah to the servants, just as He tested them with the allowed and prohibited things. So these Ayat must not be altered to imply a false meaning or be distorted from the truth."

Therefore, Allah said,

(So as for those in whose hearts there is a deviation) meaning, those who are misguided and deviate from truth to falsehood,

(they follow that which is not entirely clear thereof) meaning, they refer to the Mutashabih, because they are able to alter its meanings to conform with their false interpretation since the wordings of the Mutashabihat encompass such a wide area of meanings. As for the Muhkam Ayat, they cannot be altered because they are clear and, thus, constitute unequivocal proof against the misguided people. This is why Allah said,

(seeking Al-Fitnah) meaning, they seek to misguide their following by pretending to prove their innovation by relying on the Qur'an -- the Mutashabih of it -- but, this is proof against and not for them. For instance, Christians might claim that (`Isa is divine because) the Qur'an states that he is Ruhullah and His Word, which He gave to Mary, all the while ignoring Allah's statements,

(He (`Isa) was not more than a servant. We granted Our favor to him.) (43:59), and,

(Verily, the likeness of `Isa before Allah is the likeness of Adam. He created him from dust, then (He) said to him: "Be!" and he was.) (3:59).

There are other Ayat that clearly assert that `Isa is but one of Allah's creatures and that he is the servant and Messenger of Allah, among other Messengers.

Allah's statement,

(And seeking for its Ta'wil,) to alter them as they desire. Imam Ahmad recorded that `A'ishah said, "The Messenger of Allah recited,

(It is He Who has sent down to you the Book. In it are verses that are entirely clear, they are the foundations of the Book; and others not entirely clear,), until,

(Men of understanding) and he said,

«فَإِذَا رَأَيْتُمُ الَّذِينَ يُجَادِلُونَ فِيهِ، فَهُمُ الَّذِينَ عَنَى اللهُ، فَاحْذَرُوهُمْ»

(When you see those who argue in it (using the Mutashabihat), then they are those whom Allah meant. Therefore, beware of them.)"

Al-Bukhari recorded a similar Hadith in the Tafsir of this Ayah (3:7), as did Muslim in the book of Qadar (the Divine Will) in his Sahih, and Abu Dawud in the Sunnah section of his Sunan, from `A'ishah; "The Messenger of Allah recited this Ayah,

(It is He Who has sent down to you the Book. In it are verses that are entirely clear,) until,

(And none receive admonition except men of understanding.)

He then said,

«فَإِذَا رَأَيْتِ الَّذِينَ يَتَّبِعُونَ مَا تَشَابَهَ مِنْهُ؛ فَأُولَئِكَ الَّذِينَ سَمَّى اللهُ، فَاحْذَرُوهُمْ»

(When you see those who follow what is not so clear of the Qur'an, then they are those whom Allah described, so beware of them.)"

This is the wording recorded by Al-Bukhari.

Only Allah Knows the True Ta'wil (Interpretation) of the Mutashabihat

Allah said,

(But none knows its Ta'wil except Allah.)

Similarly, as preceded in what has been reported from Ibn `Abbas, "Tafsir is of four types: Tafsir that the Arabs know in their language; Tafsir that no one is excused of being ignorant of; Tafsir that the scholars know; and Tafsir that only Allah knows." Scholars of Qur'an recitation have different opinions about pausing at Allah's Name in this Ayah. This stop was reported from `A'ishah, `Urwah, Abu Ash-Sha`tha' and Abu Nahik.

Some pause after reciting,

(And those who are firmly grounded in knowledge) saying that the Qur'an does not address the people with what they cannot understand. Ibn Abi Najih said that Mujahid said that Ibn `Abbas said, "I am among those who are firmly grounded in its Ta'wil interpretation." The Messenger of Allah supplicated for the benefit of Ibn `Abbas,

«اللَّهُمَّ فَقِّهْهُ فِي الدِّينِ وَعَلِّمْهُ التَّأْوِيلَ»

(O Allah! Bestow on him knowledge in the religion and teach him the Ta'wil (interpretation).)

Ta'wil has two meanings in the Qur'an, the true reality of things, and what they will turn out to be. For instance, Allah said,

(And he said: "O my father! This is the Ta'wil of my dream aforetime!".) (12:100), and,

(Await they just for it's Ta'wil On the Day (Day of Resurrection) it's Ta'wil is finally fulfillled.)(7:53) refers to the true reality of Resurrection that they were told about. If this is the meaning desired in the Ayah above (3:7), then pausing after reciting Allah's Name is warranted, because only Allah knows the true reality of things. In this case, Allah's statement,

(And those who are firmly grounded in knowledge) is connected to His statement,

(say: "We believe in it") If the word Ta'wil means the second meaning, that is, explaining and describing, such as what Allah said,

((They said): "Inform us of the Ta'wil of this") meaning its explanation, then pausing after reciting,

(And those who are firmly grounded in knowledge) is warranted. This is because the scholars have general knowledge in, and understand what they were addressed with, even though they do not have knowledge of the true reality of things. Therefore, Allah's statement,

(say: "We believe in it") describes the conduct of the scholars. Similarly, Allah said,

(And your Lord comes, and the angels, in rows.) (89:22) means, your Lord will come, and the angels will come in rows.

Allah's statement that the knowledgeable people proclaim,

(We believe in it) means, they believe in the Mutashabih.

(all of it is from our Lord) meaning, both the Muhkam and the Mutashabih are true and authentic, and each one of them testifies to the truth of the other. This is because they both are from Allah and nothing that comes from Allah is ever met by contradiction or discrepancy. Allah said,

(Do they not then consider the Qur'an carefully Had it been from other than Allah, they would surely have found therein many a contradiction.) (4:82).

Allah said in his Ayah (3:7),

(And none receive admonition except men of understanding.) meaning, those who have good minds and sound comprehension, understand, contemplate and comprehend the meaning in the correct manner. Further, Ibn Al-Mundhir recorded in his Tafsir that Nafi` bin Yazid said, "Those firmly grounded in knowledge are those who are modest for Allah's sake, humbly seek His pleasure, and do not exaggerate regarding those above them, or belittle those below them."

Allah said that they supplicate to their Lord,

(Our Lord! Let not our hearts deviate (from the truth) after You have guided us.) meaning, "Do not deviate our hearts from the guidance after You allowed them to acquire it. Do not make us like those who have wickedness in their hearts, those who follow the Mutashabih in the Qur'an. Rather, make us remain firmly on Your straight path and true religion."

(And grant us from Ladunka) meaning, from You,

(Mercy) with which You make our hearts firm, and increase in our Faith and certainty,

(Truly, You are the Bestower)

Ibn Abi Hatim and Ibn Jarir recorded that Umm Salamah said that the Prophet used to supplicate,

«يَا مُقَلِّبَ الْقُلُوبِ ثَبِّتْ قَلْبِي عَلَى دِينِك»

(O You Who changes the hearts, make my heart firm on Your religion.)

He then recited,

("Our Lord! Let not our hearts deviate (from the truth) after You have guided us, and grant us mercy from You. Truly, You are the Bestower.") The Ayah continues,

("Our Lord! Verily, it is You Who will gather mankind together on the Day about which there is no doubt") meaning, they say in their supplication: O our Lord! You will gather Your creation on the Day of Return, judge between them and decide over what they disputed about. Thereafter, You will reward or punish each according to the deeds they did in this life.

Surah: 3 Ayah: 10 & Ayah: 11

﴿ إِنَّ الَّذِينَ كَفَرُواْ لَن تُغْنِىَ عَنْهُمْ أَمْوَالُهُمْ وَلاَ أَوْلَـدُهُم مِّنَ اللَّهِ شَيْئاً وَأُوْلَـئِكَ هُمْ وَقُودُ النَّارِ ﴾

10. Verily, those who disbelieve, neither their properties nor their offspring will avail them whatsoever against Allâh; and it is they who will be fuel of the Fire.

$$\bigl\{\text{كَدَأْبِ ءَالِ فِرْعَوْنَ وَٱلَّذِينَ مِن قَبْلِهِمْ ۚ كَذَّبُواْ بِـَٔايَـٰتِنَا فَأَخَذَهُمُ ٱللَّهُ بِذُنُوبِهِمْ ۗ وَٱللَّهُ شَدِيدُ ٱلْعِقَابِ}\bigl\}$$

11. Like the behavior of the people of Fir'aun (Pharaoh) and those before them; they belied Our Ayât (proofs, evidences, verses, lessons, signs, revelations, etc.). So Allâh seized (destroyed) them for their sins. And Allâh is Severe in punishment.

Transliteration

10. Inna allatheena kafaroo lan tughniya AAanhum amwaluhum wala awladuhum mina Allahi shay-an waola-ika hum waqoodu alnnari 11. Kada/bi ali firAAawna waallatheena min qablihim kaththaboo bi-ayatina faakhathahumu Allahu bithunoobihim waAllahu shadeedu alAAiqabi

Tafsir Ibn Kathir

On the Day of Resurrection, No Wealth or Offspring Shall Avail

Allah states that the disbelievers shall be fuel for the Fire,

(The Day when their excuses will be of no profit to wrongdoers. Theirs will be the curse, and theirs will be the evil abode (i.e. painful torment in Hell-fire).) (40:52).

Further, what they were granted in this life of wealth and offspring shall not avail them with Allah, or save them from His punishment and severe torment. Similarly, Allah said,

(So let not their wealth nor their children amaze you; in reality Allah's plan is to punish them with these things in the life of this world, and that their souls shall depart (die) while they are disbelievers.) (9:55), and,

(Let not the free disposal (and affluence) of the disbelievers throughout the land deceive you. A brief enjoyment; then, their ultimate abode is Hell; and worst indeed is that place for rest.) (3:196, 197).

Allah said in this Ayah (3:10),

(Verily, those who disbelieve) meaning, disbelieved in Allah's Ayat, denied His Messengers, defied His Books and did not benefit from His revelation to His Prophets,

(Neither their properties nor their offspring will avail them whatsoever against Allah; and it is they who will be fuel of the Fire.) meaning, they will be the wood with which the Fire is kindled and fed. Similarly, Allah said,

(Certainly you (disbelievers) and that which you are worshipping now besides Allah, are (but) fuel for Hell!) (21:98).

Allah said next,

(Like the Da'b of the people of Fira`wn.) Ad-Dahhak said that Ibn `Abbas said that the Ayah means, "Like the behavior of the people of Fir`awn." This is the same Tafsir of `Ikrimah, Mujahid, Abu Malik, Ad-Dahhak, and others. Other scholars said that the Ayah means, "Like the practice, conduct, likeness of the people of Fir`awn." These meanings are all plausible, for the Da'b means practice, behavior, tradition and habit. The Ayah indicates that the disbelievers will not benefit from their wealth or offspring. Rather, they will perish and be punished. This is the same end the people of Fir`awn and the previous nations met, those who rejected the Messengers, the Ayat, and proofs of Allah that they were sent with.

(And Allah is severe in punishment.) meaning, His punishment is severe and His torment is painful. None can escape Allah's grasp, nor does anything escape His knowledge. Allah does what He wills and prevails over all things, it is He to Whom everything is humbled and there is no deity worthy of worship, nor any Lord except Him.

Surah: 3 Ayah: 12 & Ayah: 13

﴿قُل لِّلَّذِينَ كَفَرُواْ سَتُغْلَبُونَ وَتُحْشَرُونَ إِلَىٰ جَهَنَّمَ وَبِئْسَ ٱلْمِهَادُ ۝﴾

12. Say (O Muhammad (peace be upon him)) to those who disbelieve: "You will be defeated and gathered together to Hell, and worst indeed is that place to rest."

﴿قَدْ كَانَ لَكُمْ ءَايَةٌ فِى فِئَتَيْنِ ٱلْتَقَتَا فِئَةٌ تُقَـٰتِلُ فِى سَبِيلِ ٱللَّهِ وَأُخْرَىٰ كَافِرَةٌ يَرَوْنَهُم مِّثْلَيْهِمْ رَأْىَ ٱلْعَيْنِ وَٱللَّهُ يُؤَيِّدُ بِنَصْرِهِۦ مَن يَشَآءُ إِنَّ فِى ذَٰلِكَ لَعِبْرَةً لِّأُوْلِى ٱلْأَبْصَـٰرِ ۝﴾

13. There has already been a sign for you (O Jews) in the two armies that met (in combat i.e. the battle of Badr). One was fighting in the Cause of Allâh, and as for the other, (they) were disbelievers. They (the believers) saw them (the disbelievers) with their own eyes twice their number (although they were thrice their number). And Allâh supports with His Victory whom He wills. Verily, in this is a lesson for those who understand. (See Verse 8:44). (Tafsir At-Tabarî)

Transliteration

12. Qul lillatheena kafaroo satughlaboona watuhsharoona ila jahannama wabi/sa almihadu 13. Qad kana lakum ayatun fee fi-atayni iltaqata fi-atun tuqatilu fee sabeeli Allahi waokhra kafiratun yarawnahum mithlayhim ra/ya alAAayni waAllahu yu-ayyidu binasrihi man yashao inna fee Thalika laAAibratan li-olee al-absari

Tafsir Ibn Kathir

Threatening the Jews With Defeat and Encouraging Them to Learn a Lesson From the Battle of Badr

Allah commanded the Prophet Muhammad to proclaim to the disbelievers,

(You will be defeated) in this life,

(And gathered together) on the Day of Resurrection,

(to Hell, and worst indeed is that place of rest)

Muhammad bin Ishaq bin Yasar recorded that `Asim bin `Umar bin Qatadah said that when the Messenger of Allah gained victory in the battle of Badr and went back to Al-Madinah, he gathered the Jews in the marketplace of Bani Qaynuqa`.

Therefore, Allah said,

(There has already been a sign for you) meaning, O Jews, who said what you said! You have an Ayah, meaning proof, that Allah will make His religion prevail, award victory to His Messenger, make His Word apparent and His religion the highest.

(In the two armies) meaning, two camps,

(that met) in combat (in Badr),

(One was fighting in the Cause of Allah) the Muslims,

(And as for the other, in disbelief) meaning, the idolators of Quraysh at Badr. Allah's statement,

(They saw them with their own eyes twice their number) means, the idolators thought that the Muslims were twice as many as they were, for Allah made this illusion a factor in the victory that Islam had over them.

It was said that the meaning of Allah's statement,

(They saw them with their own eyes twice their number) is that the Muslims saw twice as many idolators as they were, yet Allah gave them victory over the disbelievers. `Abdullah bin Mas`ud said, "When we looked at the disbelievers' forces, we found that they were twice as many as we were. When we looked at them again, we thought they did not have one man more than we had. So Allah's statement,

(And (remember) when you met, He showed them to you as few in your eyes and He made you appear as few in their eyes.) (8:44)".

When the two camps saw each other, the Muslims thought that the idolators were twice as many as they were, so that they would trust in Allah and seek His help. The idolators thought that the believers were twice as many as they were, so that they would feel fear, horror, fright and despair. When the two camps stood in lines and met in battle, Allah made each camp look smaller in the eyes of the other camp, so that they would be encouraged to fight each other,

(so that Allah might accomplish a matter already ordained.) (8:42) meaning, so that the truth and falsehood are distinguishable, and thus the word of faith prevails over disbelief and deviation, so that the believers prevail and the disbelievers are humiliated. In a similar statement, Allah said;

(And Allah has already made you victorious at Badr, when you were a weak little force) (3:123). In this Ayah (3:13) Allah said,

(And Allah supports with His victory whom He wills. Verily, in this is a lesson for those who understand.) meaning, this should be an example for those who have intelligence and sound comprehension. They should contemplate about Allah's wisdom, decisions and decree, that He gives victory to His believing servants in this life and on the Day the witnesses stand up to testify.

Surah: 3 Ayah: 14 & Ayah: 15

﴿ زُيِّنَ لِلنَّاسِ حُبُّ ٱلشَّهَوَٰتِ مِنَ ٱلنِّسَآءِ وَٱلْبَنِينَ وَٱلْقَنَٰطِيرِ ٱلْمُقَنطَرَةِ مِنَ ٱلذَّهَبِ وَٱلْفِضَّةِ وَٱلْخَيْلِ ٱلْمُسَوَّمَةِ وَٱلْأَنْعَٰمِ وَٱلْحَرْثِ ۗ ذَٰلِكَ مَتَٰعُ ٱلْحَيَوٰةِ ٱلدُّنْيَا ۖ وَٱللَّهُ عِندَهُۥ حُسْنُ ٱلْمَـَٔابِ ﴿١٤﴾ ﴾

14. Beautified for men is the love of things they covet; women, children, much of gold and silver (wealth), branded beautiful horses, cattle and well-tilled land. This is the pleasure of the present world's life; but Allâh has the excellent return (Paradise with flowing rivers) with Him.

﴿ ۞ قُلْ أَؤُنَبِّئُكُم بِخَيْرٍ مِّن ذَٰلِكُمْ ۚ لِلَّذِينَ ٱتَّقَوْاْ عِندَ رَبِّهِمْ جَنَّٰتٌ تَجْرِى مِن تَحْتِهَا ٱلْأَنْهَٰرُ خَٰلِدِينَ فِيهَا وَأَزْوَٰجٌ مُّطَهَّرَةٌ وَرِضْوَٰنٌ مِّنَ ٱللَّهِ ۗ وَٱللَّهُ بَصِيرٌۢ بِٱلْعِبَادِ ﴿١٥﴾ ﴾

15. Say: "Shall I inform you of things far better than those? For Al-Muttaqûn (the pious - see V.2:2) there are Gardens (Paradise) with their Lord, underneath which rivers flow. Therein (is their) eternal (home) and Azwâjun Mutahharatun (purified mates or wives). And Allâh will be pleased with them. And Allâh is All-Seer of the (His) slaves".

Transliteration

14. Zuyyina lilnnasi hubbu alshshahawati mina alnnisa-i waalbaneena waalqanateeri almuqantarati mina alththahabi waalfiddati waalkhayli almusawwamati waal-anAAami waalharthi thalika mataAAu alhayati alddunya waAllahu AAindahu husnu almaabi 15. Qul aonabbi-okum bikhayrin min thalikum lillatheena ittaqaw AAinda rabbihim

jannatun tajree min tahtiha al-anharu khalideena feeha waazwajun mutahharatun waridwanun mina Allahi waAllahu baseerun bialAAibadi

Tafsir Ibn Kathir

The True Value of This Earthly Life

Allah mentions the delights that He put in this life for people, such as women and children, and He started with women, because the test with them is more tempting. For instance, the Sahih recorded that the Messenger said,

«مَا تَرَكْتُ بَعْدِي فِتْنَةً أَضَرَّ عَلَى الرِّجَالِ مِنَ النِّسَاء»

(I did not leave behind me a test more tempting to men than women.)

When one enjoys women for the purpose of having children and preserving his chastity, then he is encouraged to do so. There are many Hadiths that encourage getting married, such as,

«وَإِنَّ خَيْرَ هذِهِ الْأُمَّةِ مَنْ كَانَ أَكْثَرَهَا نِسَاء»

(Verily, the best members of this Ummah are those who have the most wives) He also said,

«الدُّنْيَا مَتَاعٌ، وَخَيْرُ مَتَاعِهَا الْمَرْأَةُ الصَّالِحَة»

(This life is a delight, and the best of its delight is a righteous wife)

The Prophet said in another Hadith,

«حُبِّبَ إِلَيَّ النِّسَاءُ وَالطِّيبُ، وَجُعِلَتْ قُرَّةُ عَيْنِي فِي الصَّلَاة»

(I was made to like women and perfume, and the comfort of my eye is the prayer.)

`A'ishah, may Allah be pleased with her, said, "Nothing was more beloved to the Messenger of Allah than women, except horses," and in another narration, "...than horses except women."

The desire to have children is sometimes for the purpose of pride and boasting, and as such, is a temptation. When the purpose for having children is to reproduce and increase the Ummah of Muhammad with those who worship Allah alone without partners, then it is encouraged and praised. A Hadith states,

«تَزَوَّجُوا الْوَدُودَ الْوَلُودَ، فَإِنِّي مُكَاثِرٌ بِكُمُ الْأُمَمَ يَوْمَ الْقِيَامَة»

(Marry the Wadud (kind) and Walud (fertile) woman, for I will compare your numbers to the rest of the nations on the Day of Resurrection.)

The desire of wealth sometimes results out of arrogance, and the desire to dominate the weak and control the poor, and this conduct is prohibited. Sometimes, the want for more money is for the purpose of spending it on acts of worship, being kind to the family, the relatives, and spending on various acts of righteousness and obedience; this behavior is praised and encouraged in the religion.

Scholars of Tafsir have conflicting opinions about the amount of the Qintar, all of which indicate that the Qintar is a large amount of money, as Ad-Dahhak and other scholars said. Abu Hurayrah said "The Qintar is twelve thousand Uwqiyah, each Uwqiyah is better than what is between the heavens and earth." [This was recorded by Ibn Jarir].

The desire to have horses can be one of three types. Sometimes, owners of horses collect them to be used in the cause of Allah, and when warranted, they use their horses in battle. This type of owner shall be rewarded for this good action. Another type collects horses to boast, and out of enmity to the people of Islam, and this type earns a burden for his behavior. Another type collects horses to fulfill their needs and to collect their offspring, and they do not forget Allah's right due on their horses. This is why in this case, these horses provide a shield of sufficiency for their owner, as evident by a Hadith that we will mention, Allah willing, when we explain Allah's statement,

(And make ready against them all you can of power, including steeds of war.) (8:60).

As for the Musawwamah horses, Ibn `Abbas said that they are the branded, beautiful horses. This is the same explanation of Mujahid, `Ikrimah, Sa`id bin Jubayr, `Abdur-Rahman bin `Abdullah bin Abza, As-Suddi, Ar-Rabi` bin Anas and Abu Sinan and others. Makhul said the Musawwamah refers to the horse with a white spotted faced, and the horse with white feet. Imam Ahmad recorded that Abu Dharr said that the Messenger of Allah said,

«لَيْسَ مِنْ فَرَسٍ عَرَبِيَ إِلَّا يُؤْذَنُ لَهُ مَعَ كُلِّ فَجْرٍ يَدْعُو بِدَعْوَتَيْنِ يَقُولُ: اللَّهُمَّ إِنَّكَ خَوَّلْتَنِي مِنْ بَنِي آدَمَ، فَاجْعَلْنِي مِنْ أَحَبِّ مَالِهِ وَأَهْلِهِ إِلَيْهِ أَوْ أَحَبَّ أَهْلِهِ وَمَالِهِ إِلَيْهِ»

(Every Arabian horse is allowed to have two supplications every dawn, and the horse supplicates, `O Allah! You made me subservient to the son of Adam. Therefore, make me among the dearest of his wealth and household to him, or, ...make me the dearest of his household and wealth to him.)

Allah's statement,

(Cattle) means, camels, cows and sheep.

(And fertile land) meaning, the land that is used to farm and grow plants.

Allah then said,

(This is the pleasure of the present world's life) meaning, these are the delights of this life and its short lived joys,

(But Allah has the excellent return with Him) meaning, the best destination and reward.

The Reward of the Those Who Have Taqwa is Better Than All Joys of This World

This is why Allah said,

(Say: "Shall I inform you of things far better than those")

This Ayah means, "Say, O Muhammad, to the people, `Should I tell you about what is better than the delights and joys of this life that will soon perish'" Allah informed them of what is better when He said,

(For those who have Taqwa there are Gardens (Paradise) with their Lord, underneath which rivers flow) meaning, rivers run throughout it. These rivers carry various types of drinks: honey, milk, wine and water such that no eye has ever seen, no ear has ever heard, and no heart has ever imagined,

(Therein (is their) eternal (home)) meaning, they shall remain in it forever and ever and will not want to be removed from it.

(And Azwajun Mutahharatun (purified mates or wives)) meaning, from filth, dirt, harm, menstruation, post birth bleeding, and other things that affect women in this world.

(And Allah will be pleased with them) meaning, Allah's pleasure will descend on them and He shall never be angry with them after that. This is why Allah said in in Surah Bara`ah,

(But the pleasure of Allah is greater) (9:72), meaning, greater than the eternal delight that He has granted them. Allah then said,

(And Allah is All-Seer of the (His) servants) and, He gives each provisions according to what they deserve.

Surah: 3 Ayah: 16 & Ayah: 17

﴿ ٱلَّذِينَ يَقُولُونَ رَبَّنَآ إِنَّنَآ ءَامَنَّا فَٱغْفِرْ لَنَا ذُنُوبَنَا وَقِنَا عَذَابَ ٱلنَّارِ ۝ ﴾

16. Those who say: "Our Lord! We have indeed believed, so forgive us our sins and save us from the punishment of the Fire."

$$\text{﴿ ٱلصَّٰبِرِينَ وَٱلصَّٰدِقِينَ وَٱلْقَٰنِتِينَ وَٱلْمُنفِقِينَ وَٱلْمُسْتَغْفِرِينَ بِٱلْأَسْحَارِ ﴾}$$

17. (They are) those who are patient, those who are true (in Faith, words, and deeds), and obedient with sincere devotion in worship to Allâh. Those who spend (give the Zakât and alms in the Way of Allâh) and those who pray and beg Allâh's Pardon in the last hours of the night.

Transliteration

16. Allatheena yaqooloona rabbana innana amanna faighfir lana thunoobana waqina AAathaba alnnari 17. Alssabireena waalssadiqeena waalqaniteena waalmunfiqeena waalmustaghfireena bial-ashari

Tafsir Ibn Kathir

The Supplication and Description of Al-Muttaqin

Allah describes the Muttaqin, His pious servants, whom He promised tremendous rewards,

(Those who say: "Our Lord! We have indeed believed") in You, Your Book and Your Messenger.

(so forgive us our sins) because of our faith in You and in what You legislated for us. Therefore, forgive us our errors and shortcomings, with Your bounty and mercy,

(and save us from the punishment of the Fire.)

Allah then said,

((They are) those who are patient) while performing acts of obedience and abandoning the prohibitions.

(those who are true) concerning their proclamation of faith, by performing the difficult deeds.

(and obedient) meaning, they submit and obey Allah,

(those who spend) from their wealth on all the acts of obedience they were commanded, being kind to kith and kin, helping the needy, and comforting the destitute.

(and those who pray and beg Allah's pardon in the last hours of the night) and this testifies to the virtue of seeking Allah's forgiveness in the latter part of the night. It was reported that when Ya`qub said to his children,

(I will ask my Lord for forgiveness for you) (12:98) he waited until the latter part of the night to say his supplication.

Furthermore, the Two Sahihs, the Musnad and Sunan collections recorded through several Companions that the Messenger of Allah said,

«يَنْزِلُ اللهُ تَبَارَكَ وَتَعَالَى فِي كُلِّ لَيْلَةٍ إِلَى سَمَاءِ الدُّنْيَا حِينَ يَبْقَى ثُلُثُ اللَّيْلِ الْآخِرُ، فَيَقُولُ: هَلْ مِنْ سَائِلٍ فَأُعْطِيَهُ؟ هَلْ مِنْ دَاعٍ فَأَسْتَجِيبَ لَهُ؟ هَلْ مِنْ مُسْتَغْفِرٍ فَأَغْفِرَ لَهُ؟»

(Every night, when the last third of it remains, our Lord, the Blessed, the Superior, descends to the lowest heaven saying, "Is there anyone to ask Me, so that I may grant him his request Is there anyone to invoke Me, so that I may respond to his invocation Is there anyone seeking My forgiveness, so that I may forgive him")

The Two Sahihs recorded that `A'ishah said, "The Messenger of Allah performed Witr during the first part, the middle and latter parts of the night. Then, later (in his life), he would perform it (only) during the latter part." `Abdullah bin `Umar used to pray during the night and would ask, "O Nafi`! Is it the latter part of the night yet" and if Nafi` said, "Yes," Ibn `Umar would start supplicating to Allah and seeking His forgiveness until dawn. This Hadith was collected by Ibn Abi Hatim.

Surah: 3 Ayah: 18, Ayah: 19 & Ayah: 20

﴿شَهِدَ ٱللَّهُ أَنَّهُۥ لَآ إِلَٰهَ إِلَّا هُوَ وَٱلْمَلَٰٓئِكَةُ وَأُولُوا۟ ٱلْعِلْمِ قَآئِمًۢا بِٱلْقِسْطِ لَآ إِلَٰهَ إِلَّا هُوَ ٱلْعَزِيزُ ٱلْحَكِيمُ ۝﴾

18. Allâh bears witness that Lâ ilâha illa Huwa (none has the right to be worshipped but He), and the angels, and those having knowledge (also give this witness); (He always) maintains His creation in Justice. Lâ ilâh illa Huwa (none has the right to be worshipped but He), the All-Mighty, the All-Wise.

﴿إِنَّ ٱلدِّينَ عِندَ ٱللَّهِ ٱلْإِسْلَٰمُ ۗ وَمَا ٱخْتَلَفَ ٱلَّذِينَ أُوتُوا۟ ٱلْكِتَٰبَ إِلَّا مِنۢ بَعْدِ مَا جَآءَهُمُ ٱلْعِلْمُ بَغْيًۢا بَيْنَهُمْ ۗ وَمَن يَكْفُرْ بِـَٔايَٰتِ ٱللَّهِ فَإِنَّ ٱللَّهَ سَرِيعُ ٱلْحِسَابِ ۝﴾

19. Truly, the religion with Allâh is Islâm. Those who were given the Scripture (Jews and Christians) did not differ except, out of mutual jealousy, after knowledge had come to them. And whoever disbelieves in the Ayât (proofs, evidences, verses, signs, revelations, etc.) of Allâh, then surely, Allâh is Swift in calling to account.

﴿ فَإِنْ حَآجُّوكَ فَقُلْ أَسْلَمْتُ وَجْهِيَ لِلَّهِ وَمَنِ ٱتَّبَعَنِ ۗ وَقُل لِّلَّذِينَ أُوتُواْ ٱلْكِتَٰبَ وَٱلْأُمِّيِّـۧنَ ءَأَسْلَمْتُمْ ۚ فَإِنْ أَسْلَمُواْ فَقَدِ ٱهْتَدَواْ ۖ وَّإِن تَوَلَّوْاْ فَإِنَّمَا عَلَيْكَ ٱلْبَلَٰغُ ۗ وَٱللَّهُ بَصِيرٌۢ بِٱلْعِبَادِ ﴾ ﴿٢٠﴾

20. So if they dispute with you (Muhammad (peace be upon him)) say: "I have submitted myself to Allâh (in Islâm), and (so have) those who follow me." And say to those who were given the Scripture (Jews and Christians) and to those who are illiterates (Arab pagans): "Do you (also) submit yourselves (to Allâh in Islâm)?" If they do, they are rightly guided; but if they turn away, your duty is only to convey the Message; and Allâh is All-Seer of (His) slaves.

Transliteration

18. Shahida Allahu annahu la ilaha illa huwa waalmala-ikatu waoloo alAAilmi qa-iman bialqisti la ilaha illa huwa alAAazeezu alhakeemu 19. Inna alddeena AAinda Allahi al-islamu wama ikhtalafa allatheena ootoo alkitaba illa min baAAdi ma jaahumu alAAilmu baghyan baynahum waman yakfur bi-ayati Allahi fa-inna Allaha sareeAAu alhisabi 20. Fa-in hajjooka faqul aslamtu wajhiya lillahi wamani ittabaAAani waqul lillatheena ootoo alkitabu waal-ommiyyeena aaslamtum fa-in aslamoo faqadi ihtadaw wa-in tawallaw fa-innama AAalayka albalaghu waAllahu baseerun bialAAibadi

Tafsir Ibn Kathir

The Testimony of Tawhid

Allah bears witness, and verily, Allah is sufficient as a Witness, and He is the Most Truthful and Just Witness there is; His statement is the absolute truth,

(that La ilaha illa Huwa) meaning, He Alone is the Lord and God of all creation; everyone and everything are His servants, creation and in need of Him. Allah is the Most Rich, Free from needing anyone or anything. Allah said in another Ayah,

(But Allah bears witness to that which He has sent down (the Qur'an) unto you (O Muhammad)) (4:166).

Allah then mentioned the testimony of His angels and those who have knowledge after he mentioned His own testimony,

(Allah bears witness that none has the right to be worshipped but He), and the angels, and those having knowledge (also bear witness to this)). This Ayah emphasizes the great virtue of those who have knowledge.

((He) maintains His creation in justice) in all that He does,

(None has the right to be worshipped but He) thus emphasizing this fact,

(the Almighty, the All-Wise.) the Mighty that does not submit to weakness due to His might and greatness, the Wise in all His statements, actions, legislation and decrees.

The Religion with Allah is Islam

Allah said,

(Truly, the religion with Allah is Islam.) Allah states that there is no religion accepted with Him from any person, except Islam. Islam includes obeying all of the Messengers until Muhammad who finalized their commission, thus closing all paths to Allah except through Muhammad . Therefore, after Allah sent Muhammad , whoever meets Allah following a path other than Muhammad's, it will not be accepted of him. In another Ayah, Allah said,

(And whoever seeks a religion other than Islam, it will never be accepted of him) (3:85).

In this Ayah (3:19), Allah said, asserting that the only religion accepted with Him is Islam,

(Truly, the religion with Allah is Islam.)

Allah then states that those who were given the Scripture beforehand divided in the religion after Allah sent the Messengers and revealed the Books to them providing them the necessary proofs to not do so. Allah said,

(Those who were given the Scripture (Jews and Christians) did not differ except out of rivalry, after knowledge had come to them.) meaning, some of them wronged others. Therefore, they differed over the truth, out of envy, hatred and enmity for each other. This hatred made some of them defy those whom they hated even if they were correct. Allah then said,

(And whoever disbelieves in the Ayat of Allah) meaning, whoever rejects what Allah sent down in His Book,

(then surely, Allah is Swift in reckoning.) Allah will punish him for his rejection, reckon him for his denial, and torment him for defying His Book. Thereafter, Allah said.

(So if they dispute with you (Muhammad)) so if they argue with you about Tawhid,

(Say: "I have submitted myself to Allah (in Islam), and (so have) those who follow me") meaning, Say, `I have made my worship sincere for Allah Alone without partners, rivals, offspring or companion,

(and those who follow me) who followed my religion and embraced my creed.' In another Ayah, Allah said,

(Say (O Muhammad): "This is my way; I invite unto Allah with sure knowledge, I and whosoever follows me...") (12:108).

Islam is the Religion of Mankind and the Prophet Was Sent to all Mankind

Allah commanded His servant and Messenger, Muhammad , to call the People of the Two Scriptures and the unlettered idolators to his religion, way, Law and all that Allah sent him with. Allah said,

(And say to those who were given the Scripture (Jews and Christians) and to those who are illiterates (Arab pagans): "Do you (also) submit yourselves" If they do, they are rightly guided; but if they turn away, your duty is only to convey the Message.) meaning, their reckoning is with Allah and their return and final destination is to Him. It is He Who guides whom He wills and allows whom He wills to stray, and He has the perfect wisdom and the unequivocal proof for all of this. This is why Allah said,

(And Allah sees the servants.) for He has perfect knowledge of who deserves to be guided and who does not deserve to be guided. Verily,

(He cannot be questioned for what He does, while they will be questioned.) (21:23) because of His perfect wisdom and mercy. This and similar Ayat are clear proofs that the Message of Muhammad is universal to all creation, as it is well established in the religion, according to the various texts of the Book and Sunnah. For instance, Allah said,

(Say (O Muhammad): "O mankind! Verily, I am sent to you all as the Messenger of Allah.") (7:158), and,

(Blessed be He Who sent down the criterion to His servant that he may be a warner to the `Alamin (mankind and Jinn).) (25:1).

The Two Sahihs and other collections of Hadith recorded that the Prophet sent letters to the kings of the earth during his time and to different peoples, Arabs and non-Arabs, People of the Book and the unlettered, just as Allah had commanded him. `Abdur-Razzaq recorded that Ma`mar said, that Hammam said that Abu Hurayrah said that the Prophet said,

«وَالَّذِي نَفْسِي بِيَدِهِ، لَا يَسْمَعُ بِي أَحَدٌ مِنْ هَذِهِ الْأُمَّةِ: يَهُودِيٌّ وَلَا نَصْرَانِيٌّ، وَمَاتَ وَلَمْ يُؤْمِنْ بِالَّذِي أُرْسِلْتُ بِهِ، إِلَّا كَانَ مِنْ أَهْلِ النَّارِ»

(By He in Whose Hand is my soul! No member of this Ummah, no Jew or Christian, hears of me but dies without believing in what I was sent with, but will be among the people of the Fire.) Muslim recorded this Hadith.

The Prophet said,

«بُعِثْتُ إِلَى الْأَحْمَرِ وَالْأَسْوَد»

(I was sent to the red and black.) and,

»كَانَ النَّبِيُّ يُبْعَثُ إِلَى قَوْمِهِ خَاصَّةً، وَبُعِثْتُ إِلَى النَّاسِ عَامَّةً«

(A Prophet used to be sent to his people, but I was sent to all mankind.)

Surah: 3 Ayah: 21 & Ayah: 22

﴿ إِنَّ ٱلَّذِينَ يَكْفُرُونَ بِـَٔايَـٰتِ ٱللَّهِ وَيَقْتُلُونَ ٱلنَّبِيِّـۧنَ بِغَيْرِ حَقٍّ وَيَقْتُلُونَ ٱلَّذِينَ يَأْمُرُونَ بِٱلْقِسْطِ مِنَ ٱلنَّاسِ فَبَشِّرْهُم بِعَذَابٍ أَلِيمٍ ﴾

21. Verily! Those who disbelieve in the Ayât (proofs, evidences, verses, lessons, signs, revelations, etc.) of Allâh and kill the Prophets without right, and kill those men who order just dealings, ... then announce to them a painful torment.

﴿ أُو۟لَـٰٓئِكَ ٱلَّذِينَ حَبِطَتْ أَعْمَـٰلُهُمْ فِى ٱلدُّنْيَا وَٱلْـَٔاخِرَةِ وَمَا لَهُم مِّن نَّـٰصِرِينَ ﴾

22. They are those whose works will be lost in this world and in the Hereafter, and they will have no helpers.

Transliteration

21. Inna allatheena yakfuroona bi-ayati Allahi wayaqtuloona alnnabiyyeena bighayri haqqin wayaqtuloona Allatheena ya/muroona bialqisti mina alnnasi fabashshirhum biAAathabin aleemin 22. Ola-ika allatheena habitat aAAmaluhum fee alddunya waal-akhirati wama lahum min nasireena

Tafsir Ibn Kathir

Chastising the Jews for Their Disbelief and for Killing the Prophets and Righteous People

This Ayah chastises the People of the Book for the transgression and prohibitions they committed by their denials in the past and more recent times, of Allah's Ayat and the Messengers. They did this due to their defiance and rejection of the Messengers, denial of the truth and refusal to follow it. They also killed many Prophets when they conveyed to them what Allah legislated for them, without cause or criminal behavior committed by these Prophets, for they only called them to the truth,

(And kill those men who order just dealings) thus, demonstrating the worst type of arrogance. Indeed, the Prophet said,

»الْكِبْرُ بَطَرُ الْحَقِّ وَغَمْطُ النَّاسِ«

(Kibr (arrogance) is refusing the truth and degrading people)

This is why when they rejected the truth and acted arrogantly towards the creation, Allah punished them with humiliation and disgrace in this life, and humiliating torment in the Hereafter. Allah said,

(then announce to them a painful torment) meaning, painful and humiliating,

(They are those whose works will be lost in this world and in the Hereafter, and they will have no helpers.).

Surah: 3 Ayah: 23, Ayah: 24 & Ayah: 25

﴿ أَلَمْ تَرَ إِلَى ٱلَّذِينَ أُوتُواْ نَصِيبًا مِّنَ ٱلْكِتَـٰبِ يُدْعَوْنَ إِلَىٰ كِتَـٰبِ ٱللَّهِ لِيَحْكُمَ بَيْنَهُمْ ثُمَّ يَتَوَلَّىٰ فَرِيقٌ مِّنْهُمْ وَهُم مُّعْرِضُونَ ﴾

23. Have you not seen those who have been given a portion of the Scripture? They are being invited to the Book of Allâh to settle their dispute, then a party of them turn away, and they are averse.

﴿ ذَٰلِكَ بِأَنَّهُمْ قَالُواْ لَن تَمَسَّنَا ٱلنَّارُ إِلَّآ أَيَّامًا مَّعْدُودَٰتٍ وَغَرَّهُمْ فِى دِينِهِم مَّا كَانُواْ يَفْتَرُونَ ﴾

24. This is because they say: "The Fire shall not touch us but for a number of days." And that which they used to invent regarding their religion has deceived them.

﴿ فَكَيْفَ إِذَا جَمَعْنَـٰهُمْ لِيَوْمٍ لَّا رَيْبَ فِيهِ وَوُفِّيَتْ كُلُّ نَفْسٍ مَّا كَسَبَتْ وَهُمْ لَا يُظْلَمُونَ ﴾

25. How (will it be) when We gather them together on the Day about which there is no doubt (i.e. the Day of Resurrection). And each person will be paid in full what he has earned? And they will not be dealt with unjustly.

Transliteration

23. Alam tara ila allatheena ootoo naseeban mina alkitabi yudAAawna ila kitabi Allahi liyahkuma baynahum thumma yatawalla fareequn minhum wahum muAAridoona 24. Thalika bi-annahum qaloo lan tamassana alnnaru illa ayyaman maAAdoodatin wagharrahum fee deenihim ma kanoo yaftaroona 25. Fakayfa itha jamaAAnahum liyawmin la rayba feehi wawuffiyat kullu nafsin ma kasabat wahum la yuthlamoona

Tafsir Ibn Kathir

Chastising the People of the Book for Not Referring to the Book of Allah for Judgment

Allah criticizes the Jews and Christians who claim to follow their Books, the Tawrah and the Injil, because when they are called to refer to these Books where Allah commanded them to follow Muhammad, they turn away with aversion. This censure and criticism from Allah was all because of their defiance and rejection. Allah said next,

(This is because they say: "The Fire shall not touch us but for a number of days.") meaning, what made them dare to challenge and defy the truth is their false claim that Allah will only punish them for seven days in the Fire, a day for every one thousand years in this life. We mentioned this subject in the Tafsir of Surat Al-Baqarah.

Allah then said,

(And that which they used to invent regarding their religion has deceived them.) meaning, what caused them to remain on their false creed is that they deceived themselves, believing that the Fire will only touch them for a few days for their errors. However, it is they who have invented this notion, and Allah did not grant them authority to support this claim. Allah said, while threatening and warning them,

(How (will it be) when We gather them together on the Day about which there is no doubt (i. e. the Day of Resurrection).) meaning, what will their condition be like after they have uttered this lie about Allah, rejected His Messengers and killed His Prophets and their scholars who enjoined righteousness and forbade evil Allah will ask them about all this and punish them for what they have done. This is why Allah said,

(How (will it be) when We gather them together on the Day about which there is no doubt.) meaning, there is no doubt that this Day will come,

(And each person will be paid in full what he has earned And they will not be dealt with unjustly.).

Surah: 3 Ayah: 26 & Ayah: 27

﴿ قُلِ ٱللَّهُمَّ مَٰلِكَ ٱلْمُلْكِ تُؤْتِى ٱلْمُلْكَ مَن تَشَآءُ وَتَنزِعُ ٱلْمُلْكَ مِمَّن تَشَآءُ وَتُعِزُّ مَن تَشَآءُ وَتُذِلُّ مَن تَشَآءُ ۖ بِيَدِكَ ٱلْخَيْرُ ۖ إِنَّكَ عَلَىٰ كُلِّ شَىْءٍ قَدِيرٌ ﴿٢٦﴾ ﴾

26. Say (O Muhammad (peace be upon him)) "O Allâh! Possessor of the kingdom, You give the kingdom to whom You will, and You take the kingdom from whom You will, and You endue with honor whom You will, and You humiliate whom You will. In Your Hand is the good. Verily, You are Able to do all things.

﴿ تُولِجُ ٱلَّيْلَ فِى ٱلنَّهَارِ وَتُولِجُ ٱلنَّهَارَ فِى ٱلَّيْلِ ۖ وَتُخْرِجُ ٱلْحَىَّ مِنَ ٱلْمَيِّتِ وَتُخْرِجُ ٱلْمَيِّتَ مِنَ ٱلْحَىِّ وَتَرْزُقُ مَن تَشَآءُ بِغَيْرِ حِسَابٍ ﴿٢٧﴾ ﴾

27. You make the night to enter into the day, and You make the day to enter into the night (i.e. increase and decrease in the hours of the night and the day during winter and summer), You bring the living out of the dead, and You bring the

dead out of the living. And You give wealth and sustenance to whom You will, without limit (measure or account).

Transliteration

26. Quli allahumma malika almulki tu/tee almulka man tashao watanziAAu almulka mimman tashao watuAAizzu man tashao watuthillu man tashao biyadika alkhayru innaka AAala kulli shay-in qadeerun 27. Tooliju allayla fee alnnahari watooliju alnnahara fee allayli watukhriju alhayya mina almayyiti watukhriju almayyita mina alhayyi watarzuqu man tashao bighayri hisabin

Tafsir Ibn Kathir

Encouraging Gratitude

Allah said,

(Say) O Muhammad , while praising your Lord, thanking Him, relying in all matters upon Him and trusting in Him.

(O Allah! Possessor of the power) meaning, all sovereignty is Yours,

(You give power to whom You will, and You take power from whom You will, and You endue with honor whom You will, and You humiliate whom You will.) meaning, You are the Giver, You are the Taker, it is Your will that occurs and whatever You do not will, does not occur. This Ayah encourages thanking Allah for the favors He granted His Messenger and his Ummah. Allah transferred the prophethood from the Children of Israel to the Arab, Qurashi, Makkan, unlettered Prophet, the Final and Last of all Prophets and the Messenger of Allah to all mankind and Jinn. Allah endowed the Prophet with the best of qualities from the prophets before him. Allah also granted him extra qualities that no other Prophet or Messenger before him was endowed with, such as granting him (more) knowledge of Allah and His Law, knowledge of more of the matters of the past and the future, such as what will occur in the Hereafter. Allah allowed Muhammad's Ummah to reach the eastern and western parts of the world and gave dominance to his religion and Law over all other religions and laws. May Allah's peace and blessings be on the Prophet until the Day of Judgment, and as long as the day and night succeed each other. This is why Allah said,

(Say: "O Allah! Possessor of the power,") meaning, You decide what You will concerning Your creation and You do what you will. Allah refutes those who thought that they could decide for Allah,

(And they say: "Why is not this Qur'an sent down to some great man of the two towns (Makkah and Ta'if)") (43:31).

Allah refuted them by saying,

(Is it they who would portion out the Mercy of your Lord) (43:32), meaning, "We decide for Our creation what We will, without resistance or hindrance by anyone. We have the perfect wisdom and the unequivocal proof in all of this, and We give the prophethood to whom We will." Similarly, Allah said,

(Allah knows best with whom to place His Message) and,

(See how We prefer one above another (in this world)) (17: 21)

Allah said,

(You make the night enter into the day, and You make the day enter into the night) meaning, You take from the length of one of them and add it to the shortness of the other, so that they become equal, and take from the length of one of them and add it to the other so that they are not equal. This occurs throughout the seasons of the year: spring, summer, fall and winter. Allah's statement,

(You bring the living out of the dead, and You bring the dead out of the living.) means, You bring out the seed from the plant and the plant from the seed; the date from its seed and the date's seed from the date; the faithful from the disbeliever and the disbeliever from the faithful; the chicken from the egg and the egg from the chicken, etc.

(And You give wealth and sustenance to whom You will, without limit.) meaning, You give whomever You will innumerable amounts of wealth while depriving others from it, out of wisdom, and justice.

Surah: 3 Ayah: 28

﴿ لَّا يَتَّخِذِ ٱلْمُؤْمِنُونَ ٱلْكَٰفِرِينَ أَوْلِيَآءَ مِن دُونِ ٱلْمُؤْمِنِينَ ۖ وَمَن يَفْعَلْ ذَٰلِكَ فَلَيْسَ مِنَ ٱللَّهِ فِى شَىْءٍ إِلَّآ أَن تَتَّقُوا۟ مِنْهُمْ تُقَىٰةً ۗ وَيُحَذِّرُكُمُ ٱللَّهُ نَفْسَهُۥ ۗ وَإِلَى ٱللَّهِ ٱلْمَصِيرُ ﴿٢٨﴾

28. Let not the believers take the disbelievers as Auliyâ (supporters, helpers) instead of the believers, and whoever does that will never be helped by Allâh in any way, except if you indeed fear a danger from them. And Allâh warns you against Himself (His Punishment), and to Allâh is the final return.

Transliteration

28. La yattakhithi almu/minoona alkafireena awliyaa min dooni almu/mineena waman yafAAal Thalika falaysa mina Allahi fee shay-in illa an tattaqoo minhum tuqatan wayuhaththirukumu Allahu nafsahu wa-ila Allahi almaseeru

Tafsir Ibn Kathir

The Prohibition of Supporting the Disbelievers

Allah prohibited His believing servants from becoming supporters of the disbelievers, or to take them as comrades with whom they develop friendships, rather than the believers. Allah warned against such behavior when He said,

(And whoever does that, will never be helped by Allah in any way) meaning, whoever commits this act that Allah has prohibited, then Allah will discard him. Similarly, Allah said,

(O you who believe! Take not My enemies and your enemies as friends, showing affection towards them), until,

(And whosoever of you does that, then indeed he has gone astray from the straight path.) (60:1). Allah said,

(O you who believe! Take not for friends disbelievers instead of believers. Do you wish to offer Allah a manifest proof against yourselves) (4:144), and,

(O you who believe! Take not the Jews and the Christians as friends, they are but friends of each other. And whoever befriends them, then surely, he is one of them.) (5:51).

Allah said, after mentioning the fact that the faithful believers gave their support to the faithful believers among the Muhajirin, Ansar and Bedouins,

(And those who disbelieve are allies of one another, (and) if you do not behave the same, there will be Fitnah and oppression on the earth, and a great mischief and corruption.) (8:73).

Allah said next,

(unless you indeed fear a danger from them) meaning, except those believers who in some areas or times fear for their safety from the disbelievers. In this case, such believers are allowed to show friendship to the disbelievers outwardly, but never inwardly. For instance, Al-Bukhari recorded that Abu Ad-Darda' said, "We smile in the face of some people although our hearts curse them." Al-Bukhari said that Al-Hasan said, "The Tuqyah is allowed until the Day of Resurrection." Allah said,

(And Allah warns you against Himself.) meaning, He warns you against His anger and the severe torment He prepared for those who give their support to His enemies, and those who have enmity with His friends,

(And to Allah is the final return) meaning, the return is to Him and He will reward or punish each person according to their deeds.

Surah: 3 Ayah: 29, Ayah: 30

﴿ قُلْ إِن تُخْفُواْ مَا فِى صُدُورِكُمْ أَوْ تُبْدُوهُ يَعْلَمْهُ ٱللَّهُ وَيَعْلَمُ مَا فِى ٱلسَّمَـٰوَٰتِ وَمَا فِى ٱلْأَرْضِ وَٱللَّهُ عَلَىٰ كُلِّ شَىْءٍ قَدِيرٌ ﴿٢٩﴾ ﴾

29. Say (O Muhammad (peace be upon him)) "Whether you hide what is in your breasts or reveal it, Allâh knows it, and He knows what is in the heavens and what is in the earth. And Allâh is Able to do all things."

Chapter 3: Al-i-'Imran (The Family Of 'Imran), Verses 001-092

﴿ يَوْمَ تَجِدُ كُلُّ نَفْسٍ مَّا عَمِلَتْ مِنْ خَيْرٍ مُّحْضَرًا وَمَا عَمِلَتْ مِن سُوءٍ تَوَدُّ لَوْ أَنَّ بَيْنَهَا وَبَيْنَهُ أَمَدًا بَعِيدًا وَيُحَذِّرُكُمُ اللَّهُ نَفْسَهُ وَاللَّهُ رَءُوفٌ بِالْعِبَادِ ۞ ﴾

30. On the Day when every person will be confronted with all the good he has done, and all the evil he has done, he will wish that there were a great distance between him and his evil. And Allâh warns you against Himself (His Punishment) and Allâh is full of Kindness to the (His) slaves.

Transliteration

29. Qul in tukhfoo ma fee sudoorikum aw tubdoohu yaAAlamhu Allahu wayaAAlamu ma fee alssamawati wama fee al-ardi waAllahu AAala kulli shay-in qadeerun   30. Yawma tajidu kullu nafsin ma AAamilat min khayrin muhdaran wama AAamilat min soo-in tawaddu law anna baynaha wabaynahu amadan baAAeedan wayuhaththirukumu Allahu nafsahu waAllahu raoofun bialAAibadi

Tafsir Ibn Kathir

Allah Knows What the Hearts Conceal

Allah tells His servants that He knows the secrets and apparent matters and that nothing concerning them escapes His observation. Rather, His knowledge encompasses them in all conditions, time frames, days and instances. His knowledge encompasses all that is in heaven and earth, and nothing not even the weight of an atom, or what is smaller than that in the earth, seas and mountains, escapes His observation. Indeed,

(And Allah is able to do all things.) and His ability encompasses everything. This Ayah alerts Allah's servants that they should fear Him enough to not commit what He prohibits and dislikes, for He has perfect knowledge in all they do and is able to punish them promptly. And He gives respite to some of them, then He punishes them, and He is Swift and Mighty in taking account. This is why Allah said afterwards,

(On the Day when every person will be confronted with all the good he has done,) meaning, on the Day of Resurrection, Allah brings the good and evil deeds before the servant, just as He said,

(On that Day man will be informed of what he sent forward, and what he left behind.) (75:13).

When the servant sees his good deeds, he becomes happy and delighted. When he sees the evil deeds he committed, he becomes sad and angry. Then he will wish that he could disown his evil work and that a long distance separated it from him. He will also say to the devil who used to accompany him in this life, and who used to encourage him to do evil;

("Would that between me and you were the distance of the two easts - a horrible companion (indeed)!) (43:38).

Allah then said, while threatening and warning,

(And Allah warns you against Himself) meaning, He warns you against His punishment. Allah then said, while bringing hope to His servants, so that they do not despair from His mercy or feel hopeless of His kindness,

(And Allah is full of kindness with the servants)

Al-Hasan Al-Basri said, "Allah is so kind with them that He warns them against Himself." Others commented, "He is merciful with His creation and likes for them to remain on His straight path and chosen religion, and to follow His honorable Messenger."

Surah: 3 Ayah: 31 & Ayah: 32

﴿ قُلْ إِن كُنتُمْ تُحِبُّونَ ٱللَّهَ فَٱتَّبِعُونِى يُحْبِبْكُمُ ٱللَّهُ وَيَغْفِرْ لَكُمْ ذُنُوبَكُمْ ۗ وَٱللَّهُ غَفُورٌ رَّحِيمٌ ﴾

31. Say (O Muhammad (peace be upon him) to mankind): "If you (really) love Allâh then follow me (i.e. accept Islâmic Monotheism, follow the Qur'ân and the Sunnah), Allâh will love you and forgive you your sins. And Allâh is Oft-Forgiving, Most Merciful."

﴿ قُلْ أَطِيعُوا۟ ٱللَّهَ وَٱلرَّسُولَ ۖ فَإِن تَوَلَّوْا۟ فَإِنَّ ٱللَّهَ لَا يُحِبُّ ٱلْكَٰفِرِينَ ﴾

32. Say (O Muhammad (peace be upon him)) "Obey Allâh and the Messenger (Muhammad (peace be upon him))" But if they turn away, then Allâh does not like the disbelievers.

Transliteration

31. Qul in kuntum tuhibboona Allaha faittabiAAoonee yuhbibkumu Allahu wayaghfir lakum thunoobakum waAllahu ghafoorun raheemun   32. Qul ateeAAoo Allaha waalrrasoola fa-in tawallaw fa-inna Allaha la yuhibbu alkafireena

Tafsir Ibn Kathir

Allah's Love is Attained by Following the Messenger

This honorable Ayah judges against those who claim to love Allah, yet do not follow the way of Muhammad . Such people are not true in their claim until they follow the Shari`ah (Law) of Muhammad and his religion in all his statements, actions and conditions. It is recorded in the Sahih that the Messenger of Allah said,

«مَنْ عَمِلَ عَمَلًا لَيْسَ عَلَيْهِ أَمْرُنَا فَهُوَ رَدٌّ»

(Whoever commits an act that does not conform with our matter (religion), then it will be rejected of him.)

This is why Allah said here,

(Say (O Muhammad to mankind): "If you (really) love Allah, then follow me, Allah will love you...") meaning, what you will earn is much more than what you sought in loving Him, for Allah will love you. Al-Hasan Al-Basri and several scholars among the Salaf commented, "Some people claimed that they love Allah. So Allah tested them with this Ayah;

(Say (O Muhammad to mankind): "If you (really) love Allah, then follow me, Allah will love you..."). "

Allah then said,

("And forgive you your sins. And Allah is Oft-Forgiving, Most Merciful.") meaning, by your following the Messenger, you will earn all this with the blessing of his mission. Allah next commands everyone,

(Say: "Obey Allah and the Messenger." But if they turn away) by defying the Prophet,

(then Allah does not like the disbelievers.) thus, testifying that defiance of the Messenger's way constitutes Kufr. Indeed, Allah does not like whoever does this, even if he claims that he loves Allah and seeks a means of approach to Him, unless, and until, he follows the unlettered Prophet, the Final Messenger from Allah to the two creations: mankind and the Jinn. This is the Prophet who, if the previous Prophets and mighty Messengers were to have been alive during his time, they would have no choice but to follow, obey him, and to abide by his Law. We will mention this fact when we explain the Ayah,

(And (remember) when Allah took the Covenant of the Prophets) (3:81), Allah willing.

Surah: 3 Ayah: 33, Ayah: 34

﴿ ۞ إِنَّ ٱللَّهَ ٱصْطَفَىٰٓ ءَادَمَ وَنُوحًا وَءَالَ إِبْرَٰهِيمَ وَءَالَ عِمْرَٰنَ عَلَى ٱلْعَٰلَمِينَ ۞ ﴾

33. Allâh chose Adam, Nûh (Noah), the family of Ibrâhim (Abraham) and the family of 'Imrân above the 'Alamîn (mankind and jinn) (of their times).

﴿ ذُرِّيَّةً بَعْضُهَا مِنْ بَعْضٍ ۗ وَٱللَّهُ سَمِيعٌ عَلِيمٌ ۞ ﴾

34. Offspring, one of the other, and Allâh is the All-Hearer, All-Knower.

Transliteration

33. Inna Allaha istafa adama wanoohan waala ibraheema waala AAimrana AAala alAAalameena 34. Thurriyyatan baAAduha min baAAdin waAllahu sameeAAun AAaleemun

Tafsir Ibn Kathir

The Chosen Ones Among the People of the Earth

Allah states that He has chosen these households over the people of the earth. For instance, Allah chose Adam, created him with His Hand and blew life into him. Allah commanded the angels to prostrate before Adam, taught him the names of everything and allowed him to dwell in Paradise, but then sent him down from it out of His wisdom. Allah chose Nuh and made him the first Messenger to the people of the earth, when the people worshipped idols and associated others with Allah in worship. Allah avenged the way Nuh was treated, for he kept calling his people day and night, in public and in secret, for a very long time. However, his calling them only made them shun him more, and this is when Nuh supplicated against them. So Allah caused them to drown, and none among them was saved, except those who followed the religion that Allah sent to Nuh. Allah also chose the household of Ibrahim, including the master of all mankind, and the Final Prophet, Muhammad, peace be upon him. Allah also chose the household of `Imran, the father of Marym bint `Imran, the mother of `Isa, peace be upon them. So `Isa is from the offspring of Ibrahim, as we will mention in the Tafsir of Surat Al-An`am, Allah willing, and our trust is in Him.

Surah: 3 Ayah: 35 & Ayah: 36

﴿ إِذْ قَالَتِ ٱمْرَأَتُ عِمْرَانَ رَبِّ إِنِّى نَذَرْتُ لَكَ مَا فِى بَطْنِى مُحَرَّرًا فَتَقَبَّلْ مِنِّى إِنَّكَ أَنتَ ٱلسَّمِيعُ ٱلْعَلِيمُ ﴾

35. (Remember) when the wife of 'Imrân said: "O my Lord! I have vowed to You what (the child that) is in my womb to be dedicated for Your services (free from all worldly work; to serve Your Place of worship), so accept this, from me. Verily, You are the All-Hearer, the All-Knowing."

﴿ فَلَمَّا وَضَعَتْهَا قَالَتْ رَبِّ إِنِّى وَضَعْتُهَآ أُنثَىٰ وَٱللَّهُ أَعْلَمُ بِمَا وَضَعَتْ وَلَيْسَ ٱلذَّكَرُ كَٱلْأُنثَىٰ وَإِنِّى سَمَّيْتُهَا مَرْيَمَ وَإِنِّى أُعِيذُهَا بِكَ وَذُرِّيَّتَهَا مِنَ ٱلشَّيْطَٰنِ ٱلرَّجِيمِ ﴾

36. Then when she delivered her (child Maryam (Mary)) she said: "O my Lord! I have given birth to a female child," - and Allâh knew better what she brought forth, - "And the male is not like the female, and I have named her Maryam (Mary), and I seek refuge with You (Allâh) for her and for her offspring from Shaitan (Satan), the outcast."

Transliteration

35. Ith qalati imraatu AAimrana rabbi innee nathartu laka ma fee batnee muharraran fataqabbal minnee innaka anta alssameeAAu alAAaleemu 36. Falamma wadaAAat-ha qalat rabbi innee wadaAAtuha ontha waAllahu aAAlamu bima wadaAAat walaysa

alththakaru kaalontha wa-innee sammaytuha maryama wa-innee oAAeethuha bika wathurriyyataha mina alshshaytani alrrajeemi

Tafsir Ibn Kathir

The Story of Maryam's Birth

The wife of `Imran mentioned here is the mother of Maryam, and her name is Hannah bint Faqudh. Muhammad bin Ishaq mentioned that Hannah could not have children and that one day, she saw a bird feeding its chick. She wished she could have children and supplicated to Allah to grant her offspring. Allah accepted her supplication, and when her husband slept with her, she became pregnant. She vowed to make her child concentrate on worship and serving Bayt Al-Maqdis (the Masjid in Jerusalem), when she became aware that she was pregnant. She said,

(O my Lord! I have vowed to You what is in my womb to be dedicated for Your services, so accept this from me. Verily, You are the All-Hearer, the All-Knowing.) meaning, You hear my supplication and You know my intention. She did not know then what she would give birth to, a male or a female.

(Then when she gave birth to her, she said: "O my Lord! I have given birth to a female child, - and Allah knew better what she bore.)

(And the male is not like the female,) in strength and the commitment to worship Allah and serve the Masjid in Jerusalem.

(And I have named her Maryam,) thus, testifying to the fact that it is allowed to give a name to the newly born the day it is born, as is apparent from the Ayah, which is also a part of the law of those who were before us. Further, the Sunnah of the Messenger of Allah mentioned that the Prophet said,

«وُلِدَ لِيَ اللَّيْلَةَ وَلَدٌ، سَمَّيْتُهُ بِاسْمِ أَبِي إِبْرَاهِيم»

(This night, a son was born for me and I called him by my father's name, Ibrahim.) Al-Bukhari and Muslim collected this Hadith.

They also recorded that Anas bin Malik brought his newborn brother to the Messenger of Allah who chewed a piece of date and put it in the child's mouth and called him `Abdullah. Other new born infants were also given names on the day they were born.

Qatadah narrated that Al-Hasan Al-Basri said, that Samurah bin Jundub said that the Messenger of Allah said,

«كُلُّ غُلَامٍ رَهِينٌ بِعَقِيقَتِهِ، يُذْبَحُ عَنْهُ يَوْمَ سَابِعِهِ، وَيُسَمَّى وَيُحْلَقُ رَأْسُه»

(Every new born boy held in security by his `Aqiqah, until his seventh day, a sacrifice is offered on his behalf, he is given a name, and the hair on his head is shaved.)

This Hadith was collected by Ahmad and the collectors of the Sunan, and was graded Sahih by At-Tirmidhi. We should mention that another narration for this Hadith contained the wording, "and blood is offered on his behalf," which is more famous and established than the former narration, and Allah knows best.

Allah's statement that Maryam's mother said,

("...And I seek refuge with You for her and for her offspring from Shaytan, the outcast.") means, that she sought refuge with Allah from the evil of Shaytan, for her and her offspring, i.e., `Isa, peace be upon him. Allah accepted her supplication, for `Abdur-Razzaq recorded that Abu Hurayrah said that the Messenger of Allah said,

«مَا مِنْ مَوْلُودٍ يُولَدُ إِلَّا مَسَّهُ الشَّيْطَانُ حِينَ يُولَدُ، فَيَسْتَهِلُّ صَارِخًا مِنْ مَسِّهِ إِيَّاهُ، إِلَّا مَرْيَمَ وَابْنَهَا»

(Every newly born baby is touched by Shaytan when it is born, and the baby starts crying because of this touch, except Maryam and her son.)

Abu Hurayrah then said, "Read if you will,

(And I seek refuge with You for her and for her offspring from Shaytan, the outcast)." The Two Sahihs recorded this Hadith.

Surah: 3 Ayah: 37

﴿ فَتَقَبَّلَهَا رَبُّهَا بِقَبُولٍ حَسَنٍ وَأَنْبَتَهَا نَبَاتًا حَسَنًا وَكَفَّلَهَا زَكَرِيَّا ۖ كُلَّمَا دَخَلَ عَلَيْهَا زَكَرِيَّا الْمِحْرَابَ وَجَدَ عِنْدَهَا رِزْقًا ۖ قَالَ يَا مَرْيَمُ أَنَّىٰ لَكِ هَٰذَا ۖ قَالَتْ هُوَ مِنْ عِنْدِ اللَّهِ ۖ إِنَّ اللَّهَ يَرْزُقُ مَنْ يَشَاءُ بِغَيْرِ حِسَابٍ ﴾

37. So her Lord (Allâh) accepted her with goodly acceptance. He made her grow in a good manner and put her under the care of Zakariyâ (Zachariya). Every time he entered Al-Mihrâb to (visit) her, he found her supplied with sustenance. He said: "O Maryam (Mary)! From where have you got this?" She said, "This is from Allâh." Verily, Allâh provides sustenance to whom He wills, without limit."

Transliteration

37. Fataqabbalaha rabbuha biqaboolin hasanin waanbataha nabatan hasanan wakaffalaha zakariyya kullama dakhala AAalayha zakariyya almihraba wajada AAindaha rizqan qala ya maryamu anna laki hatha qalat huwa min AAindi Allahi inna Allaha yarzuqu man yashao bighayri hisabin

Tafsir Ibn Kathir

Maryam Grows Up; Her Honor is with Allah

Allah states that He has accepted Maryam as a result of her mother's vow and that He,

(made her grow in a good manner) meaning, made her conduct becoming, her mannerism delightful and He made her well liked among people. He also made her accompany the righteous people, so that she learned righteousness, knowledge and religion.

(And put her under the care of Zakariyya) meaning, Allah made Zakariyya her sponsor. Allah made Zakariyya Maryam's guardian for her benefit, so that she would learn from his tremendous knowledge and righteous conduct. He was the husband of her maternal aunt, as Ibn Ishaq and Ibn Jarir stated, or her brother-in-law, as mentioned in the Sahih,

«فَإِذَا بِيَحْيَى وَعِيسَى، وَهُمَا ابْنَا الْخَالَة»

(I saw John and `Isa, who are maternal cousins.)

We should state that in general terms, what Ibn Ishaq said is plausible, and in this case, Maryam was under the care of her maternal aunt. The Two Sahihs recorded that the Messenger of Allah decided that `Amarah, the daughter of Hamzah, be raised by her maternal aunt, the wife of Ja`far bin Abi Talib, saying,

«الْخَالَةُ بِمَنْزِلَةِ الْأُمِّ»

(The maternal aunt is just like the mother.)

Allah then emphasizes Maryam's honor and virtue at the place of worship she attended,

(Every time he entered the Mihrab to (visit) her, he found her supplied with sustenance.)

Mujahid, `Ikrimah, Sa`id bin Jubayr, Abu Ash-Sha`tha, Ibrahim An-Nakha`i, Ad-Dahhak, Qatadah, Ar-Rabi` bin Anas, `Atiyah Al-`Awfi and As-Suddi said, "He would find with her the fruits of the summer during winter, and the fruits of the winter during summer." When Zakariyya would see this; d

(He said: "O Maryam! From where have you gotten this") meaning, where did you get these fruits from

(She said, "This is from Allah." Verily, Allah provides sustenance to whom He wills, without limit.)

Surah: 3 Ayah: 38, Ayah: 39, Ayah: 40 & Ayah: 41

﴿ هُنَالِكَ دَعَا زَكَرِيَّا رَبَّهُۥ قَالَ رَبِّ هَبْ لِى مِن لَّدُنكَ ذُرِّيَّةً طَيِّبَةً إِنَّكَ سَمِيعُ ٱلدُّعَآءِ ۝ ﴾

38. At that time Zakariyâ (Zachariya) invoked his Lord, saying: "O my Lord! Grant me from You, a good offspring. You are indeed the All-Hearer of invocation."

﴿ فَنَادَتْهُ ٱلْمَلَٰٓئِكَةُ وَهُوَ قَآئِمٌ يُصَلِّى فِى ٱلْمِحْرَابِ أَنَّ ٱللَّهَ يُبَشِّرُكَ بِيَحْيَىٰ مُصَدِّقًۢا بِكَلِمَةٍ مِّنَ ٱللَّهِ وَسَيِّدًا وَحَصُورًا وَنَبِيًّا مِّنَ ٱلصَّٰلِحِينَ ۝ ﴾

39. Then the angels called him, while he was standing in prayer in Al-Mihrâb (a praying place or a private room), (saying): "Allâh gives you glad tidings of Yahya (John), confirming (believing in) the Word from Allâh (i.e. the creation of 'Isâ (Jesus) (peace be upon him), the Word from Allâh ("Be!" - and he was!)) noble, keeping away from sexual relations with women, a Prophet, from among the righteous."

﴿ قَالَ رَبِّ أَنَّىٰ يَكُونُ لِى غُلَٰمٌ وَقَدْ بَلَغَنِىَ ٱلْكِبَرُ وَٱمْرَأَتِى عَاقِرٌ قَالَ كَذَٰلِكَ ٱللَّهُ يَفْعَلُ مَا يَشَآءُ ۝ ﴾

40. He said: "O my Lord! How can I have a son when I am very old, and my wife is barren?" Allâh said: "Thus Allâh does what He wills."

﴿ قَالَ رَبِّ ٱجْعَل لِّىٓ ءَايَةً قَالَ ءَايَتُكَ أَلَّا تُكَلِّمَ ٱلنَّاسَ ثَلَٰثَةَ أَيَّامٍ إِلَّا رَمْزًا وَٱذْكُر رَّبَّكَ كَثِيرًا وَسَبِّحْ بِٱلْعَشِىِّ وَٱلْإِبْكَٰرِ ۝ ﴾

41. He said: "O my Lord! Make a sign for me." Allâh said: "Your sign is that you shall not speak to mankind for three days except with signals. And remember your Lord much (by praising Him again and again), and glorify (Him) in the afternoon and in the morning."

Transliteration

38. Hunalika daAAa zakariyya rabbahu qala rabbi hab lee min ladunka thurriyyatan tayyibatan innaka sameeAAu aldduAAa/-I 39. Fanadat-hu almala-ikatu wahuwa qa-imun yusallee fee almihrabi anna Allaha yubashshiruka biyahya musaddiqan bikalimatin mina Allahi wasayyidan wahasooran wanabiyyan mina alssaliheena 40. Qala rabbi anna yakoonu lee ghulamun waqad balaghaniya alkibaru waimraatee AAaqirun qala kathalika Allahu yafAAalu ma yasha/o 41. Qala rabbi ijAAal lee ayatan qala ayatuka alla tukallima alnnasa thalathata ayyamin illa ramzan waothkur rabbaka katheeran wasabbih bialAAashiyyi waal-ibkari

Tafsir Ibn Kathir

The Supplication of Zakariyya, and the Good News of Yahya's Birth

When Zakariyya saw that Allah provided sustenance for Maryam by giving her the fruits of winter in summer and the fruits of summer in winter, he was eager to have a child of his own. By then, Zakariyya had become an old man, his bones feeble and his head full of gray hair. His wife was an old women who was barren. Yet, he still supplicated to Allah and called Him in secret,

(O my Lord! Grant me from Ladunka,) from You,

(A good offspring) meaning, a righteous offspring,

(You are indeed the All-Hearer of invocation.) Allah said,

(Then the angels called him, while he was standing in prayer in the Mihrab,) meaning, the angels spoke to him directly while he was secluded, standing in prayer at his place of worship. Allah told us about the good news that the angels delivered to Zakariyya,

(Allah gives you glad tidings of Yahya,) of a child from your offspring, his name is Yahya. Qatadah and other scholars said that he was called Yahya (literally, `he lives') because Allah filled his life with faith.

Allah said next,

(believing in the Word from Allah) Al-`Awfi reported that Ibn `Abbas said, and also Al-Hasan, Qatadah, `Ikrimah, Mujahid, Abu Ash-Sha`tha, As-Suddi, Ar-Rabi` bin Anas, Ad-Dahhak, and several others said that the Ayah,

(believing in the Word from Allah) means, "Believing in `Isa, son of Maryam."

Abu Al-`Aliyah, Ar-Rabi` bin Anas, Qatadah and Sa`id bin Jubayr said that Allah's statement,

(And Sayyidan) means, a wise man. Ibn `Abbas, Ath-Thawri and Ad-Dahhak said that Sayyidan means, "The noble, wise and pious man." Sa`id bin Al-Musayyib said that Sayyid is the scholar and Faqih. `Atiyah said that Sayyid is the man noble in behavior and piety. `Ikrimah said that it refers to a person who is not overcome by anger, while Ibn Zayd said that it refers to the noble man. Mujahid said that Sayyidan means, honored by Allah.

Allah's statement,

(And Hasuran) does not mean he refrains from sexual relations with women, but that he is immune from illegal sexual relations. This does not mean that he does not marry women and have legal sexual relations with them, for Zakariyya said in his supplication for the benefit of Yahya,

(Grant me from You, a good offspring), meaning, grant me a son who will have offspring, and Allah knows best.

Allah's statement,

(A Prophet, from among the righteous) delivers more good news of sending Yahya as Prophet after the good news that he will be born. This good news was even better than the news of Yahya's birth. In a similar statement, Allah said to the mother of Musa,

(Verily, We shall bring him back to you, and shall make him one of the Messengers.) (28:7)

When Zakariyya heard the good news, he started contemplating about having children at his age. He said,

("O my Lord! How can I have a son when I am very old, and my wife is barren" (He) said...) meaning the angel said,

("Thus Allah does what He wills.") meaning, this is Allah's matter, He is so Mighty that nothing escapes His power, nor is anything beyond His ability.

(He said: "O my Lord! Make a sign for me") meaning make a sign that alerts me that the child will come,

((Allah) said: "Your sign is that you shall not speak to the people for three days except by signals.") meaning, you will not be able to speak except with signals, although you are not mute. In another Ayah, Allah said,

(For three nights, though having no bodily defect.) (19:10)

Allah then commanded Zakariyya to supplicate, thank and praise Him often in that condition,

(And remember your Lord much and glorify (Him) in the afternoon and in the morning.)

We will elaborate more on this subject in the beginning of Surah Maryam (chapter 19), Allah willing.

Surah: 3 Ayah: 42, Ayah: 43 & Ayah: 44

﴿ وَإِذْ قَالَتِ ٱلْمَلَٰٓئِكَةُ يَٰمَرْيَمُ إِنَّ ٱللَّهَ ٱصْطَفَىٰكِ وَطَهَّرَكِ وَٱصْطَفَىٰكِ عَلَىٰ نِسَآءِ ٱلْعَٰلَمِينَ ۝ ﴾

42. And (remember) when the angels said: "O Maryam (Mary)! Verily, Allâh has chosen you, purified you (from polytheism and disbelief), and chosen you above the women of the 'Alamîn (mankind and jinn) (of her lifetime)."

﴿ يَٰمَرْيَمُ ٱقْنُتِى لِرَبِّكِ وَٱسْجُدِى وَٱرْكَعِى مَعَ ٱلرَّٰكِعِينَ ۝ ﴾

43. O Mary! "Submit yourself with obedience to your Lord (Allâh, by worshipping none but Him Alone) and prostrate yourself, and Irkâ'i (bow down) along with Ar-Râki'ûn (those who bow down)."

﴿ ذَٰلِكَ مِنْ أَنۢبَآءِ ٱلْغَيْبِ نُوحِيهِ إِلَيْكَ ۚ وَمَا كُنتَ لَدَيْهِمْ إِذْ يُلْقُونَ أَقْلَـٰمَهُمْ أَيُّهُمْ يَكْفُلُ مَرْيَمَ وَمَا كُنتَ لَدَيْهِمْ إِذْ يَخْتَصِمُونَ ﴾

44. This is a part of the news of the Ghaib (unseen, i.e. the news of the past nations of which you have no knowledge) which We reveal to you (O Muhammad (peace be upon him)) You were not with them, when they cast lots with their pens as to which of them should be charged with the care of Maryam (Mary); nor were you with them when they disputed.

Transliteration

42. Wa-ith qalati almala-ikatu ya maryamu inna Allaha istafaki watahharaki waistafaki AAala nisa-I alAAalameena 43. Ya maryamu oqnutee lirabbiki waosjudee wairkaAAee maAAa alrrakiAAeena 44. Thalika min anba-i alghaybi nooheehi ilayka wama kunta ladayhim ith yulqoona aqlamahum ayyuhum yakfulu maryama wama kunta ladayhim ith yakhtasimoona

Tafsir Ibn Kathir

The Virtue of Maryam Over the Women of Her Time

Allah states that the angels spoke to Maryam by His command and told her that He chose her because of her service to Him, because of her modesty, honor, innocence, and conviction. Allah also chose her because of her virtue over the women of the world. At-Tirmidhi recorded that `Ali bin Abi Talib said, "I heard the Messenger of Allah say,

«خَيْرُ نِسَائِهَا مَرْيَمُ بِنْتُ عِمْرَانَ، وَخَيْرُ نِسَائِهَا خَدِيجَةُ بِنْتُ خُوَيْلِد»

(The best woman (in her time) was Maryam, daughter of `Imran, and the best woman (of the Prophet's time) is Khadijah (his wife), daughter of Khuwaylid.)"

The Two Sahihs recorded this Hadith. Ibn Jarir recorded that Abu Musa Al-Ash`ari said that the Messenger of Allah said,

«كَمُلَ مِنَ الرِّجَالِ كَثِيرٌ، وَلَمْ يَكْمُلْ مِنَ النِّسَاءِ إِلَّا مَرْيَمُ بِنْتُ عِمْرَانَ وَ آسِيَةُ امْرَأَةُ فِرْعَوْن»

(Many men achieved perfection, but among women, only Maryam the daughter of `Imran and Asiah, the wife of Fir`awn, achieved perfection.)

The Six -- with the exception of Abu Dawud - recorded it. Al-Bukhari's wording for it reads,

«كَمُلَ مِنَ الرِّجَالِ كَثِيرٌ، وَلَمْ يَكْمُلْ مِنَ النِّسَاءِ إِلَّا آسِيَةُ امْرَأَةُ فِرْعَوْنَ، وَمَرْيَمُ بِنْتُ عِمْرَانَ، وَإِنَّ فَضْلَ عَائِشَةَ عَلَى النِّسَاءِ كَفَضْلِ الثَّرِيدِ عَلَى سَائِرِ الطَّعَامِ»

(Many men reached the level of perfection, but no woman reached such a level except Asiah, the wife of Fir`awn, and Maryam, the daughter of `Imran. The superiority of `A'ishah (his wife) to other women, is like the superiority of Tharid (meat and bread dish) to other meals.)

We mentioned the various chains of narration and wordings for this Hadith in the story of `Isa, son of Maryam, in our book, Al-Bidayah wan-Nihayah, all the thanks are due to Allah.

Allah states that the angels commanded Maryam to increase acts of worship, humbleness, submission, prostration, bowing, and so forth, so that she would acquire what Allah had decreed for her, as a test for her. Yet, this test also earned her a higher grade in this life and the Hereafter, for Allah demonstrated His might by creating a son inside her without male intervention. Allah said,

("O Maryam! Submit yourself with obedience (Aqnuti) and prostrate yourself, and bow down along with Ar-Raki`in.")

As for Qunut (Aqnuti in the Ayah), it means to submit with humbleness. In another Ayah, Allah said,

(Nay, to Him belongs all that is in the heavens and on earth, and all surrender with obedience (Qanitun) to Him.) (2:116)

Allah next said to His Messenger after He mentioned Maryam's story,

(This is a part of the news of the Ghayb which We reveal.) "and narrate to you (O Muhammad), "

(You were not with them, when they cast lots with their pens as to which of them should be charged with the care of Maryam; nor were you with them when they disputed.) meaning, "You were not present, O Muhammad, when this occurred, so you cannot narrate what happened to the people as an eye witness. Rather, Allah disclosed these facts to you as if you were a witness, when they conducted a lottery to choose the custodian of Maryam, seeking the reward of this good deed."

Ibn Jarir recorded that `Ikrimah said, "Maryam's mother left with Maryam, carrying her in her infant cloth, and took her to the rabbis from the offspring of Aaron, the brother of Musa. They were responsible for taking care of Bayt Al-Maqdis (the Masjid) at that time, just as there were those who took care of the Ka`bah. Maryam's mother said to them, `Take this child whom I vowed (to serve the Masjid), I have set her free, since she is my daughter, for no menstruating woman should enter the Masjid, and I shall not take her back home.' They said, `She is the daughter of our Imam,' as `Imran used to lead them in prayer, `who took care of our sacrificial rituals.' Zakariyya said, `Give her to me, for her maternal aunt is my wife.' They said, `Our hearts cannot bear that you take her, for she is the daughter of our Imam.' So they conducted a lottery with the pens with which they wrote the Tawrah, and Zakariyya won the lottery and took Maryam into his care.'". `Ikrimah, As-Suddi, Qatadah, Ar-Rabi` bin Anas, and several others said that the rabbis went into the Jordan river and conducted a lottery there, deciding to throw their pens into the river. The pen that remained afloat and idle would indicate that its owner would take care of Maryam. When they threw their pens into the river, the water took all the pens under, except Zakariyya's pen, which remained afloat in its place. Zakariyya was also their master, chief, scholar, Imam and Prophet, may Allah's peace and blessings be on him and the rest of the Prophets.

Surah: 3 Ayah: 45, Ayah: 46 & Ayah: 47

﴿ إِذْ قَالَتِ ٱلْمَلَٰٓئِكَةُ يَٰمَرْيَمُ إِنَّ ٱللَّهَ يُبَشِّرُكِ بِكَلِمَةٍ مِّنْهُ ٱسْمُهُ ٱلْمَسِيحُ عِيسَى ٱبْنُ مَرْيَمَ وَجِيهًا فِى ٱلدُّنْيَا وَٱلْأَخِرَةِ وَمِنَ ٱلْمُقَرَّبِينَ ۝ ﴾

45. (Remember) when the angels said: "O Maryam (Mary)! Verily, Allâh gives you the glad tidings of a Word ("Be!" - and he was! i.e. 'Isâ (Jesus) the son of Maryam (Mary)) from Him, his name will be the Messiah 'Isâ (Jesus), the son of Maryam (Mary), held in honor in this world and in the Hereafter, and will be one of those who are near to Allâh."

﴿ وَيُكَلِّمُ ٱلنَّاسَ فِى ٱلْمَهْدِ وَكَهْلًا وَمِنَ ٱلصَّٰلِحِينَ ۝ ﴾

46. "He will speak to the people in the cradle and in manhood, and he will be one of the righteous."

﴿ قَالَتْ رَبِّ أَنَّىٰ يَكُونُ لِى وَلَدٌ وَلَمْ يَمْسَسْنِى بَشَرٌ قَالَ كَذَٰلِكِ ٱللَّهُ يَخْلُقُ مَا يَشَآءُ إِذَا قَضَىٰٓ أَمْرًا فَإِنَّمَا يَقُولُ لَهُۥ كُن فَيَكُونُ ۝ ﴾

47. She said: "O my Lord! How shall I have a son when no man has touched me." He said: "So (it will be) for Allâh creates what He wills. When He has decreed something, He says to it only: "Be!" - and it is.

Transliteration

45. Ith qalati almala-ikatu ya maryamu inna Allaha yubashshiruki bikalimatin minhu ismuhu almaseehu AAeesa ibnu maryama wajeehan fee alddunya waal-akhirati wamina almuqarrabeena 46. Wayukallimu alnnasa fee almahdi wakahlan wamina alssaliheena 47. Qalat rabbi anna yakoonu lee waladun walam yamsasnee basharun qala kathaliki Allahu yakhluqu ma yashao itha qada amran fa-innama yaqoolu lahu kun fayakoonu

Tafsir Ibn Kathir

Delivering the Good News to Maryam of `Isa's Birth

This Ayah contains the glad tidings the angels brought to Maryam that she would give birth to a mighty son who will have a great future. Allah said,

((Remember) when the angels said: "O Maryam! Verily, Allah gives you the glad tidings of a Word from Him,) a son who will come into existence with a word from Allah, `Be', and he was. This is the meaning of Allah's statement (about Yahya)

(Believing in the Word from Allah.) (3:39), according to the majority of the scholars.

(His name will be Al-Masih, `Isa, the son of Maryam) and he will be known by this name in this life, especially by the believers. `Isa was called "Al-Masih" (the Messiah) because when he touched (Mash) those afflicted with an illness, they would be healed by Allah's leave. Allah's statement,

(`Isa, the son of Maryam) relates `Isa to his mother, because he did not have a father.

(Held in honor in this world and in the Hereafter, and will be one of those who are near to Allah.) meaning, he will be a leader and honored by Allah in this life, because of the Law that Allah will reveal to him, sending down the Scripture to him, along with the other bounties that Allah will grant him with. `Isa will be honored in the Hereafter and will intercede with Allah, by His leave, on behalf of some people, just as is the case with his brethren the mighty Messengers of Allah, peace be upon them all.

`Isa Spoke When He was Still in the Cradle

Allah said,

(He will speak to the people, in the cradle and in manhood,) calling to the worship of Allah Alone without partners, while still in the cradle, as a miracle from Allah, and when he is a man, by Allah's revelation to him.

Muhammad bin Ishaq recorded that Abu Hurayrah said that the Messenger of Allah said,

«مَا تَكَلَّمَ مَوْلُودٌ فِي صِغَرِهِ إِلَّا عِيسَى وَصَاحِبُ جُرَيْجٍ»

(No infant spoke in the cradle except `Isa and the companion of Jurayj.)

Ibn Abi Hatim recorded that Abu Hurayrah said that the Prophet said,

«لَمْ يَتَكَلَّمْ فِي الْمَهْدِ إِلَّا ثَلَاثَةٌ: عِيسَى، وَصَبِيٌّ كَانَ فِي زَمَنِ جُرَيْجٍ، وَصَبِيٌّ آخَرُ»

(No infant spoke in the cradle except three, `Isa, the boy during the time of Jurayj, and another boy.)

(And he will be one of the righteous.) in his statements and actions, for he will possess, pure knowledge and righteous works.

`Isa was Created Without a Father

When Maryam heard the good news that the angels conveyed from Allah, she said;

("O my Lord! How shall I have a son when no man has touched me.")

Mary said, "How can I have a son while I did not marry, nor intend to marry, nor am I an indecent woman, may Allah forbid" The angel conveyed to Maryam, Allah's answer,

(So (it will be) for Allah creates what He wills.)

He is Mighty in power and nothing escapes His ability. Allah used the word `create' here instead of the word `does' as in the tale about Zakariyya (3:40), to eradicate any evil thought concerning `Isa. Allah next emphasized this fact when He said,

(When He has decreed something, He says to it only: "Be! - and it is.) meaning, what Allah wills, comes into existence instantly and without delay. In another Ayah, Allah said,

(And Our commandment is but one as the twinkling of an eye.) (54:50), meaning, "We only issue the command once, and it comes into existence instantly, as fast as, and faster than, a blink of the eye."

Surah: 3 Ayah: 48, Ayah: 49, Ayah: 50 & Ayah: 51

﴿وَيُعَلِّمُهُ ٱلْكِتَٰبَ وَٱلْحِكْمَةَ وَٱلتَّوْرَىٰةَ وَٱلْإِنجِيلَ ۝﴾

48. And He (Allâh) will teach him ('Isâ (Jesus)) the Book and Al-Hikmah (i.e. the Sunnah, the faultless speech of the Prophets, wisdom), (and) the Taurât (Torah) and the Injeel (Gospel).

﴿وَرَسُولًا إِلَىٰ بَنِىٓ إِسْرَٰٓءِيلَ أَنِّى قَدْ جِئْتُكُم بِـَٔايَةٍ مِّن رَّبِّكُمْ ۖ أَنِّىٓ أَخْلُقُ لَكُم مِّنَ ٱلطِّينِ كَهَيْـَٔةِ ٱلطَّيْرِ فَأَنفُخُ فِيهِ فَيَكُونُ طَيْرًۢا بِإِذْنِ ٱللَّهِ ۖ وَأُبْرِئُ ٱلْأَكْمَهَ وَٱلْأَبْرَصَ وَأُحْىِ ٱلْمَوْتَىٰ بِإِذْنِ ٱللَّهِ ۖ وَأُنَبِّئُكُم بِمَا تَأْكُلُونَ وَمَا تَدَّخِرُونَ فِى بُيُوتِكُمْ ۚ إِنَّ فِى ذَٰلِكَ لَءَايَةً لَّكُمْ إِن كُنتُم مُّؤْمِنِينَ ۝﴾

49. And will make him ('Isâ (Jesus)) a Messenger to the Children of Israel (saying): "I have come to you with a sign from your Lord, that I design for you out of clay, a figure like that of a bird, and breathe into it, and it becomes a bird by Allâh's Leave; and I heal him who was born blind, and the leper, and I bring the dead to

life by Allâh's Leave. And I inform you of what you eat, and what you store in your houses. Surely, therein is a sign for you, if you believe.

﴿وَمُصَدِّقًا لِّمَا بَيْنَ يَدَىَّ مِنَ ٱلتَّوْرَىٰةِ وَلِأُحِلَّ لَكُم بَعْضَ ٱلَّذِى حُرِّمَ عَلَيْكُمْ وَجِئْتُكُم بِـَٔايَةٍ مِّن رَّبِّكُمْ فَٱتَّقُوا۟ ٱللَّهَ وَأَطِيعُونِ ۝﴾

50. And I have come confirming that which was before me of the Taurât (Torah), and to make lawful to you part of what was forbidden to you, and I have come to you with a proof from your Lord. So fear Allâh and obey me.

﴿إِنَّ ٱللَّهَ رَبِّى وَرَبُّكُمْ فَٱعْبُدُوهُ ۗ هَـٰذَا صِرَٰطٌ مُّسْتَقِيمٌ ۝﴾

51. Truly! Allâh is my Lord and your Lord, so worship Him (Alone). This is the Straight Path.

Transliteration

48. WayuAAallimuhu alkitaba waalhikmata waalttawrata waal-injeela 49. Warasoolan ila banee isra-eela annee qad ji/tukum bi-ayatin min rabbikum annee akhluqu lakum mina altteeni kahay-ati alttayri faanfukhu feehi fayakoonu tayran bi-ithni Allahi waobri-o al-akmaha waal-abrasa waohyee almawta bi-ithni Allahi waonabbi-okum bima ta/kuloona wama taddakhiroona fee buyootikum inna fee thalika laayatan lakum in kuntum mu/mineena 50. Wamusaddiqan lima bayna yadayya mina alttawrati wali-ohilla lakum baAAda allathee hurrima AAalaykum waji/tukum bi-ayatin min rabbikum faittaqoo Allaha waateeAAooni 51. Inna Allaha rabbee warabbukum faoAAbudoohu hatha siratun mustaqeemun

Tafsir Ibn Kathir

The Description of `Isa and the Miracles He Performed

Allah states that the good news brought to Maryam about `Isa was even better because Allah would teach him,

(the Book and Al-Hikmah). It appears that the `Book' the Ayah mentioned here refers to writing. We explained the meaning of Al-Hikmah in the Tafsir of Surat Al-Baqarah.

(the Tawrah and the Injil). The Tawrah is the Book that Allah sent down to Musa, son of `Imran, while the Injil is what Allah sent down to `Isa, son of Maryam, peace be upon them, and `Isa memorized both Books. Allah's statement,

(And will make him a Messenger to the Children of Israel) means, that Allah will send `Isa as a Messenger to the Children of Israel, proclaiming to them,

(I have come to you with a sign from your Lord, that I design for you out of clay, a figure like that of a bird, and breathe into it, and it becomes a bird by Allah's leave). These are the miracles that `Isa performed; he used to make the shape of a bird from clay and blow into it, and it became a bird by Allah's leave. Allah made this a miracle for `Isa to testify that He had sent him.

(And I heal him who is Akmah) meaning, `a person who was born blind,' which perfects this miracle and makes the challenge more daring.

(And the leper) which is a known disease,

(And I bring the dead to life by Allah's leave).

Many scholars stated that Allah sent every Prophet with a miracle suitable to his time. For instance, in the time of Musa, magic was the trade of the time, and magicians held a high position. So Allah sent Musa with a miracle that captured the eyes and bewildered every magician. When the magicians realized that Musa's miracle came from the Almighty, Most Great, they embraced Islam and became pious believers. As for `Isa, he was sent during a time when medicine and knowledge in physics were advancing. `Isa brought them the types of miracles that could not be performed, except by one sent by Allah. How can any physician bring life to clay, cure blindness and leprosy and bring back to life those entrapped in the grave Muhammad was sent during the time of eloquent people and proficient poets. He brought them a Book from Allah; if mankind and the Jinn tried to imitate ten chapters, or even one chapter of it, they will utterly fail in this task, even if they tried to do it by collective cooperation. This is because the Qur'an is the Word of Allah and is nothing like that of the creatures.

`Isa's statement,

(And I inform you of what you eat, and what you store in your houses) means, I tell you about what one of you has just eaten and what he is keeping in his house for tomorrow.

(Surely, therein), all these miracles,

(is a sign for you) testifying to the truth of what I was sent to you with,

(If you believe. And I have come confirming that which was before me of the Tawrah,) affirming the Tawrah and upholding it,

(and to make lawful to you part of what was forbidden to you.)

This part of the Ayah indicates that `Isa abrogated some of the Laws of the Tawrah and informed the Jews of the truth regarding some issues that they used to dispute about. In another Ayah;

(And in order to make clear to you some of the (points) in which you differ) (43:63).

`Isa said next,

(And I have come to you with a proof from your Lord.) "Containing affirmation and evidence to the truth of what I am conveying to you."

(So have Taqwa of Allah and obey me. Truly, Allah is my Lord and your Lord, so worship Him (Alone).) for I and you are equal in our servitude, submission and humbleness to Him,

(This is the straight path.)

Surah: 3 Ayah: 52, Ayah: 53 & Ayah: 54

﴿ ۞ فَلَمَّآ أَحَسَّ عِيسَىٰ مِنْهُمُ ٱلْكُفْرَ قَالَ مَنْ أَنصَارِىٓ إِلَى ٱللَّهِ ۖ قَالَ ٱلْحَوَارِيُّونَ نَحْنُ أَنصَارُ ٱللَّهِ ءَامَنَّا بِٱللَّهِ وَٱشْهَدْ بِأَنَّا مُسْلِمُونَ ﴾

52. Then when 'Isâ (Jesus) came to know of their disbelief, he said: "Who will be my helpers in Allâh's Cause?" Al-Hawâriûn (the disciples) said: "We are the helpers of Allâh; we believe in Allâh, and bear witness that we are Muslims (i.e. we submit to Allâh)."

﴿ رَبَّنَآ ءَامَنَّا بِمَآ أَنزَلْتَ وَٱتَّبَعْنَا ٱلرَّسُولَ فَٱكْتُبْنَا مَعَ ٱلشَّـٰهِدِينَ ﴾

53. Our Lord! We believe in what You have sent down, and we follow the Messenger ('Isâ (Jesus)) so write us down among those who bear witness (to the truth i.e. Lâ ilâha illallâh - none has the right to be worshipped but Allâh).

﴿ وَمَكَرُواْ وَمَكَرَ ٱللَّهُ ۖ وَٱللَّهُ خَيْرُ ٱلْمَـٰكِرِينَ ﴾

54. And they (disbelievers) plotted (to kill 'Isâ (Jesus) peace be upon him), and Allâh plotted too. And Allâh is the Best of those who plot.

Transliteration

52. Falamma ahassa AAeesa minhumu alkufra qala man ansaree ila Allahi qala alhawariyyoona nahnu ansaru Allahi amanna biAllahi waishhad bi-anna muslimoona 53. Rabbana amanna bima anzalta waittabaAAna alrrasoola faoktubna maAAa alshshahideena 54. Wamakaroo wamakara Allahu waAllahu khayru almakireena

Tafsir Ibn Kathir

The Disciples Give Their Support to `Isa

Allah said,

(Then when `Isa came to know), meaning, `Isa felt that they were adamant in disbelief and continuing in misguidance. He said to them,

(Who will be my helper in Allah's cause) Mujahid commented, "Meaning, who would follow me to Allah" However, it appears that `Isa was asking, "Who would help me convey the Message of Allah"

The Prophet said during the Hajj season, before the Hijrah,

$$\text{«مَنْ رَجُلٌ يُؤْوِينِي حَتَّى أُبَلِّغَ كَلَامَ رَبِّي؟، فَإِنَّ قُرَيْشًا قَدْ مَنَعُونِي أَنْ أُبَلِّغَ كَلَامَ رَبِّي»}$$

(Who will give me asylum so that I can convey the Speech of my Lord, for the Quraysh have prevented me from conveying the Speech of my Lord.) until he found the Ansar. The Ansar helped the Prophet and gave him refuge. He later migrated to them, they comforted the Prophet and protected him from all his enemies, may Allah be pleased with them all. This is similar to what happened with `Isa, for some of the Children of Israel believed in him, gave him their aid and support and followed the light that was sent with him. This is why Allah said about them;

(Al-Hawariyyun said: "We are the helpers of Allah; we believe in Allah, and bear witness that we are Muslims. Our Lord! We believe in what You have sent down, and we follow the Messenger; so write us down among those who bear witness.") Hawari in Arabic - means `support'. The Two Sahihs recorded that when the Prophet encouraged the people to fight during the battle of Al-Ahzab, Az-Zubayr came forward, and again, when the Prophet asked for fighters a second time. The Prophet said,

$$\text{«إِنَّ لِكُلِّ نَبِيٍّ حَوَارِيًّا، وَحَوَارِيِّ الزُّبَيْرِ»}$$

(Every Prophet has a Hawari, and Az-Zubayr is my Hawari)

Ibn Abi Hatim recorded that Ibn `Abbas said about,

(so write us down among those who bear witness) "Meaning among the Ummah of Muhammad." This Hadith has a good chain of narration.

The Jews Plot to Kill `Isa

Allah states that the Children of Israel tried to kill `Isa by conspiring to defame him and crucify him. They complained about him to the king who was a disbeliever. They claimed that `Isa was a man who misguided people, discouraged them from obeying the king, caused division, and separated between man and his own son. They also said other lies about `Isa, which they will carry on their necks, including accusing him of being an illegitimate son. The king became furious and sent his men to capture `Isa to torture and crucify him. When they surrounded `Isa's home and he thought that they would surely capture him, Allah saved him from them, raising him up from the house to heaven. Allah put the image of `Isa on a man who was in the house; when the unjust people went in the house while it was still dark, they thought that he was `Isa. They captured that man, humiliated and crucified him. They also placed thorns on his head. However, Allah deceived these people. He saved and raised His Prophet from them, leaving them in disarray in the darkness of their transgression, thinking that they had successfully achieved their goal. Allah made their hearts hard, and defiant of the truth, disgracing them in such disgrace that it will remain with them until the Day of Resurrection. This is why Allah said,

(And they plotted, and Allah planned too. And Allah is the Best of those who plot.)

Surah: 3 Ayah: 55, Ayah: 56, Ayah: 57 & Ayah: 58

﴿ إِذْ قَالَ ٱللَّهُ يَـٰعِيسَىٰٓ إِنِّى مُتَوَفِّيكَ وَرَافِعُكَ إِلَىَّ وَمُطَهِّرُكَ مِنَ ٱلَّذِينَ كَفَرُواْ وَجَاعِلُ ٱلَّذِينَ ٱتَّبَعُوكَ فَوْقَ ٱلَّذِينَ كَفَرُوٓاْ إِلَىٰ يَوْمِ ٱلْقِيَـٰمَةِ ثُمَّ إِلَىَّ مَرْجِعُكُمْ فَأَحْكُمُ بَيْنَكُمْ فِيمَا كُنتُمْ فِيهِ تَخْتَلِفُونَ ۝ ﴾

55. And (remember) when Allâh said: "O 'Isâ (Jesus)! I will take you and raise you to Myself and clear you (of the forged statement that 'Isâ (Jesus) is Allâh's son) of those who disbelieve, and I will make those who follow you (Monotheists, who worship none but Allâh) superior to those who disbelieve (in the Oneness of Allâh, or disbelieve in some of His Messengers, e.g. Muhammad (peace be upon him) 'Isâ (Jesus), Mûsâ (Moses), etc., or in His Holy Books, e.g. the Taurât (Torah), the Injeel (Gospel), the Qur'ân) till the Day of Resurrection. Then you will return to Me and I will judge between you in the matters in which you used to dispute."

﴿ فَأَمَّا ٱلَّذِينَ كَفَرُواْ فَأُعَذِّبُهُمْ عَذَابًا شَدِيدًا فِى ٱلدُّنْيَا وَٱلْـَٔاخِرَةِ وَمَا لَهُم مِّن نَّـٰصِرِينَ ۝ ﴾

56. "As to those who disbelieve, I will punish them with a severe torment in this world and in the Hereafter, and they will have no helpers."

﴿ وَأَمَّا ٱلَّذِينَ ءَامَنُواْ وَعَمِلُواْ ٱلصَّـٰلِحَـٰتِ فَيُوَفِّيهِمْ أُجُورَهُمْ وَٱللَّهُ لَا يُحِبُّ ٱلظَّـٰلِمِينَ ۝ ﴾

57. And as for those who believe (in the Oneness of Allâh) and do righteous good deeds, Allâh will pay them their reward in full. And Allâh does not like the Zâlimûn (polytheists and wrong-doers).

﴿ ذَٰلِكَ نَتْلُوهُ عَلَيْكَ مِنَ ٱلْـَٔايَـٰتِ وَٱلذِّكْرِ ٱلْحَكِيمِ ۝ ﴾

58. This is what We recite to you (O Muhammad (peace be upon him)) of the Verses and the Wise Reminder (i.e. the Qur'ân).

Transliteration

55. Ith qala Allahu ya AAeesa innee mutawaffeeka warafiAAuka ilayya wamutahhiruka mina allatheena kafaroo wajaAAilu allatheena ittabaAAooka fawqa allatheena kafaroo ila yawmi alqiyamati thumma ilayya marjiAAukum faahkumu baynakum feema kuntum

feehi takhtalifoona 56. Faamma allatheena kafaroo faoAAaththibuhum AAathaban shadeedan fee alddunya waal-akhirati wama lahum min nasireena 57. Waamma allatheena amanoo waAAamiloo alssalihati fayuwaffeehim ojoorahum waAllahu la yuhibbu alththalimeena 58. Thalika natloohu AAalayka mina al-ayati waalththikri alhakeemi

Tafsir Ibn Kathir

Meaning of 'Take You'

Allah said,

(I will take you and raise you to Myself) while you are asleep. Allah said in a similar Ayat,

(It is He Who takes your souls by night (when you are asleep).) (6:60), and,

(It is Allah Who takes away the souls at the time of their death, and those that die not during their sleep.) (39:42).

The Messenger of Allah used to recite the following words when he would awaken;

«الْحَمْدُ لِلَّهِ الَّذِي أَحْيَانَا بَعْدَ مَا أَمَاتَنَا، وَإِلَيْهِ النُّشُورُ»

(All the thanks are due to Allah Who brought us back to life after He had caused us to die (sleep), and the Return is to Him).

Allah said,

(And because of their disbelief and allegations against Maryam and because of their saying "We killed Al-Masih `Isa, son of Maryam, the Messenger of Allah, - but they killed him not, nor crucified him, but it appeared that way to them) until,

(For surely; they killed him not But Allah raised him up unto Himself. And Allah is Ever All-Powerful, All-Wise. And there is none of the people of the Scripture (Jews and Christians) but must believe in him before his death. And on the Day of Resurrection, he (`Isa) will be a witness against them.) (4:156-159)

`His death' refers to `Isa, and the Ayah means that the People of the Book will believe in `Isa, before `Isa dies. This will occur when `Isa comes back to this world before the Day of Resurrection, as we will explain. By that time, all the People of the Book will believe in `Isa, for he will annul the Jizyah and he will only accept Islam from people. Ibn Abi Hatim recorded that Al-Hasan said that Allah's statement,

(I will take you) is in reference to sleep, for Allah raised `Isa while he was asleep.

Altering the Religion of `Isa

Allah said,

(And purify (save) you from those who disbelieve) by raising you to heaven,

(And I will make those who follow you superior to those who disbelieve, till the Day of Resurrection)

This is what happened. When Allah raised `Isa to heaven, his followers divided into sects and groups. Some of them believed in what Allah sent `Isa as, a servant of Allah, His Messenger, and the son of His female-servant.

However, some of them went to the extreme over `Isa, believing that he was the son of Allah. Some of them said that `Isa was Allah Himself, while others said that he was one of a Trinity. Allah mentioned these false creeds in the Qur'an and refuted them. The Christians remained like this until the third century CE, when a Greek king called, Constantine, became a Christian for the purpose of destroying Christianity. Constantine was either a philosopher, or he was just plain ignorant. Constantine changed the religion of `Isa by adding to it and deleting from it. He established the rituals of Christianity and the so-called Great Trust, which is in fact the Great Treachery. He also allowed them to eat the meat of swine, changed the direction of the prayer that `Isa established to the east, built churches for `Isa, and added ten days to the fast as compensation for a sin that he committed, as claimed. So the religion of `Isa became the religion of Constantine, who built more then twelve thousand churches, temples and monasteries for the Christians as well as the city that bears his name, Constantinople (Istanbul). Throughout this time, the Christians had the upper hand and dominated the Jews. Allah aided them against the Jews because they used to be closer to the truth than the Jews, even though both groups were and still are disbelievers, may Allah's curse descend on them.

When Allah sent Muhammad , those who believed in him also believed in Allah, His Angels, Books and Messengers in the correct manner. So they were the true followers of every Prophet who came to earth. They believed in the unlettered Prophet , the Final Messenger and the master of all mankind, who called them to believe in the truth in its entirety. This is why they had more right to every Prophet than his own nation, especially those who claim to follow their Prophet's way and religion, yet change and alter his religion. Furthermore, Allah abrogated all the laws that were sent down to the Prophets with the Law He sent Muhammad with, which consists of the true religion that shall never change or be altered until the commencement of the Last Hour. Muhammad's religion shall always be dominant and victorious over all other religions. This is why Allah allowed Muslims to conquer the eastern and western parts of the world and the kingdoms of the earth. Furthermore, all countries submitted to them; they demolished Kisra (king of Persia) and destroyed the Czar, ridding them of their treasures and spending these treasures for Allah's sake. All this occurred just as their Prophet told them it would, when he conveyed Allah's statement,

(Allah has promised those among you who believe and do righteous good deeds, that He will certainly grant them succession in the land, as He granted it to those before them, and that He will grant them the authority to practice their religion which He has chosen for them. And He will surely give them in exchange a safe security after their fear (provided) they worship Me and do not associate anything with Me.) (24:55).

Therefore, Muslims are the true believers in `Isa. The Muslims then acquired Ash-Sham from the Christians, causing them to evacuate to Asia Minor, to their fortified city in Constantinople. The Muslims will be above them until the Day of Resurrection. Indeed, he, Muhammad , who is truthful and who received the true news, has conveyed to Muslims that they will conquer Constantinople in the future, and seize its treasures.

Threatening the Disbelievers with Torment in This Life and the Hereafter

Allah said,

(And I will make those who follow you superior to those who disbelieve till the Day of Resurrection. Then you will return to Me and I will judge between you in the matters in which you used to dispute. As to those who disbelieve, I will punish them with a severe torment in this world and in the Hereafter, and they will have no helpers.)

This is what Allah did to the Jews who disbelieved in `Isa and the Christians who went to the extreme over him. Allah tormented them in this life; they were killed, captured, and lost their wealth and kingdoms. Their torment in the Hereafter is even worse and more severe,

(And they have no Waq (defender or protector) against Allah) (13:34).

(And as for those who believe and do righteous good deeds, Allah will pay them their reward in full) in this life, with victory and domination, and in the Hereafter, with Paradise and high grades,

(And Allah does not like the wrongdoers.)

Allah then said,

(This is what We recite to you of the verses and the Wise Reminder.) meaning, "What We narrated to you, O Muhammd, regarding `Isa, his birth and his life, is what Allah conveyed and revealed to you, sent down from the Al-Lawh Al-Mahfuz (The Preserved Tablet). So there is no doubt in it. Similarly, Allah said in Surah Maryam;

(Such is `Isa, son of Maryam. (It is) a statement of truth, about which they doubt (or dispute). It befits not Allah that He should beget a son. Glorified be He. When He decrees a thing, He only says to it: "Be!" and it is.)

Surah: 3 Ayah: 59, Ayah: 60, Ayah: 61, Ayah: 62 & Ayah: 63

﴿ إِنَّ مَثَلَ عِيسَىٰ عِندَ ٱللَّهِ كَمَثَلِ ءَادَمَ ۖ خَلَقَهُۥ مِن تُرَابٍ ثُمَّ قَالَ لَهُۥ كُن فَيَكُونُ ۝ ﴾

59. Verily, the likeness of 'Isâ (Jesus) before Allâh is the likeness of Adam. He created him from dust, then (He) said to him: "Be!" - and he was.

$$\left\{ \text{ٱلْحَقُّ مِن رَّبِّكَ فَلَا تَكُن مِّنَ ٱلْمُمْتَرِينَ} \right\}$$

60. (This is) the truth from your Lord, so be not of those who doubt.

$$\left\{ \text{فَمَنْ حَآجَّكَ فِيهِ مِنۢ بَعْدِ مَا جَآءَكَ مِنَ ٱلْعِلْمِ فَقُلْ تَعَالَوْاْ نَدْعُ أَبْنَآءَنَا وَأَبْنَآءَكُمْ وَنِسَآءَنَا وَنِسَآءَكُمْ وَأَنفُسَنَا وَأَنفُسَكُمْ ثُمَّ نَبْتَهِلْ فَنَجْعَل لَّعْنَتَ ٱللَّهِ عَلَى ٱلْكَٰذِبِينَ} \right\}$$

61. Then whoever disputes with you concerning him ('Isâ (Jesus)) after (all this) knowledge that has come to you, (i.e. 'Isâ (Jesus)) being a slave of Allâh, and having no share in Divinity) say: (O Muhammad (peace be upon him)) "Come, let us call our sons and your sons, our women and your women, ourselves and yourselves - then we pray and invoke (sincerely) the Curse of Allâh upon those who lie."

$$\left\{ \text{إِنَّ هَٰذَا لَهُوَ ٱلْقَصَصُ ٱلْحَقُّ وَمَا مِنْ إِلَٰهٍ إِلَّا ٱللَّهُ وَإِنَّ ٱللَّهَ لَهُوَ ٱلْعَزِيزُ ٱلْحَكِيمُ} \right\}$$

62. Verily! This is the true narrative (about the story of 'Isâ (Jesus)), and, Lâ ilâha ill-Allâh (none has the right to be worshipped but Allâh, the One and the Only True God, Who has neither a wife nor a son). And indeed, Allâh is the All-Mighty, the All-Wise.

$$\left\{ \text{فَإِن تَوَلَّوْاْ فَإِنَّ ٱللَّهَ عَلِيمٌۢ بِٱلْمُفْسِدِينَ} \right\}$$

63. And if they turn away (and do not accept these true proofs and evidences), then surely, Allâh is All-Aware of those who do mischief.

Transliteration

59. Inna mathala AAeesa AAinda Allahi kamathali adama khalaqahu min turabin thumma qala lahu kun fayakoonu   60. Alhaqqu min rabbika fala takun mina almumtareena   61. Faman hajjaka feehi min baAAdi ma jaaka mina alAAilmi faqul taAAalaw nadAAu abnaana waabnaakum wanisaana wanisaakum waanfusana waanfusakum thumma nabtahil fanajAAal laAAnata Allahi AAala alkathibeena   62. Inna hatha lahuwa alqasasu alhaqqu wama min ilahin illa Allahu wa-inna Allaha lahuwa alAAazeezu alhakeemu   63. Fa-in tawallaw fa-inna Allaha AAaleemun bialmufsideena

Tafsir Ibn Kathir

The Similarities Between the Creation of Adam and the Creation of `Isa

Allah said,

(Verily, the likeness of `Isa before Allah) regarding Allah's ability, since He created him without a father,

(is the likeness of Adam), for Allah created Adam without a father or a mother. Rather,

(He created him from dust, then (He) said to him: "Be!" and he was.)

Therefore, He Who created Adam without a father or a mother is able to create `Isa, as well, without a father. If the claim is made that `Isa is Allah's son because he was created without a father, then the same claim befits Adam even more. However, since such a claim regarding Adam is obviously false, then making the same claim about `Isa is even more false.

Furthermore, by mentioning these facts, Allah emphasizes His ability, by creating Adam without a male or female, Hawa' from a male without a female, and `Isa from a mother without a father, compared to His creating the rest of creation from male and female. This is why Allah said in Surah Maryam,

(And We made him a sign for mankind) (19: 21).

Allah said in this Ayah,

((This is) the truth from your Lord, so be not of those who doubt.) meaning, this is the only true story about `Isa, and what is beyond truth save falsehood Allah next commands His Messenger to call those who defy the truth, regarding `Isa, to the Mubahalah (the curse).

The Challenge to the Mubahalah

(Then whoever disputes with you concerning him after the knowledge that has come to you, say: "Come, let us call our sons and your sons, our women and your women, ourselves and yourselves") for the Mubahalah,

(then we pray), supplicate,

(and we invoke Allah's curse upon the liars) among the two of us.

The reason for the call to Mubahalah and the revelation of the Ayat from the beginning of this Surah until here, is that a delegation from the Christians of Najran (in Yemen) came to Al-Madinah to argue about `Isa, claiming that he was divine and the son of Allah. Allah sent down the beginning of this Surah until here, to refute their claims, as Imam Muhammad bin Ishaq bin Yasar and other scholars stated.

Muhammad bin Ishaq bin Yasar said in his famous Sirah, "The delegation of Christians from Najran came to the Messenger of Allah . The delegation consisted of sixty horsemen, including fourteen of their chiefs who make decisions. These men were Al-`Aqib, also known as `Abdul-Masih, As-Sayyid, also known as Al-Ayham, Abu Harithah bin `Alqamah, of (the family of) Bakr bin Wa`il and Uways bin Al-Harith. They also included, Zayd, Qays, Yazid, Nabih, Khuwaylid, `Amr, Khalid, `Abdullah and

Yuhannas. Three of these men were chiefs of this delegation, Al-`Aqib, their leader and to whom they referred for advice and decision; As-Sayyid, their scholar and leader in journeys and social gatherings; and Abu Harithah bin `Alqamah, their patriarch, priest and religious leader. Abu Harithah was an Arab man from (the family of) Bakr bin Wa`il, but when he embraced Christianity, the Romans and their kings honored him and built churches for him (or in his honor). They also supported him financially and gave him servants, because they knew how firm his faith in their religion was." Abu Harithah knew the description of the Messenger of Allah from what he read in earlier divine Books. However, his otherwise ignorance led him to insist on remaining a Christian, because he was honored and had a high position with the Christians. Ibn Ishaq said, "Muhammad bin Ja`far bin Az-Zubayr said that, `The (Najran) delegation came to the Messenger of Allah in Al-Madinah, entered his Masjid wearing robes and garments, after the Prophet had prayed the `Asr prayer. They accompanied a caravan of camels led by Bani Al-Harith bin Ka`b. The Companions of the Messenger of Allah who saw them said that they never saw a delegation like them after that... Then Abu Harithah bin `Alqamah and Al-`Aqib `Abdul-Masih or As-Sayyid Al-Ayham spoke to the Messenger of Allah , and they were Christians like the king (Roman King). However, they disagreed about `Isa; some of them said, `He is Allah,' while some said, `He is the son of Allah,' and some others said, `He is one of a trinity.' Allah is far from what they attribute to Him."

Indeed, these are the creeds of the Christians. They claim that `Isa is God, since he brought the dead back to life, healed blindness, leprosy and various illnesses, told about matters of the future, created the shape of birds and blew life into them, bringing them to life. However, all these miracles occurred by Allah's leave, so that `Isa would be a sign from Allah for people.

They also claim that `Isa is the son of Allah, since he did not have a father and he spoke when he was in the cradle, a miracle which had not occurred by any among the Children of Adam before him, so they claim. They also claim that `Isa is one of a trinity, because Allah would say, `We did, command, create and demand.' They said, `If Allah were one, he would have said, `I did, command, create and decide.' This is why they claim that `Isa and Allah are one (Trinity). Allah is far from what they attribute to Him, and we should mention that the Qur'an refuted all these false Christian claims.

Ibn Ishaq continued, "When these Ayat came to the Messenger from Allah , thus judging between him and the People of the Book, Allah also commanded the Prophet to call them to the Mubahalah if they still refused the truth. The Prophet called them to the Mubahalah. They said, `O Abu Al-Qasim! Let us think about this matter and get back to you with our decision to what we want to do.' They left the Prophet and conferred with Al-`Aqib, to whom they referred to for advice. They said to him, `O `Abdul-Masih! What is your advice' He said, `By Allah, O Christian fellows! You know that Muhammad is a Messenger and that he brought you the final word regarding your fellow (`Isa). You also know that no Prophet conducted Mubahalah with any people, and the old persons among them remained safe and the young people grew up. Indeed, it will be the end of you if you do it. If you have already decided that you will remain in your religion and your creed regarding your fellow (`Isa), then conduct a treaty with the man (Muhammad) and go back to your land.' They came to the Prophet and said, `O Abu Al-Qasim! We decided that we cannot do Mubahalah with you and that you remain on your religion, while we remain on our religion. However, send with us a man from your Companions whom you are pleased with to judge between us regarding our monetary disputes, for you are acceptable to us in this regard.'"

Al-Bukhari recorded that Hudhayfah said, "Al-`Aqib and As-Sayyid, two leaders from Najran, came to the Messenger of Allah seeking to invoke Allah for curses (against whoever is unjust among them), and one of them said to the other, `Let us not do that. By Allah, if he were truly a Prophet and we invoke Allah for curses, we and our offspring shall never succeed afterwards.' So they said, `We will give you what you asked and send a trusted man with us, just a trusted man.' The Messenger of Allah said;

»لَأَبْعَثَنَّ مَعَكُمْ رَجُلًا أَمِينًا حَقَّ أَمِينٍ«

("Verily, I will send a trusted man with you, a truly trustworthy man." The Companions of the Messenger of Allah all felt eager to be that man. The Messenger said,

»قُمْ يَا أَبَا عُبَيْدَةَ بْنَ الْجَرَّاحِ«

"O Abu `Ubaydah bin Al-Jarrah! Stand up." When Abu `Ubaydah stood up, the Messenger of Allah said,

»هَذَا أَمِينُ هَذِهِ الْأُمَّةِ«

"This is the trustee of this Ummah.'")

Al-Bukhari recorded that Anas said that the Messenger of Allah said on another occasion,

»لِكُلِّ أُمَّةٍ أَمِينٌ، وَأَمِينُ هَذِهِ الْأُمَّةِ أَبُو عُبَيْدَةَ بْنُ الْجَرَّاحِ«

(Every Ummah has a trustee, and the trustee of this Ummah is Abu `Ubaydah bin Al-Jarrah.)

Imam Ahmad recorded that Ibn `Abbas said, "Abu Jahl, may Allah curse him, said, `If I see Muhammad praying next to the Ka`bah, I will step on his neck.' The Prophet later said,

»لَوْ فَعَلَ لَأَخَذَتْهُ الْمَلَائِكَةُ عِيَانًا، وَلَوْ أَنَّ الْيَهُودَ تَمَنَّوُا الْمَوْتَ لَمَاتُوا، وَرَأَوْا

مقاعدهم من النار، ولو خرج الذين يباهلون رسول اللهصلى الله عليه وسلّم لرجعوا لا يجدون مالًا ولا أهلًا»

(Had he tried to do it, the angels would have taken him publicly. Had the Jews wished for death, they would have perished and would have seen their seats in the Fire. Had those who sought Mubahalah with the Messenger of Allah, went ahead with it, they would not have found estates or families when they returned home)." Al-Bukhari, At-Tirmidhi and An-Nasa'i also recorded this Hadith, which At-Tirmidhi graded Hasan Sahih.

Allah then said,

(Verily, this is the true narrative) meaning, what we narrated to you, O Muhammad, about `Isa is the plain truth that cannot be avoided,

(and none has the right to be worshipped but Allah. And indeed, Allah is the All-Mighty, the All-Wise. And if they turn away,) by abandoning this truth,

(then surely, Allah is All-Aware of those who do mischief.) for those who abandon the truth for falsehood commit mischief, and Allah has full knowledge of them and will subject them to the worst punishment. Verily, Allah is able to control everything, all praise and thanks are due to Him, and we seek refuge with Him from His revenge.

Surah: 3 Ayah: 64

﴿ قُلْ يَٰٓأَهْلَ ٱلْكِتَٰبِ تَعَالَوْاْ إِلَىٰ كَلِمَةٍ سَوَآءٍۭ بَيْنَنَا وَبَيْنَكُمْ أَلَّا نَعْبُدَ إِلَّا ٱللَّهَ وَلَا نُشْرِكَ بِهِۦ شَيْـًٔا وَلَا يَتَّخِذَ بَعْضُنَا بَعْضًا أَرْبَابًا مِّن دُونِ ٱللَّهِ ۚ فَإِن تَوَلَّوْاْ فَقُولُواْ ٱشْهَدُواْ بِأَنَّا مُسْلِمُونَ ۝ ﴾

64. Say (O Muhammad (peace be upon him)) "O people of the Scripture (Jews and Christians): Come to a word that is just between us and you, that we worship none but Allâh (Alone), and that we associate no partners with Him, and that none of us shall take others as lords besides Allâh. Then, if they turn away, say: "Bear witness that we are Muslims."

Transliteration

64. Qul ya ahla alkitabi taAAalaw ila kalimatin sawa-in baynana wabaynakum alla naAAbuda illa Allaha wala nushrika bihi shay-an wala yattakhitha baAAduna baAAdan arbaban min dooni Allahi fain tawallaw faqooloo ishhadoo bi-anna muslimoona

Tafsir Ibn Kathir

Every Person Knows about Tawhid

This Ayah includes the People of the Book, the Jews and Christians, and those who follow their ways.

(Say: "O people of the Scripture! Come to a word")

`Word' - in Arabic - also means a complete sentence, as evident from this Ayah. Allah described this word as being one,

(that is the same between us and you), an honest and righteous word that is fair to both parties. Allah then explained this word,

(that we worship none but Allah (Alone), and that we associate no partners with Him,) we worship neither a statue, cross, idol, Taghut (false gods), fire or anything else. Rather, we worship Allah Alone without partners, and this is the message of all of Allah's Messengers. Allah said,

(And We did not send any Messenger before you but We revealed to him (saying): "None has the right to be worshipped but I (Allah)), so worship Me (Alone and none else).") (21:25) and,

(And verily, We have sent among every Ummah a Messenger (proclaiming): "Worship Allah (Alone), and avoid (or keep away from) Taghut (all false deities).") (16:36). Allah said next,

("and that none of us shall take others as lords besides Allah.") Ibn Jurayj commented, "We do not obey each other in disobedience to Allah."

(Then, if they turn away, say: "Bear witness that we are Muslims.") if they abandon this fair call, then let them know that you will remain in Islam as Allah has legislated for you.

We should mention that the letter that the Prophet sent to Heraclius reads, "In the Name of Allah, the Most Gracious, the Most Merciful. From Muhammad, the Messenger of Allah, to Heraclius, Leader of the Romans: peace be upon those who follow the true guidance. Embrace Islam and you will acquire safety, embrace Islam and Allah will grant you a double reward. However, if you turn away from it, then you will carry the burden of the peasants, and,

("O people of the Scripture: Come to a word that is the same between us and you, that we worship none but Allah (Alone), and that we associate no partners with Him, and that none of us shall take others as lords besides Allah." Then, if they turn away, say: "Bear witness that we are Muslims.")"

Muhammad bin Ishaq and other scholars said that the beginning of Surah Al `Imran, and more than eighty verses thereafter; were revealed about the delegation of Najran. Az-Zuhri stated that the people of Najran were the first people to pay the Jizyah (tax money paid to the Muslim State). However, there is no disagreement that the Ayah that ordained the Jizyah (9:29) was revealed after the Fath (conquering Makkah, and therefore, after the delegation of Najran came to Al-Madinah). So, how can this Ayah (3:64) be contained in the Prophet's letter to Heraclius before the victory of Makkah, and how can we harmonize between the statements of Muhammad bin Ishaq and Az-Zuhri The answer is that the delegation of Najran came before Al-Hudaybiyyah (before the victory of Makkah), and what they paid was in lieu of the Mubahalah; not as Jizyah. The Ayah about the Jizyah was later revealed, and its ruling supported what occurred with the Najran people. In support of this opinion, we should mention that in another instance, the ruling on dividing the booty into one - fifth (for the Prophet) and four-fifths (for the fighters) agreed with the practice of `Abdullah bin Jahsh during the raid that he led before Badr. An Ayah later on upheld the way `Abdullah divided the booty. Therefore, it is possible that the Prophet wrote this statement (Say, "O People of the Scripture. ..") in his letter to Heraclius before the Ayah was revealed. Later on, the Qur'an agreed with the Prophet's statement, word by word. It is also a fact that the Qur'an was revealed in agreement with what `Umar said regarding the captured disbelievers at Badr, the Hijab (Muslim woman code of dress), refraining from performing prayer for the hypocrites, and regarding his statements:

(And take you the Maqam (place) of Ibrahim as a place of prayer.) (2:125), and, (It may be if he divorced you (all) that his Lord will give him instead of you, wives better than you.) (66:5).

Surah: 3 Ayah: 65, Ayah: 66, Ayah: 67 & Ayah: 68

﴿ يَٰٓأَهْلَ ٱلْكِتَٰبِ لِمَ تُحَآجُّونَ فِىٓ إِبْرَٰهِيمَ وَمَآ أُنزِلَتِ ٱلتَّوْرَىٰةُ وَٱلْإِنجِيلُ إِلَّا مِنۢ بَعْدِهِۦٓ ۚ أَفَلَا تَعْقِلُونَ ﴾

65. O people of the Scripture (Jews and Christians)! Why do you dispute about Ibrâhim (Abraham), while the Taurât (Torah) and the Injeel (Gospel) were not revealed till after him? Have you then no sense?

﴿ هَٰٓأَنتُمْ هَٰٓؤُلَآءِ حَٰجَجْتُمْ فِيمَا لَكُم بِهِۦ عِلْمٌ فَلِمَ تُحَآجُّونَ فِيمَا لَيْسَ لَكُم بِهِۦ عِلْمٌ ۚ وَٱللَّهُ يَعْلَمُ وَأَنتُمْ لَا تَعْلَمُونَ ﴾

66. Verily, you are those who have disputed about that of which you have knowledge. Why do you then dispute concerning that of which you have no knowledge? It is Allâh Who knows, and you know not.

﴿ مَا كَانَ إِبْرَٰهِيمُ يَهُودِيًّا وَلَا نَصْرَانِيًّا وَلَٰكِن كَانَ حَنِيفًا مُّسْلِمًا وَمَا كَانَ مِنَ ٱلْمُشْرِكِينَ ﴾

67. Ibrâhim (Abraham) was neither a Jew nor a Christian, but he was a true Muslim Hanifa (Islâmic Monotheism - to worship none but Allâh Alone) and he was not of Al-Mushrikûn (See V.2:105).

﴿ إِنَّ أَوْلَى ٱلنَّاسِ بِإِبْرَٰهِيمَ لَلَّذِينَ ٱتَّبَعُوهُ وَهَـٰذَا ٱلنَّبِىُّ وَٱلَّذِينَ ءَامَنُوا۟ ۗ وَٱللَّهُ وَلِىُّ ٱلْمُؤْمِنِينَ ﴿٦٨﴾ ﴾

68. Verily, among mankind who have the best claim to Ibrâhim (Abraham) are those who followed him, and this Prophet (Muhammad (peace be upon him)) and those who have believed (Muslims). And Allâh is the Walî (Protector and Helper) of the believers.

Transliteration

65. Ya ahla alkitabi lima tuhajjoona fee ibraheema wama onzilati alttawratu waal-injeelu illa min baAAdihi afala taAAqiloona   66. Ha antum haola-i hajajtum feema lakum bihi AAilmun falima tuhajjoona feema laysa lakum bihi AAilmun waAllahu yaAAlamu waantum la taAAlamoona   67. Ma kana ibraheemu yahoodiyyan wala nasraniyyan walakin kana haneefan musliman wama kana mina almushrikeena   68. Inna awla alnnasi bi-ibraheema lallatheena ittabaAAoohu wahatha alnnabiyyu waallatheena amanoo waAllahu waliyyu almu/mineena

Tafsir Ibn Kathir

Disputing with the Jews and Christians About the Religion of Ibrahim

Allah censures the Jews and Christians for their dispute with Muslims over Ibrahim Al-Khalil and the claim each group made that he was one of them. Muhammad bin Ishaq bin Yasar reported that Ibn `Abbas said, "The Christians of Najran and Jewish rabbis gathered before the Messenger of Allah and disputed in front of him. The rabbis said, `Ibrahim was certainly Jewish.' The Christians said, `Certainly, Ibrahim was Christian.' So Allah sent down,

(O people of the Scripture (Jews and Christians)! Why do you dispute about Ibrahim,) meaning, `How is it that you, Jews, claim that Ibrahim was Jew, although he lived before Allah sent down the Tawrah to Musa How is it that you, Christians, claim that Ibrahim was Christian, although Christianity came after his time" This is why Allah said,

(Have you then no sense)

Allah then said,

c(Verily, you are those who have disputed about that of which you have knowledge. Why do you then dispute concerning that of which you have no knowledge)

This Ayah criticizes those who argue and dispute without knowledge, just as the Jews and Christians did concerning Ibrahim. Had they disputed about their religions, which they had knowledge of, and about the Law that was legislated for them until Muhammad was sent, it would have been better for them. Rather, they disputed about what they had no knowledge of, so Allah criticized them for this behavior. Allah commanded them to refer what they have no knowledge of to He Who knows the seen and unseen matters and Who knows the true reality of all things. This is why Allah said,

(It is Allah Who knows, and you know not.)

Allah said,

(Ibrahim was neither a Jew nor a Christian, but he was a true Muslim Hanifa), shunning Shirk and living in Iman,

(and he was not of the Mushrikin.)

This Ayah is similar to the Ayah in Surat Al-Baqarah,

(And they say, "Be Jews or Christians, then you will be guided...") (2:135).

Allah said next,

(Verily, among mankind who have the best claim to Ibrahim are those who followed him, and this Prophet and those who have believed. And Allah is the Wali (Protector and Helper) of the believers.)

This Ayah means, "The people who have the most right to be followers of Ibrahim are those who followed his religion and this Prophet, Muhammad , and his Companions from the Muhajirin, Ansar and those who followed their lead." Sa`id bin Mansur recorded that Ibn Mas`ud said that the Messenger of Allah said,

«إِنَّ لِكُلِّ نَبِيٍّ وُلَاةً مِنَ النَّبِيِّينَ، وَإِنَّ وَلِيِّي مِنْهُمْ أَبِي وَخَلِيلُ رَبِّي عَزَّ وَجَل»

(Every Prophet had a Wali (supporter, best friend) from among the Prophets. My Wali among them is my father Ibrahim, the Khalil (intimate friend) of my Lord, the Exalted and Most Honored)

The Prophet then recited,

(Verily, among mankind who have the best claim to Ibrahim are those who followed him...)

Allah's statement,

(And Allah is the Wali (Protector and Helper) of the believers.) means, Allah is the Protector of all those who believe in His Messengers.

Surah: 3 Ayah: 69, Ayah: 70, Ayah: 71, Ayah: 72, Ayah: 73 & Ayah: 74

﴿ وَدَّت طَّآئِفَةٌ مِّنْ أَهْلِ ٱلْكِتَٰبِ لَوْ يُضِلُّونَكُمْ وَمَا يُضِلُّونَ إِلَّآ أَنفُسَهُمْ وَمَا يَشْعُرُونَ ۝ ﴾

69. A party of the people of the Scripture (Jews and Christians) wish to lead you astray. But they shall not lead astray anyone except themselves, and they perceive not.

﴿ يَٰٓأَهْلَ ٱلْكِتَٰبِ لِمَ تَكْفُرُونَ بِـَٔايَٰتِ ٱللَّهِ وَأَنتُمْ تَشْهَدُونَ ۝ ﴾

70. O people of the Scripture! (Jews and Christians): "Why do you disbelieve in the Ayât of Allâh, (the Verses about Prophet Muhammad (peace be upon him) present in the Taurât (Torah) and the Injeel (Gospel)) while you (yourselves) bear witness (to their truth)."

﴿ يَٰٓأَهْلَ ٱلْكِتَٰبِ لِمَ تَلْبِسُونَ ٱلْحَقَّ بِٱلْبَٰطِلِ وَتَكْتُمُونَ ٱلْحَقَّ وَأَنتُمْ تَعْلَمُونَ ۝ ﴾

71. O people of the Scripture (Jews and Christians): "Why do you mix truth with falsehood and conceal the truth while you know?"

﴿ وَقَالَت طَّآئِفَةٌ مِّنْ أَهْلِ ٱلْكِتَٰبِ ءَامِنُوا۟ بِٱلَّذِىٓ أُنزِلَ عَلَى ٱلَّذِينَ ءَامَنُوا۟ وَجْهَ ٱلنَّهَارِ وَٱكْفُرُوٓا۟ ءَاخِرَهُۥ لَعَلَّهُمْ يَرْجِعُونَ ۝ ﴾

72. And a party of the people of the Scripture say: "Believe in the morning in that which is revealed to the believers (Muslims), and reject it at the end of the day, so that they may turn back.

﴿ وَلَا تُؤْمِنُوٓا۟ إِلَّا لِمَن تَبِعَ دِينَكُمْ قُلْ إِنَّ ٱلْهُدَىٰ هُدَى ٱللَّهِ أَن يُؤْتَىٰٓ أَحَدٌ مِّثْلَ مَآ أُوتِيتُمْ أَوْ يُحَآجُّوكُمْ عِندَ رَبِّكُمْ قُلْ إِنَّ ٱلْفَضْلَ بِيَدِ ٱللَّهِ يُؤْتِيهِ مَن يَشَآءُ وَٱللَّهُ وَٰسِعٌ عَلِيمٌ ۝ ﴾

73. And believe no one except the one who follows your religion. Say (O Muhammad (peace be upon him)) "Verily! Right guidance is the Guidance of Allâh" and do not believe that anyone can receive like that which you have received (of Revelation) except when he follows your religion, otherwise they would engage you in argument before your Lord. Say (O Muhammad (peace be upon him)) "All the bounty is in the Hand of Allâh; He grants to whom He wills. And Allâh is All-Sufficient for His creatures' needs, All-Knower."

$$\left\{ \text{يَخْتَصُّ بِرَحْمَتِهِۦ مَن يَشَآءُ ۚ وَٱللَّهُ ذُو ٱلْفَضْلِ ٱلْعَظِيمِ} \right\}$$

74. He selects for His Mercy (Islâm and the Qur'ân with Prophethood) whom He wills and Allâh is the Owner of Great Bounty.

Transliteration

69. Waddat ta-ifatun min ahli alkitabi law yudilloonakum wama yudilloona illa anfusahum wama yashAAuroona 70. Ya ahla alkitabi lima takfuroona bi-ayati Allahi waantum tashhadoona 71. Ya ahla alkitabi lima talbisoona alhaqqa bialbatili wataktumoona alhaqqa waantum taAAlamoona 72. Waqalat ta-ifatun min ahli alkitabi aminoo biallathee onzila AAala allatheena amanoo wajha alnnahari waokfuroo akhirahu laAAallahum yarjiAAoona 73. Wala tu/minoo illa liman tabiAAa deenakum qul inna alhuda huda Allahi an yu/ta ahadun mithla ma ooteetum aw yuhajjookum AAinda rabbikum qul inna alfadla biyadi Allahi yu/teehi man yashao waAllahu wasiAAun AAaleemun

Tafsir Ibn Kathir

The Envy the Jews Feel Towards Muslims; Their Wicked Plots Against Muslims

Allah states that the Jews envy the faithful and wish they could misguide them. Allah states that the punishment of this behavior will fall back upon them, while they are unaware. Allah criticizes them,

(O People of the Scripture!: Why do you disbelieve in the Ayat of Allah, while you bear witness.)

You know for certain that Allah's Ayat are true and authentic,

(O People of the Scripture: Why do you mix truth with falsehood and conceal the truth while you know) by hiding what is in your Books about the description of Muhammad , while you know what you do.

(And a party of the People of the Scripture say: "Believe in the morning in that which is revealed to the believers, and reject it at the end of the day,)

This is a wicked plan from the People of the Book to deceive Muslims who are weak in the religion. They decided that they would pretend to be believers in the beginning of the day, by attending the dawn prayer with the Muslims. However, when the day ended, they would revert to their old religion so that the ignorant people would say, "They reverted to their old religion because they uncovered some shortcomings in the Islamic religion." This is why they said next.

(so that they may turn back.) Ibn Abi Najih said that Mujahid commented about this Ayah, which refers to the Jews, "They attended the dawn prayer with the Prophet and disbelieved in the end of the day in order to misguide the people. This way, people would think that they have uncovered shortcomings in the religion that they briefly followed."

Chapter 3: Al-i-'Imran (The Family Of 'Imran), Verses 001-092

("And believe no one except the one who follows your religion.")

They said, do not trust anyone with your secret knowledge, except those who follow your religion. Therefore, they say, do not expose your knowledge to Muslims in order to prevent them from believing in it and, thus, use it as proof against you. Allah replied,

(Say: (O Prophet) "Verily, right guidance is the guidance of Allah.")

Allah guides the hearts of the faithful to the perfect faith through the clear Ayat, plain proofs and unequivocal evidence that He has sent down to His servant and Messenger Muhammad . This occurs, O you Jews, even though you hide the description of Muhammad . the unlettered Prophet whom you find in your Books that you received from the earlier Prophets. Allah's statement;

((And they say:) "Do not believe that anyone can receive like that which you have received, otherwise they would engage you in argument before your Lord.")

They say, "Do not disclose the knowledge that you have to the Muslims, to prevent them from learning it and thus becoming your equals. They will be even better because they will believe in it or will use it against you as evidence with your Lord, and thus establish Allah's proof against you in this life and the Hereafter." Allah said,

(Say: "All the bounty is in the Hand of Allah; He grants to whom He wills.) meaning, all affairs are under His control, and He gives and takes. Verily, Allah gives faith, knowledge and sound comprehension to whomever He wills. He also misguides whomever He wills by blinding his sight, mind, sealing his heart, hearing and stamping his eyes closed. Allah has the perfect wisdom and the unequivocal proofs.

(And Allah is All-Sufficient for His creatures' needs, All-Knower." He selects for His mercy whom He wills and Allah is the Owner of great bounty.) meaning, He has endowed you, O believers, with tremendous virtue, in that He honored your Prophet Muhammad over all other prophets, and by directing you to the best Shari`ah there is.

Surah: 3 Ayah: 75 & Ayah: 76

﴿ ۞ وَمِنْ أَهْلِ ٱلْكِتَبِ مَنْ إِن تَأْمَنْهُ بِقِنطَارٍ يُؤَدِّهِۦٓ إِلَيْكَ وَمِنْهُم مَّنْ إِن تَأْمَنْهُ بِدِينَارٍ لَّا يُؤَدِّهِۦٓ إِلَيْكَ إِلَّا مَا دُمْتَ عَلَيْهِ قَآئِمًا ۗ ذَٰلِكَ بِأَنَّهُمْ قَالُوا۟ لَيْسَ عَلَيْنَا فِى ٱلْأُمِّيِّۦنَ سَبِيلٌ وَيَقُولُونَ عَلَى ٱللَّهِ ٱلْكَذِبَ وَهُمْ يَعْلَمُونَ ۩ ﴾

75. Among the people of the Scripture (Jews and Christians) is he who, if entrusted with a Qintar (a great amount of wealth, etc.), will readily pay it back; and among them there is he who, if entrusted with a single silver coin, will not repay it unless you constantly stand demanding, because they say: "There is no blame

on us to betray and take the properties of the illiterates (Arabs)." But they tell a lie against Allâh while they know it.

$$\bulletبَلَىٰ مَنْ أَوْفَىٰ بِعَهْدِهِ وَٱتَّقَىٰ فَإِنَّ ٱللَّهَ يُحِبُّ ٱلْمُتَّقِينَ ۝$$

76. Yes, whoever fulfils his pledge and fears Allâh much; verily, then Allâh loves those who are Al-Muttaqûn (the pious - see V.2:2).

Transliteration

75. Wamin ahli alkitabi man in ta/manhu biqintarin yu-addihi ilayka waminhum man in ta/manhu bideenarin la yu-addihi ilayka illa ma dumta AAalayhi qa-iman thalika bi-annahum qaloo laysa AAalayna fee al-ommiyyeena sabeelun wayaqooloona AAala Allahi alkathiba wahum yaAAlamoona 76. Bala man awfa biAAahdihi waittaqa fa-inna Allaha yuhibbu almuttaqeena

Tafsir Ibn Kathir

How Trustworthy Are the Jews

Allah states that there are deceitful people among the Jews. He also warns the faithful against being deceived by them, because some of them,

(if entrusted with a Qintar (a great amount)) of money,

(will readily pay it back;) This Ayah indicates that this type would likewise give what is less than a Qintar, as is obvious. However,

(and among them there is he who, if entrusted with a single silver coin, will not repay it unless you constantly stand demanding,) and insisting on acquiring your rightful property. If this is what he would do with one Dinar, then what about what is more than a Dinar We mentioned the meaning of Qintar in the beginning of this Surah, while the value of Dinar is well known. Allah's statement,

(because they say: "There is no blame on us to betray and take the properties of the illiterates (Arabs).") means, what made them reject the truth (or what they owed) is that they said, "There is no harm in our religion if we eat up the property of the unlettered ones, the Arabs, for Allah has allowed it for us." Allah replied,

(But they tell a lie against Allah while they know it.) for they invented this lie and word of misguidance. Rather, Allah would not allow this money for them unless they had a right to it.

`Abdur-Razzaq recorded that Sa`sa`ah bin Yazid said that a man asked Ibn `Abbas, "During battle, we capture some property belonging to Ahl Adh-Dhimmah, such as chickens and sheep." Ibn `Abbas said, "What do you do in this case" The man said, "We say that there is no sin (if we confiscate them) in this case." He said, "That is what the People of the Book said,

(There is no blame on us to betray and take the properties of the illiterates (Arabs).)

Verily, if they pay the Jizyah, then you are not allowed their property, except when they willingly give it up."

Allah then said,

(Yes, whoever fulfills his pledge and fears Allah much,) fulfills his promise and fears Allah among you, O People of the Book, regarding the covenant Allah took from you to believe in Muhammad when he is sent, just as He took the same covenant from all Prophets and their nations. Whoever avoids Allah's prohibitions, obeys Him and adheres to the Shari`ah that He sent with His Final Messenger and the master of all mankind.

(verily, then Allah loves the Muttaqin.)

Surah: 3 Ayah: 77

﴿ إِنَّ ٱلَّذِينَ يَشْتَرُونَ بِعَهْدِ ٱللَّهِ وَأَيْمَٰنِهِمْ ثَمَنًا قَلِيلًا أُو۟لَٰٓئِكَ لَا خَلَٰقَ لَهُمْ فِى ٱلْأَٰخِرَةِ وَلَا يُكَلِّمُهُمُ ٱللَّهُ وَلَا يَنظُرُ إِلَيْهِمْ يَوْمَ ٱلْقِيَٰمَةِ وَلَا يُزَكِّيهِمْ وَلَهُمْ عَذَابٌ أَلِيمٌ ﴿٧٧﴾

77. Verily, those who purchase a small gain at the cost of Allâh's Covenant and their oaths, they shall have no portion in the Hereafter (Paradise). Neither will Allâh speak to them, nor look at them on the Day of Resurrection, nor will He purify them, and they shall have a painful torment.

Transliteration

77. Inna allatheena yashtaroona biAAahdi Allahi waaymanihim thamanan qaleelan olaika la khalaqa lahum fee al-akhirati wala yukallimuhumu Allahu wala yanthuru ilayhim yawma alqiyamati wala yuzakkeehim walahum AAathabun aleemun

Tafsir Ibn Kathir

There is No Share in the Hereafter for Those Who Break Allah's Covenant

Allah states that whoever prefers the small things of this short, soon to end life, instead of fulfilling what they have promised Allah by following Muhammad , announcing his description (from their books) to people and affirming his truth, then,

(they shall have no portion in the Hereafter.)

They will not have a share or part in the Hereafter's rewards,

(Neither will Allah speak to them nor look at them on the Day of Resurrection) with His mercy. This Ayah indicates that Allah will not speak words of kindness nor look at them with any mercy,

(nor will He purify them) from sins and impurities. Rather, He will order them to the Fire,

(and they shall have a painful torment.)

There are several Hadiths on the subject of this Ayah, some of which follow. The First Hadith

Imam Ahmad recorded that Abu Dharr said, "The Messenger of Allah said,

«ثَلَاثَةٌ لَا يُكَلِّمُهُمُ اللهُ، وَلَا يَنْظُرُ إِلَيْهِمْ يَوْمَ الْقِيَامَةِ، وَلَا يُزَكِّيهِمْ، وَلَهُمْ عَذَابٌ أَلِيم»

(There are three persons whom Allah will not speak to, look at on the Day of Resurrection or purify, and they shall taste a painful torment. I said, `O Messenger of Allah! Who are they, may they gain failure and loss' He said, repeating this statement thrice,

«الْمُسْبِلُ، وَالْمُنَفِّقُ سِلْعَتَهُ بِالْحَلِفِ الْكَاذِبِ، وَالْمَنَّان»

`The Musbil (man whose clothes reach below the ankles), he who swears while lying so as to sell his merchandize and the one who gives charity and reminds people of it).')" This was also recorded by Muslim, and the collectors of the Sunan. Another Hadith

Imam Ahmad recorded that `Adi bin `Amirah Al-Kindi said, "Imru' Al-Qays bin `Abis, a man from Kindah, disputed with a man from Hadramut in front of the Messenger of Allah concerning a piece of land. The Prophet required the man from Hadramut to present his evidence, but he did not have any. The Prophet required Imru' Al-Qays to swear to his truthfulness, but the man from Hadramut said, `O Messenger of Allah! If you only require him to swear, then by the Lord of the Ka`bah (Allah), my land is lost.' The Messenger of Allah said,

«مَنْ حَلَفَ عَلَى يَمِينٍ كَاذِبَةٍ لِيَقْتَطِعَ بِهَا مَالَ أَحَدٍ، لَقِيَ اللهَ عَزَّ وَجَلَّ وَهُوَ عَلَيْهِ غَضْبَان»

(Whoever swears while lying to acquire the property of others, will meet Allah while He is angry with him.)" Raja' one of the narrators of the Hadith, said that the Messenger of Allah then recited,

[إِنَّ الَّذِينَ يَشْتَرُونَ بِعَهْدِ اللَّهِ وَأَيْمَنِهِمْ ثَمَنًا قَلِيلًا]

(Verily, those who purchase a small gain at the cost of Allah's covenant and their oaths...)

Imru' Al-Qays said, `What if one forfeits this dispute, what will he gain, O Messenger of Allah' The Prophet answered, `Paradise.' Imru' Al-Qays said, `Bear witness that I forfeit all the land for him.'" An-Nasa'i also recorded this Hadith. Another Hadith

Imam Ahmad recorded that `Abdullah said that the Messenger of Allah said,

«مَنْ حَلَفَ عَلَى يَمِينٍ هُوَ فِيهَا فَاجِرٌ، لِيَقْتَطِعَ بِهَا مَالَ امْرِى مُسْلِمٍ، لَقِيَ اللهَ عَزَّ وَجَلَّ وَهُوَ عَلَيْهِ غَضْبَانُ»

(Whoever takes a false oath to deprive a Muslim of his property will meet Allah while He is angry with him.)

Al-Ash`ath said, "By Allah! This verse was revealed concerning me. I owned some land with a Jewish man who denied my right, and I complained against him to the Messenger of Allah. The Prophet asked me, `Do you have evidence' I said, `I don't have evidence.' He said to the Jew, `Take an oath then.' I said, `O Allah's Messenger! He will take a (false) oath immediately, and I will lose my property.' Allah revealed the verse,

(Verily, those who purchase a small gain at the cost of Allah's covenant and their oaths...)"

The Two Sahihs recorded this Hadith. Another Hadith

Imam Ahmad recorded that Abu Hurayrah said that the Messenger of Allah said,

«ثَلَاثَةٌ لَا يُكَلِّمُهُمُ اللهُ يَوْمَ الْقِيَامَةِ، وَلَا يَنْظُرُ إِلَيْهِمْ، وَلَا يُزَكِّيهِمْ، وَلَهُمْ عَذَابٌ أَلِيمٌ: رَجُلٌ مَنَعَ ابْنَ السَّبِيلِ فَضْلَ مَاءٍ عِنْدَهُ، وَرَجُلٌ حَلَفَ عَلَى سِلْعَةٍ بَعْدَ الْعَصْرِ يَعْنِي كَاذِبًا وَرَجُلٌ بَايَعَ إِمَامًا، فَإِنْ أَعْطَاهُ وَفَى لَهُ، وَإِنْ لَمْ يُعْطِهِ لَمْ يَفِ لَهُ»

(Three persons whom Allah shall not speak to on the Day of Resurrection, or look at, or purify them, and they shall taste a painful torment. (They are) a man who does not give the wayfarer some of the water that he has; a man who swears, while lying, in order to complete a sales transaction after the `Asr prayer; and a man who gives his pledge of allegiance to an Imam (Muslim Ruler), and if the Imam gives him (something), he fulfills the pledge, but if the Imam does not give him, he does not fulfill the pledge).

Abu Dawud and At-Tirmidhi also recorded this Hadith, and At-Tirmidhi graded it Hasan Sahih.

Surah: 3 Ayah: 78

﴿ وَإِنَّ مِنْهُمْ لَفَرِيقًا يَلْوُونَ أَلْسِنَتَهُم بِٱلْكِتَٰبِ لِتَحْسَبُوهُ مِنَ ٱلْكِتَٰبِ وَمَا هُوَ مِنَ ٱلْكِتَٰبِ وَيَقُولُونَ هُوَ مِنْ عِندِ ٱللَّهِ وَمَا هُوَ مِنْ عِندِ ٱللَّهِ وَيَقُولُونَ عَلَى ٱللَّهِ ٱلْكَذِبَ وَهُمْ يَعْلَمُونَ ﴾

78. And verily, among them is a party who distort the Book with their tongues (as they read), so that you may think it is from the Book, but it is not from the Book, and they say: "This is from Allâh," but it is not from Allâh; and they speak a lie against Allâh while they know it.

Transliteration

78. Wa-inna minhum lafareeqan yalwoona alsinatahum bialkitabi litahsaboohu mina alkitabi wama huwa mina alkitabi wayaqooloona huwa min AAindi Allahi wama huwa min AAindi Allahi wayaqooloona AAala Allahi alkathiba wahum yaAAlamoona

Tafsir Ibn Kathir

The Jews Alter Allah's Words

Allah states that some Jews, may Allah's curses descend on them, distort Allah's Words with their tongues, change them from their appropriate places, and alter their intended meanings. They do this to deceive the ignorant people by making it appear that their words are in the Book of Allah. They attribute their own lies to Allah, even though they know that they have lied and invented falsehood. Therefore, Allah said,

(and they speak a lie against Allah while they know it.)

Mujahid, Ash-Sha`bi, Al-Hasan, Qatadah and Ar-Rabi` bin Anas said that,

(who distort the Book with their tongues,) means, "They alter them (Allah's Words)."

Al-Bukhari reported that Ibn `Abbas said that the Ayah means they alter and add although none among Allah's creation can remove the Words of Allah from His Books, they alter and distort their apparent meanings. Wahb bin Munabbih said, "The Tawrah and the Injil remain as Allah revealed them, and no letter in them was removed. However, the people misguide others by addition and false interpretation, relying on books that they wrote themselves. Then,

(they say: "This is from Allah," but it is not from Allah;)

As for Allah's Books, they are still preserved and cannot be changed." Ibn Abi Hatim recorded this statement. However, if Wahb meant the books that are currently in the hands of the People of the Book, then we should state that there is no doubt that they altered, distorted, added to and deleted from them. For instance, the Arabic versions of these books contain tremendous error, many additions and deletions and enormous misinterpretation. Those who rendered these translations have incorrect comprehension in most, rather, all of these translations. If Wahb meant the Books of Allah that He has with Him, then indeed, these Books are preserved and were never changed.

Surah: 3 Ayah: 79 & Ayah: 80

﴿ مَا كَانَ لِبَشَرٍ أَن يُؤْتِيَهُ ٱللَّهُ ٱلْكِتَٰبَ وَٱلْحُكْمَ وَٱلنُّبُوَّةَ ثُمَّ يَقُولَ لِلنَّاسِ كُونُوا۟ عِبَادًا لِّى مِن دُونِ ٱللَّهِ وَلَٰكِن كُونُوا۟ رَبَّٰنِيِّۦنَ بِمَا كُنتُمْ تُعَلِّمُونَ ٱلْكِتَٰبَ وَبِمَا كُنتُمْ تَدْرُسُونَ ﴾ ﴿٧٩﴾

79. It is not (possible) for any human being to whom Allâh has given the Book and Al-Hukm (the knowledge and understanding of the laws of religion) and Prophethood to say to the people: "Be my worshippers rather than Allâh's." On the contrary (he would say): "Be you Rabbaniyun (learned men of religion who practice what they know and also preach others), because you are teaching the Book, and you are studying it."

﴿ وَلَا يَأْمُرَكُمْ أَن تَتَّخِذُوا۟ ٱلْمَلَٰٓئِكَةَ وَٱلنَّبِيِّۦنَ أَرْبَابًا ۗ أَيَأْمُرُكُم بِٱلْكُفْرِ بَعْدَ إِذْ أَنتُم مُّسْلِمُونَ ﴾ ﴿٨٠﴾

80. Nor would he order you to take angels and Prophets for lords (gods). Would he order you to disbelieve after you have submitted to Allâh's Will? (Tafsir At-Tabarî).

Transliteration

79. Ma kana libasharin an yu/tiyahu Allahu alkitaba waalhukma waalnnubuwwata thumma yaqoola lilnnasi koonoo AAibadan lee min dooni Allahi walakin koonoo rabbaniyyeena bima kuntum tuAAallimoona alkitaba wabima kuntum tadrusoona 80. Wala ya/murakum an tattakhithoo almala-ikata waalnnabiyyeena arbaban aya/murukum bialkufri baAAda ith antum muslimoona

Tafsir Ibn Kathir

No Prophet Ever Called People to Worship him or to Worship Other Than Allah

This Ayah (3:79) means, it is not for a person whom Allah has given the Book, knowledge in the Law and prophethood to proclaim to the people, "Worship me instead of Allah," meaning, along with Allah. If this is not the right of a Prophet or a Messenger, then indeed, it is not the right of anyone else to issue such a claim.

This criticism refers to the ignorant rabbis, priests and teachers of misguidance, unlike the Messengers and their sincere knowledgeable followers who implement their knowledge; for they only command what Allah commands them, as their honorable Messengers conveyed to them. They also forbid what Allah forbade for them, by the words of His honorable Messengers. The Messengers, may Allah's peace and blessings be on all of them, are the emissaries between Allah and His creation, conveying Allah's Message and Trust. The messengers indeed fulfilled their mission, gave sincere advice to creation and conveyed the truth to them. Allah's statement,

(On the contrary (he would say), "Be you Rabbaniyyun, because you are teaching the Book, and you are studying it.") means, the Messenger recommends the people to be Rabbaniyyun. Ibn `Abbas, Abu Razin and several others said that Rabbaniyyun means, "Wise, learned, and forbearing." Ad-Dahhak commented concerning Allah's statement,

(because you are teaching the Book, and you are studying it.) "Whoever learns the Qur'an deserves to become a Faqih (learned)."

(and you are studying it), preserving its words.

Allah then said,

(Nor would he order you to take angels and Prophets for lords.) The Prophet does not command worshipping other than Allah, whether a sent Messenger or an angel.

(Would he order you to disbelieve after you have submitted to Allah's will) meaning, he would not do that, for whoever calls to worshipping other than Allah, will have called to Kufr. The Prophets only call to Iman which commands worshipping Allah Alone without partners. Allah said in other Ayat,

(And We did not send any Messenger before you (O Muhammad) but We revealed to him (saying): "None has the right to be worshipped but I, so worship Me".) (21:25),

(And verily, We have sent among every Ummah a Messenger (proclaiming): "Worship Allah (Alone), and avoid Taghut (all false deities).") (16:36), and,

(And ask those of Our Messengers whom We sent before you: "Did We ever appoint gods to be worshipped besides the Most Gracious (Allah)") (43:45)

Allah said concerning the angels,

(And if any of them should say: "Verily, I am a god besides Him (Allah)," such a one We should recompense with Hell. Thus We recompense the wrongdoers.) (21:29).

Surah: 3 Ayah: 81 & Ayah: 82

﴿ وَإِذْ أَخَذَ ٱللَّهُ مِيثَٰقَ ٱلنَّبِيِّـۧنَ لَمَآ ءَاتَيْتُكُم مِّن كِتَٰبٍ وَحِكْمَةٍ ثُمَّ جَآءَكُمْ رَسُولٌ مُّصَدِّقٌ لِّمَا مَعَكُمْ لَتُؤْمِنُنَّ بِهِۦ وَلَتَنصُرُنَّهُۥ ۚ قَالَ ءَأَقْرَرْتُمْ وَأَخَذْتُمْ عَلَىٰ ذَٰلِكُمْ إِصْرِى ۖ قَالُوٓا۟ أَقْرَرْنَا ۚ قَالَ فَٱشْهَدُوا۟ وَأَنَا۠ مَعَكُم مِّنَ ٱلشَّٰهِدِينَ ﴾

81. And (remember) when Allâh took the Covenant of the Prophets, saying: "Take whatever I gave you from the Book and Hikmah (understanding of the Laws of

Allâh), and afterwards there will come to you a Messenger (Muhammad (peace be upon him)) confirming what is with you; you must, then, believe in him and help him." Allâh said: "Do you agree (to it) and will you take up My Covenant (which I conclude with you)?" They said: "We agree." He said: "Then bear witness; and I am with you among the witnesses (for this)."

﴿ فَمَن تَوَلَّىٰ بَعْدَ ذَٰلِكَ فَأُو۟لَـٰٓئِكَ هُمُ ٱلْفَـٰسِقُونَ ۝ ﴾

82. Then whoever turns away after this, they are the Fâsiqûn (rebellious: those who turn away from Allâh's Obedience).

Transliteration

81. Wa-ith akhatha Allahu meethaqa alnnabiyyeena lama ataytukum min kitabin wahikmatin thumma jaakum rasoolun musaddiqun lima maAAakum latu/minunna bihi walatansurunnahu qala aaqrartum waakhathtum AAala thalikum isree qaloo aqrarna qala faishhadoo waana maAAakum mina alshshahideena 82. Faman tawalla baAAda thalika faola-ika humu alfasiqoona

Tafsir Ibn Kathir

Taking a Pledge From the Prophets to Believe in Our Prophet, Muhammad

Allah states that He took a pledge from every Prophet whom He sent from Adam until `Isa, that when Allah gives them the Book and the Hikmah, thus acquiring whatever high grades they deserve, then a Messenger came afterwards, they would believe in and support him. Even though Allah has given the Prophets the knowledge and the prophethood, this fact should not make them refrain from following and supporting the Prophet who comes after them. This is why Allah, the Most High, Most Honored, said

(And (remember) when Allah took the covenant of the Prophets, saying: "Take whatever I gave you from the Book and Hikmah.") meaning, if I give you the Book and the Hikmah,

("and afterwards there will come to you a Messenger confirming what is with you; you must, then, believe in him and help him." Allah said, "Do you agree (to it) and will you take up Isri")

Ibn `Abbas, Mujahid, Ar-Rabi`, Qatadah and As-Suddi said that `Isri' means, "My covenant." Muhammad bin Ishaq said that,

(Isri) means, "The responsibility of My covenant that you took," meaning, the ratified pledge that you gave Me.

(They said: "We agree." He said: "Then bear witness; and I am with you among the witnesses." then whoever turns away after this,") from fulfilling this pledge and covenant, c

(they are the rebellious.) `Ali bin Abi Talib and his cousin `Abdullah bin `Abbas said, "Allah never sent a Prophet but after taking his pledge that if Muhammad were sent in his lifetime, he would believe in and support him." Allah commanded each Prophet to take a pledge from his nation that if Muhammad were sent in their time, they would believe in and support him. Tawus, Al-Hasan Al-Basri and Qatadah said, "Allah took the pledge from the Prophets that they would believe in each other", and this statement does not contradict what `Ali and Ibn `Abbas stated.

Therefore, Muhammad is the Final Prophet until the Day of Resurrection. He is the greatest Imam, who if he existed in any time period, deserves to be obeyed, rather than all other Prophets. This is why Muhammad led the Prophets in prayer during the night of Isra' when they gathered in Bayt Al-Maqdis (Jerusalem). He is the intercessor on the Day of Gathering, when the Lord comes to judge between His servants. This is Al-Maqam Al-Mahmud (the praised station) (refer to 17:79) that only Muhammad deserves, a responsibility which the mighty Prophets and Messengers will decline to assume. However, Muhammad will carry the task of intercession, may Allah's peace and blessings be on him.

Surah: 3 Ayah: 83, Ayah: 84 & Ayah: 85

﴿ أَفَغَيْرَ دِينِ ٱللَّهِ يَبْغُونَ وَلَهُۥٓ أَسْلَمَ مَن فِى ٱلسَّمَٰوَٰتِ وَٱلْأَرْضِ طَوْعًا وَكَرْهًا وَإِلَيْهِ يُرْجَعُونَ ۝ ﴾

83. Do they seek other than the religion of Allâh (the true Islâmic Monotheism - worshipping none but Allâh Alone), while to Him submitted all creatures in the heavens and the earth, willingly or unwillingly. And to Him shall they all be returned.

﴿ قُلْ ءَامَنَّا بِٱللَّهِ وَمَآ أُنزِلَ عَلَيْنَا وَمَآ أُنزِلَ عَلَىٰٓ إِبْرَٰهِيمَ وَإِسْمَٰعِيلَ وَإِسْحَٰقَ وَيَعْقُوبَ وَٱلْأَسْبَاطِ وَمَآ أُوتِىَ مُوسَىٰ وَعِيسَىٰ وَٱلنَّبِيُّونَ مِن رَّبِّهِمْ لَا نُفَرِّقُ بَيْنَ أَحَدٍ مِّنْهُمْ وَنَحْنُ لَهُۥ مُسْلِمُونَ ۝ ﴾

84. Say (O Muhammad (peace be upon him)) "We believe in Allâh and in what has been sent down to us, and what was sent down to Ibrâhim (Abraham), Ismâ'il (Ishmael), Ishâque (Isaac), Ya'qûb (Jacob) and Al-Asbât (the offspring of the twelve sons of Ya'qûb (Jacob)) and what was given to Mûsâ (Moses), 'Isâ (Jesus) and the Prophets from their Lord. We make no distinction between one another among them and to Him (Allâh) we have submitted (in Islâm)."

﴿ وَمَن يَبْتَغِ غَيْرَ ٱلْإِسْلَٰمِ دِينًا فَلَن يُقْبَلَ مِنْهُ وَهُوَ فِى ٱلْأَخِرَةِ مِنَ ٱلْخَٰسِرِينَ ۝ ﴾

85. And whoever seeks a religion other than Islâm, it will never be accepted of him, and in the Hereafter he will be one of the losers.

Transliteration

83. Afaghayra deeni Allahi yabghoona walahu aslama man fee alssamawati waal-ardi tawAAan wakarhan wa-ilayhi yurjaAAoona 84. Qul amanna biAllahi wama onzila AAalayna wama onzila AAala ibraheema wa-ismaAAeela waishaqa wayaAAqooba waal-asbati wama ootiya moosa waAAeesa waalnnabiyyoona min rabbihim la nufarriqu bayna ahadin minhum wanahnu lahu muslimoona 85. Waman yabtaghi ghayra al-islami deenan falan yuqbala minhu wahuwa fee al-akhirati mina alkhasireena

Tafsir Ibn Kathir

The Only Valid Religion To Allah is Islam

Allah rebukes those who prefer a religion other than the religion that He sent His Books and Messengers with, which is the worship of Allah Alone without partners, to Whom,

(submitted all creatures in the heavens and the earth,) Willingly, or not. Allah said in other Ayat,

(And unto Allah (Alone) falls in prostration whoever is in the heavens and the earth, willingly or unwillingly.) (13:15), and,

(Have they not observed things that Allah has created: (how) their shadows incline to the right and to the left, making prostration unto Allah, and they are lowly And to Allah prostrate all that is in the heavens and all that is in the earth, of the moving creatures and the angels, and they are not proud. They fear their Lord above them, and they do what they are commanded) (16: 48-50).

Therefore, the faithful believer submits to Allah in heart and body, while the disbeliever unwillingly submits to Him in body only, since he is under Allah's power, irresistible control and mighty kingship that cannot be repelled or resisted. Waki` reported that Mujahid said that the Ayah,

(While to Him submitted all creatures in the heavens and the earth, willingly or unwillingly), is similar to the Ayah,

(And verily, if you ask them: "Who created the heavens and the earth" Surely, they will say: "Allah") (39:38).

He also reported that Ibn `Abbas said about,

(while to Him submitted all creatures in the heavens and the earth, willingly or unwillingly.)

"When He took the covenant from them."

(And to Him shall they all be returned) on the Day of Return, when He will reward or punish each person according to his or her deeds.

Allah then said,

(Say: "We believe in Allah and in what has been sent down to us) the Qur'an,

(and what was sent down to Ibrahim, Ismai`Ol, Ishaq, Ya`qub) the scriptures and revelation,

(and the Asbat,) the Asbat are the twelve tribes who originated from the twelve children of Israel (Ya`qub).

(and what was given to Musa, `Isa) the Tawrah and the Injil,

(and the Prophets from their Lord.) and this encompasses all of Allah's Prophets.

(We make no distinction between one another among them) we believe in all of them,

(And to Him (Allah) we have submitted (in Islam))

Therefore, faithful Muslims believe in every Prophet whom Allah has sent and in every Book He revealed, and never disbelieve in any of them. Rather, they believe in what was revealed by Allah, and in every Prophet sent by Allah. Allah said next,

(And whoever seeks a religion other than Islam, it will never be accepted of him,) whoever seeks other than what Allah has legislated, it will not be accepted from him,

(and in the Hereafter he will be one of the losers.)

As the Prophet said in an authentic Hadith,

«مَنْ عَمِلَ عَمَلًا لَيْسَ عَلَيْهِ أَمْرُنَا، فَهُوَ رَدٌّ»

(Whoever commits an action that does not conform to our matter (religion) then it is rejected).

Surah: 3 Ayah: 86, Ayah: 87, Ayah: 88 & Ayah: 89

﴿كَيْفَ يَهْدِى ٱللَّهُ قَوْمًا كَفَرُوا۟ بَعْدَ إِيمَٰنِهِمْ وَشَهِدُوٓا۟ أَنَّ ٱلرَّسُولَ حَقٌّ وَجَآءَهُمُ ٱلْبَيِّنَٰتُ وَٱللَّهُ لَا يَهْدِى ٱلْقَوْمَ ٱلظَّٰلِمِينَ ۝﴾

86. How shall Allâh guide a people who disbelieved after their belief and after they bore witness that the Messenger (Muhammad (peace be upon him)) is true and after clear proofs had come unto them? And Allâh guides not the people who are Zâlimûn (polytheists and wrong-doers).

﴿أُو۟لَٰٓئِكَ جَزَآؤُهُمْ أَنَّ عَلَيْهِمْ لَعْنَةَ ٱللَّهِ وَٱلْمَلَٰٓئِكَةِ وَٱلنَّاسِ أَجْمَعِينَ ۝﴾

87. They are those whose recompense is that on them (rests) the Curse of Allâh, of the angels, and of all mankind.

﴿ خَٰلِدِينَ فِيهَا لَا يُخَفَّفُ عَنْهُمُ ٱلْعَذَابُ وَلَا هُمْ يُنظَرُونَ ۝ ﴾

88. They will abide therein (Hell). Neither will their torment be lightened, nor will it be delayed or postponed (for a while).

﴿ إِلَّا ٱلَّذِينَ تَابُوا۟ مِنۢ بَعْدِ ذَٰلِكَ وَأَصْلَحُوا۟ فَإِنَّ ٱللَّهَ غَفُورٌ رَّحِيمٌ ۝ ﴾

89. Except for those who repent after that and do righteous deeds. Verily, Allâh is Oft-Forgiving, Most Merciful.

Transliteration

86. Kayfa yahdee Allahu qawman kafaroo baAAda eemanihim washahidoo anna alrrasoola haqqun wajaahumu albayyinatu waAllahu la yahdee alqawma aiththalimeena 87. Ola-ika jazaohum anna AAalayhim laAAnata Allahi waalmala-ikati waalnnasi ajmaAAeena 88. Khalideena feeha la yukhaffafu AAanhumu alAAathabu wala hum yuntharoona 89. Illa allatheena taboo min baAAdi thalika waaslahoo fa-inna Allaha ghafoorun raheemun

Tafsir Ibn Kathir

Allah Does Not Guide People Who Disbelieve After they Believed, Unless They Repent

Ibn Jarir recorded that Ibn `Abbas said, "A man from the Ansar embraced Islam, but later reverted and joined the polytheists. He later on became sorry and sent his people to, `Ask the Messenger of Allah for me, if I can repent.' Then,

(How shall Allah guide a people who disbelieved after their belief) until,

(Verily, Allah is Oft-Forgiving, Most Merciful.) was revealed and his people sent word to him and he re-embraced Islam."

This is the wording recorded by An-Nasa'i, Al-Hakim and Ibn Hibban. Al-Hakim said, "Its chain is Sahih and they did not record it."

Allah's statement,

(How shall Allah guide a people who disbelieved after their belief and after they bore witness that the Messenger is true and after clear proofs came to them)

means, the proofs and evidences were established, testifying to the truth of what the Messenger was sent with. The truth was thus explained to them, but they reverted to the darkness of polytheism. Therefore, how can such people deserve guidance after they willingly leapt into utter blindness This is why Allah said,

(And Allah guides not the people who are wrongdoers.)

He then said,

(They are those whose recompense is that on them (rests) the curse of Allah, of the angels and of all mankind.)

Allah curses them and His creation also curses them.

(They will abide therein) in the curse,

(Neither will their torment be lightened nor will it be delayed or postponed.) for, the torment will not be lessened, not even for an hour. After that, Allah said,

(Except for those who repent after that and do righteous deeds. Verily, Allah is Oft-Forgiving, Most Merciful.)

This Ayah indicates Allah's kindness, graciousness, compassion, mercy and favor on His creatures when they repent to Him, for He forgives them in this case.

Surah: 3 Ayah: 90 & Ayah: 91

﴿ إِنَّ ٱلَّذِينَ كَفَرُواْ بَعْدَ إِيمَٰنِهِمْ ثُمَّ ٱزْدَادُواْ كُفْرًا لَّن تُقْبَلَ تَوْبَتُهُمْ وَأُوْلَٰٓئِكَ هُمُ ٱلضَّآلُّونَ ﴾

90. Verily, those who disbelieved after their Belief and then went on increasing in their disbelief (i.e. disbelief in the Qur'ân and in Prophet Muhammad (peace be upon him)) - never will their repentance be accepted (because they repent only by their tongues and not from their hearts). And they are those who are astray.

﴿ إِنَّ ٱلَّذِينَ كَفَرُواْ وَمَاتُواْ وَهُمْ كُفَّارٌ فَلَن يُقْبَلَ مِنْ أَحَدِهِم مِّلْءُ ٱلْأَرْضِ ذَهَبًا وَلَوِ ٱفْتَدَىٰ بِهِۦٓ أُوْلَٰٓئِكَ لَهُمْ عَذَابٌ أَلِيمٌ وَمَا لَهُم مِّن نَّٰصِرِينَ ﴾

91. Verily, those who disbelieved, and died while they were disbelievers, the (whole) earth full of gold will not be accepted from anyone of them even if they offered it as a ransom. For them is a painful torment and they will have no helpers.

Transliteration

90. Inna allatheena kafaroo baAAda eemanihim thumma izdadoo kufran lan tuqbala tawbatuhum waola-ika humu alddalloona 91. Inna allatheena kafaroo wamatoo wahum kuffarun falan yuqbala min ahadihim milo al-ardi thahaban walawi iftada bihi ola-ika lahum AAathabun aleemun wama lahum min nasireena

Tafsir Ibn Kathir

Neither Repentance of the Disbeliever Upon Death, Nor His Ransoming Himself on the Day of Resurrection Shall be Accepted

Allah threatens and warns those who revert to disbelief after they believed and who thereafter insist on disbelief until death. He states that in this case, no repentance shall be accepted from them upon their death. Similarly, Allah said,

(And of no effect is the repentance of those who continue to do evil deeds until death faces one of them) (4:18).

This is why Allah said,

(never will their repentance be accepted. And they are those who went astray.) to those who abandon the path of truth for the path of wickedness. Al-Hafiz Abu Bakr Al-Bazzar recorded that Ibn `Abbas said that some people embraced Islam, reverted to disbelief, became Muslims again, then reverted from Islam. They sent their people inquiring about this matter and they asked the Messenger of Allah . On that, this Ayah was revealed,

(Verily, those who disbelieved after their belief and then went on increasing in their disbelief never will their repentance be accepted). The chain of narration is satisfactory. Thereafter, Allah said,

(Verily, those who disbelieved, and died while they were disbelievers, the (whole) earth full of gold will not be accepted from anyone of them even if they offered it as a ransom.)

Those who die while disbelievers, shall have no good deed ever accepted from them, even if they spent the earth's fill of gold in what was perceived to be an act of obedience. The Prophet was asked about `Abdullah bin Jud`an, who used to be generous to guests, helpful to the indebted and who gave food (to the poor); will all that benefit him The Prophet said,

«لَا، إِنَّهُ لَمْ يَقُلْ يَوْمًا مِنَ الدَّهْرِ: رَبِّ اغْفِرْ لِي خَطِيئَتِي يَوْمَ الدِّين»

(No, for not even one day during his life did he pronounce, `O my Lord! Forgive my sins on the Day of Judgment.)

Similarly, if the disbeliever gave the earth's full of gold as ransom, it will not be accepted from him. Allah said,

(...nor shall compensation be accepted from him, nor shall intercession be of use to him,)(2:123), and

(...on which there will be neither mutual bargaining nor befriending.) (14:31), and,

(Verily, those who disbelieve, if they had all that is in the earth, and as much again therewith to ransom themselves thereby from the torment on the Day of Resurrection, it would never be accepted of them, and theirs would be a painful torment) (5:36).

This is why Allah said here,

,(Verily, those who disbelieved, and died while they were disbelievers, the (whole) earth full of gold will not be accepted from anyone of them if they offered it as a ransom).

The implication of this Ayah is that the disbeliever shall never avoid the torment of Allah, even if he spent the earth's fill of gold, or if he ransoms himself with the earth's fill of gold, - all of its mountains, hills, sand, dust, valleys, forests, land and sea.

Imam Ahmad recorded that Anas said that the Messenger of Allah said,

«يُؤْتَى بِالرَّجُلِ مِنْ أَهْلِ الْجَنَّةِ فَيَقُولُ لَهُ: يَا ابْنَ آدَمَ، كَيْفَ وَجَدْتَ مَنْزِلَكَ؟ فَيَقُولُ: أَيْ رَبِّ خَيْرَ مَنْزِلٍ، فَيَقُولُ: سَلْ وَتَمَنَّ، فَيَقُولُ: مَا أَسْأَلُ وَلَا أَتَمَنَّى إِلَّا أَنْ تَرُدَّنِي إِلَى الدُّنْيَا فَأُقْتَلَ فِي سَبِيلِكَ عَشْرَ مِرَارٍ، لِمَا يَرَى مِنْ فَضْلِ الشَّهَادَةِ، وَيُؤْتَى بِالرَّجُلِ مِنْ أَهْلِ النَّارِ فَيَقُولُ لَهُ: يَا ابْنَ آدَمَ، كَيْفَ وَجَدْتَ مَنْزِلَكَ؟ فَيَقُولُ: يَا رَبِّ شَرَّ مَنْزِلٍ، فَيَقُولُ لَهُ: تَفْتَدِي مِنِّي بِطِلَاعِ الْأَرْضِ ذَهَبًا؟ فَيَقُولُ: أَيْ رَبِّ نَعَمْ، فَيَقُولُ: كَذَبْتَ، قَدْ سَأَلْتُكَ أَقَلَّ مِنْ ذَلِكَ وَأَيْسَرَ فَلَمْ تَفْعَلْ، فَيُرَدُّ إِلَى النَّارِ»

(A man from among the people of Paradise will be brought and Allah will ask him, "O son of Adam! How did you find your dwelling" He will say, "O Lord, it is the best dwelling." Allah will say, "Ask and wish." The man will say, "I only ask and wish that You send me back to the world so that I am killed ten times in Your cause," because of the honor of martyrdom he would experience. A man from among the people of the Fire will be brought, and Allah will say to him, "O son of Adam! How do you find your dwelling" He will say, "It is the worst dwelling, O Lord." Allah will ask him, "Would you ransom yourself from Me with the earth's fill of gold" He will say, "Yes, O Lord." Allah will say, "You have lied. I asked you to do what is less and easier than that, but you did not do it," and he will be sent back to the Fire.)

This is why Allah said,

(For them is a painful torment and they will have no helpers.) for they shall not have anyone who will save them from the torment of Allah or rescue them from His painful punishment.

Surah: 3 Ayah: 92

﴿ لَن تَنَالُوا۟ ٱلْبِرَّ حَتَّىٰ تُنفِقُوا۟ مِمَّا تُحِبُّونَ ۚ وَمَا تُنفِقُوا۟ مِن شَىْءٍ فَإِنَّ ٱللَّهَ بِهِۦ عَلِيمٌ ﴾

Chapter 3: Al-i-'Imran (The Family Of 'Imran), Verses 001-092

92. By no means shall you attain Al-Birr (piety, righteousness - here it means Allâh's Reward, i.e. Paradise), unless you spend (in Allâh's Cause) of that which you love; and whatever of good you spend, Allâh knows it well.

Transliteration

92. Lan tanaloo albirra hatta tunfiqoo mimma tuhibboona wama tunfiqoo min shay-in fa-inna Allaha bihi AAaleemun

Tafsir Ibn Kathir

Al-Birr is Spending from the Best of One's Wealth

In his Tafsir, Waki` reported, that `Amr bin Maymun said that (By no means shall you attain Al-Birr) is in reference to attaining Paradise. Imam Ahmad reported that Anas bin Malik said, "Abu Talhah had more property than any other among the Ansar in Al-Madinah, and the most beloved of his property to him was Bayruha' garden, which was in front of the (Messenger's) Masjid. Sometimes, Allah's Messenger used to go to the garden and drink its fresh water." Anas added, "When these verses were revealed,

(By no means shall you attain Al-Birr unless You spend of that which you love,) Abu Talhah said, `O Allah's Messenger! Allah says, (By no means shall you attain Al-Birr, unless you spend of that which you love;) No doubt, Bayruha' garden is the most beloved of all my property to me. So I want to give it in charity in Allah's cause, and I expect its reward and compensation from Allah. O Allah's Messenger! Spend it where Allah makes you think is feasible.' On that, Allah's Messenger said,

»بَخٍ بَخٍ، ذَاكَ مَالٌ رَابِحٌ، ذَاكَ مَالٌ رَابِحٌ، وَقَدْ سَمِعْتُ، وَأَنَا أَرَى أَنْ تَجْعَلَهَا فِي الْأَقْرَبِين«

(Well-done! It is profitable property, it is profitable property. I have heard what you have said, and I think it would be proper if you gave it to your kith and kin.) Abu Talhah said, `I will do so, O Allah's Messenger.' Then Abu Talhah distributed that garden among his relatives and cousins." This Hadith was recorded in the Two Sahihs. They also recorded that `Umar said, "O Messenger of Allah! I never gained possession of a piece of property more precious to me than my share in Khaybar. Therefore, what do you command me to do with it" The Prophet said,

»حَبِّسِ الْأَصْلَ وَسَبِّلِ الثَّمَرَة«

(Retain the land to give its fruits in Allah's cause.)

www.ingramcontent.com/pod-product-compliance
Ingram Content Group UK Ltd.
Pitfield, Milton Keynes, MK11 3LW, UK
UKHW051250180426
11947UKWH00020B/1640